Sheriff Ballard turned on the TV and VCR. He ran the tape.

He and the officer with him listened to Leonard Lake, on the tape, rant about the survival of the fittest. The officer watched silently as a second tape began. A woman was chained to a chair. Lake paced in front of her. Charlie Ng stood off to the side. Lake began talking about how the woman should "cooperate," or be buried with a round in her head in the same place they "buried Mike."

Lake proclaimed he was not going to be caught—because there were no witnesses. He called it a little "crude," but shrugged it off as the reality of the situation.

The tape ran on. Lake chastised the helpless young woman for beating on the door of the cell in the concrete bunker. She was told not to do that again, or she'd get a severe whipping.

Ballard pushed the pause button. "We now have substantial proof of the identity of the woman you're looking at.

"She was seen leaving work with a stranger on April fourteenth. A coworker asked where she was going. She said she was going to the mountains, her boyfriend was in trouble. This guy was just giving her a lift. She got into a car, and was never seen or heard from again. . . ."

EYE OF EVIL

JOSEPH HARRINGTON
and ROBERT BURGER

SMP
ST. MARTIN'S PAPERBACKS

EYE OF EVIL

Cover photographs by AP/Wide World Photos.

ISBN: 0-312-95175-2

Printed in the United States of America

St. Martin's Paperbacks edition/December 1993

10 9 8 7 6 5 4 3 2 1

AUTHOR'S NOTE

Eye of Evil is a true account of Leonard Lake's and Charles Ng's alleged involvement in the mass-murder case discovered in Wilseyville, California in 1985, the subsequent flight of Ng to Canada, his trial there, his eventual extradition to the United States in 1991, his preliminary hearing in San Andreas in 1992, and motions for his trial in 1993. There is no way to predict at the time of this publication when or where his trial will occur. Because Mr. Ng has not had the benefit of a trial in the United States, the authors have scrupulously maintained his right to presumption of innocence in the telling of this story.

All of the events reported here are based on published information and court documents. Much of the dialogue has been reconstructed from testimony or created based on published accounts. In particular, the police interviews of Claralyn Balazs have been derived from facts contained in press accounts. The presumed thoughts and imagined words of the participants were written in consonance with the actions of those people. In no case has a substantive claim been made without reliance on published accounts or testimony at Ng's preliminary hearing.

With one exception, all of the persons named in this book are actual. The exception is the ubiquitous reporter, Tomasina Boyd Clancy, who is inspired by many of the reporters involved in this case, including the authors. Her adventures in covering the story are fictitious. The story, however, is all too real.

—Joseph Harrington and Robert Burger
August 1993

This book is dedicated to law enforcement agencies throughout North America, whose work we were able to see in a new light in the complexity of this case.

It is impossible in a work of this scope to include details of all the agencies that aided in this investigation. But this is a representative list of those involved.

South San Francisco Police Department
San Francisco Police Department
Calaveras Sheriff's Department
Calaveras County District Attorney's Office
Royal Canadian Mounted Police
Calaveras/Tuolumne CDF
Stockton Police Department
Ventura Police Department
San Jose Police Department
Milpitas Police Department
Morgan Hill Police Department
Watsonville Police Department
Chicago Police Department
Skokie Police Department
Cook County Police Department
Capitola Police Department
San Diego Police Department
San Diego Sheriff's Department
Calgary Police Department
Humboldt County Sheriff's Department
Mendocino County Sheriff's Department
Washoe County Sheriff's Department
Alameda County Sheriff's Department

Alameda County District Attorney's Office
San Luis Obispo Police Department
Merced Police Department
Los Angeles Police Department
Palo Alto Police Department
California Highway Patrol
Fresno Police Department
Sunnyvale Police Department
San Francisco District Attorney's Office
United States Attorney's Office, Chicago and
Washington D. C.
El Dorado Sheriff's Office
Douglas County Sheriff's Office
South Lake Tahoe Police Department
Hollister Police Department
Placer County Sheriff's Department
Daly City Police Department
Office of the Attorney General, Alberta, Canada
Los Angeles Sheriff's Department
San Francisco Chief Coroner/Medical Examiner
Federal Bureau of Investigation

Prologue

TUESDAY, JANUARY 12, 1993, 9:00 A.M.

THE RAIN SWEPT DOWN IN WAVES AGAINST the windshield. During the night a storm had funneled up from the coast and the valley into the Sierra, and now with the dawn its eye began to unleash its torrents.

The countryside was still as beautiful as she remembered it—a peaceful land of cattle ranchers and dairymen and now grape growers. It was so unlike the terror and bestial evil of eight years ago.

Tomasina Boyd Clancy had never thought of herself as beautiful, nor even peaceful. Her reddish hair, shoulder-length and unruly, defined her disposition toward men and women alike. It was an attitude like a chip on her shoulder, the "show me" challenge of her native Missouri. And in her business she needed every bit of it, for she was a rare live-by-your-wits reporter. She was a free-lancer paid by no one until she delivered something that was irresistible.

Clancy was drawn to disaster and mayhem, the bigger the better. A plane crashes in the Andes, Clancy stirs herself to be there first, looking over the shoulders of rescuers, angling for quotes from survivors. The tabloids bought her work from time to time, but her staple was the daily newspaper—the bigger the better.

Her nickname was inevitable: Tom Boy Clancy, or T.B., depending on whether the person using it liked her or not. Tom Boy for friends, T.B. for jealous rivals.

Most of the time she was called T.B.

She was driving south from Sacramento on State Highway 49, the road that follows the route of the gold miners, snaking through canyons that once rang with pickaxes and shovels. She was headed for the small town of San Andreas.

"San Andreas" resonates throughout California. For reasons of geography it is the name of an earthquake fault that runs almost the length of the state. It is the name of the county seat of Calaveras, the home of the "Big Trees" that startled the world in the late nineteenth century as the oldest living things on the planet. Mark Twain celebrated the annual competition of the giant leaping frogs of Calaveras, an innocence unmarred by riotous exploits of harlotry, drunkenness, and mayhem that were the divine right of the forty-niners. In 1885 the gentleman bandit Black Bart held up his last stagecoach, and was tried and convicted at the San Andreas Courthouse.

The town of San Andreas is about 120 miles, as the crow flies, due east of San Francisco Bay. It is one of those intermediate places that catches some of the tourists headed south for Yosemite National Park, or east to the ski slopes off State Highway 88.

The foothills here are a no-man's-land between the stately Sierra and the lush San Joaquin Valley. Just north of San Andreas, at Sutter Creek, the cry of "Gold!" went out in 1848.

Here the riverbeds are worn smooth from centuries of run-off of the snow fields above. Every canyon is cut with a network of rivulets, searching for a common path to the flatlands. At times the crystal liquid plunges into motionless pools, at times it washes over sandstone or cuts into mineral-laden banks. Each rock field is a sluice that sucks heavier metals into its web of silica and quartz, working and reworking the heaviest metal into flecks, sometimes globules. The relentless pounding of water on stone for millennia leeches out and gathers in. In time the stone surfaces become set, and there is gold.

Yet there are badlands here. Below the timberline of pine, fir, and sequoia there is little water: a pond here, a slough there. Hydraulic mining a century ago has thrown up massive beds of wasteland: bleached rocks that are the bones of this earth's crust lie under an uncaring sun. Bluffs jut up as remnants of another geological era. Stone walls built by shepherds of the last century carve out imaginary kingdoms.

The scenery swam in T. B. Clancy's peripheral vision. What a story, she thought, and remembered her byline eight years ago: Into this remote area came two men. The law claimed that they had been intent on living out fantasies of cruelty that even their Vietnam duty as Marines could not have taught them.

These mountains were just remote enough to allow the sadistic games to go undetected for more than three years. In that time, victims were hunted down, tortured, hacked up, and killed: men, women, children. This was the story of a descent into evil—and a reckoning.

Great story, she thought. Compelling. Violent. Gruesomely unusual. Death and a reckoning. At least that's what she thought when she first stumbled on the case.

Leonard Lake, she thought, dealt himself a reckoning —no courts, no lawyers, no circus. His alleged partner, on the other hand, had deftly managed to maneuver things for years.

Eight years . . . eight years the citizens of California had waited; the courts had waited; the victims' relatives had waited.

And now, finally, tomorrow the trial was to begin.

The rain started coming down heavily again. The respite was over. At first the windshield wipers managed to handle the water—as if coming from a garden hose. Then the garden hose turned into a fireman's four-inch nozzle.

She slowed the car—forty-five . . . thirty-five . . . fifteen.

Good Lord, she thought, I can barely see the road.

Tentatively, she edged to the shoulder. She glanced at her watch: nine A.M. I have to be in court in half an hour, she thought. The county clerk had told her there was to be one final motion today before the trial which would begin tomorrow. *No way am I missing the kick-off of this case.*

Eight years ago I was here early too, the first reporter on the scene. Unfortunately, damn it, I wasn't the first one to file the story.

She remembered Sheriff Claud Ballard with his big moon face and shining eyes. She smiled. *He caught me. I had it, right in my hand, and Ballard—with deft professionalism mixed with humor—took it from me. A scoop to dream about—lost.*

The rain stopped—as the story had in 1985. One second blinding, the next—gone. She pulled out onto the highway, glanced at her watch, and sped toward San Andreas.

The courthouse was on the south end of town. She passed the local stores and recalled a quaint fact: there were no stoplights in San Andreas—unbelievably, no stoplights in the whole county.

She turned off Highway 49, drove a few blocks and pulled into the parking lot of the county's government buildings.

She looked at her watch: nine-twenty. Where, she thought, are the sound trucks? The TV trucks? The satellite dishes?

The accused is not here!

Maybe he didn't have to appear for the motion. Maybe he wouldn't arrive until tomorrow. Then she saw a deputy sheriff on the roof. He was carrying a sniper rifle.

The accused has to be here.

She drove to the rear parking lot. A nondescript, unmarked white van was parked at the rear, its doors nuzzled against the back entrance of the courthouse.

He's here, she repeated to herself.

She noticed the Folsom prison guard lounging by the white van. He had an Uzi slung over his shoulder.

The trial's on! Finally, after the interminable delays, the surviving partner accused of the most heinous crimes I've ever investigated in my journalistic career is going to be tried by the state.

But where, she wondered, the shadow of uncertainty coming over her once more, is the press?

Four months ago, when the preliminary hearing started, the fourth estate had multiple-tiered representation: TV, press, radio, news magazines. And not just from California, but from back East. There had even been a photographer from the *London Globe and Sun.*

The weather? she speculated. No way, not for this case. Maybe she had missed a news report. Possible, but then why the armed guards?

Maybe the press was waiting for the blood and guts of the trial to begin. Marsden motions and Simmons admonitions bored most of the fourth estate. Not her. She thrived on details.

She walked to the front of the courthouse. Through the glass windows she could see four deputy sheriffs standing by the large metal detector. Leaning against the wall, arms crossed, was Sheriff Nutall. He seems to have lost some of the sparkle in his eyes, she thought, but he was still the consummate cop—lean, lanky, tough, with only a few more gray hairs after eight years. There were only two people waiting in line. Both men emptied their pockets.

She recognized them: Webster and Marovich—court-appointed lawyers for the defendant. Both had put on some weight, she noted, and the gangly Marovich seemed more stooped, as if from constantly conferring with his bantam-rooster partner.

T. B. Clancy entered the building. She remembered the drill from the preliminary hearing. The metal detector was set at its most sensitive level. Her earrings set off the machine. The tiny brads that had been used to hold her high heels together did likewise. The screws that held the armatures of her reading glasses, the metal tip of her plastic ballpoint pen, any metal at all set off the alarm, the solemn warning that someone potentially dangerous was trying to enter the courtroom.

She nodded at the female deputy sheriff. Off came Clancy's earrings, her shoes, her pen. Out came the contents of her purse.

The deputy sheriff meticulously examined the items, then waved her through the metal detector.

The alarm went off—a shrill whine.

Clancy smiled helplessly. "I thought I removed everything metal—"

The man wearing sergeant stripes said in a gruff voice, "You can't enter."

Clancy sighed and returned to the walk-through point.

The deputy sheriff was in her mid-fifties, wore her hair close-cropped. She smiled. "I remember you."

"From the preliminary hearing?"

"Yes, that too. But from the original investigation. Wow, did you cause a stir. The sheriff was so angry."

"Sheriff Ballard."

"Yes. He passed away a few years ago."

"I know. I heard during the preliminary hearing."

"You're a reporter."

"Free-lance."

The woman smiled again and nodded toward the hallway. "Still have to pat you down."

T. B. Clancy followed her to a vacant office, where she was frisked. The officer volunteered, "No way are they going to start the trial tomorrow."

"You've heard something?" Clancy asked, trying to keep the disappointment out of her voice.

"Nope, just that there's too many lawyers here."

"I saw Webster and Marovich."

"Ephraim Margolin may be here."

"What for?"

The deputy sheriff shrugged. "Sorry, gag order."

Damn, Clancy thought. The gag order on this case was driving her crazy. Margolin was big-time, national. He was representing John Gotti, the New York convicted gangster, on his appeal.

Why would Margolin be here again?

Clancy hated not knowing what was going on.

She entered the rear of the courtroom and sat in the last row of seats. It was small for a courtroom: six double rows of seats, with a capacity of sixty spectators.

Beyond the bar that separated spectators from the officers of the court sat four men and one woman.

James Webster and Thomas Marovich had taken their places at the defense table. The woman, Sharlene Honnaka, the state deputy attorney general, was whispering with John Martin, the prosecuting attorney, appointed by Calaveras County. Margolin was not in evidence.

There was only one other person in the room who was not a guard or a lawyer. The bright-faced, stocky young man sat in the back row.

I know that guy. Matt, she remembered, Matt Hedgers, the local reporter who worked for the San Andreas newspaper. He was working on some sort of screenplay, about a local historical character. She searched her memory. The data surfaced: Joaquin Murrietta and Three-Fingered Jack—two very notorious western bandits.

He noticed her, grinned and waved.

She smiled back. Local sources are invaluable. She moved down the row and sat beside him. "How's the screenplay going?"

He beamed at her for remembering. "Slow, but great—if you know what I mean."

"Is the San Francisco lawyer coming?"

"Margolin's representing Lew and Burt. He's filed papers with the court."

Lew and Burt? She thought they'd been long forgotten. She knew that Garrick Lew had been the accused's personal lawyer in 1985. Michael Burt had been the court-appointed lawyer from San Francisco's Public Attorney's Office.

Judge Mewhinney had fired Burt and Lew a year and a half ago, in October of '91. His reasoning was that Burt had a time problem—as he was handling the appeals in the Los Angeles case known as "Night Stalker"—and that Lew had never tried a capital case.

She asked, "Margolin must be asking to—"

"He's petitioning the court to fire Marovich and Webster and reinstate Lew and Burt."

"But the trial's supposed to start tomorrow."

"Want to bet on it? The only people here are the attorneys and the guards."

Clancy looked around the courtroom. This is when real stories came out; when no one else was poking around.

The security was the same as in the preliminary hearing. Two uniformed deputy sheriffs flanked the judge's bench. Two more, dressed in civilian clothes, sat at the rear of the courtroom. Each had his coat off, folded over his lap, concealing a sawed-off shotgun.

Four months ago this room had been packed with reporters and victims' relatives, and even the standing room along the wall was taken.

Now, she thought, just me and Matt and enough firepower to guarantee food delivery to the starving Somalians.

Plus the lawyers.

She went to the bar that separated the spectators from the jury and officers of the court. She placed her hands on the walnut rail and made mental notes. The judge's bench was to her left, the jury box to her right. The defendant's table was in front of the judge's bench, the prosecutors in front of the empty jury box.

On the wall to her left was a map detailing the remote country property where the "alleged" crimes occurred. Next to the map was a list of the charges. She read:

1. Murder	Kathy Allen
2. Murder	Brenda O'Connor
3. Murder	Michael Carroll
4. Murder	Lonnie Bond Sr.
5. Murder	Robin Stapley
6. Murder	Paul Cosner
7. Murder	Clifford Peranteau
8. Murder	Jeffrey Gerald
9. Murder	Lonnie Bond Jr.

10. Burglary (Spec. allegation)	Dubs family
11. Murder	Sean Dubs
12. Murder	Deborah Dubs
13. Murder	Harvey Dubs

The door by the jury box opened. A Folsom prison guard entered. He was holding a chain that was attached to the waist of the defendant. A second chain was held by a Calaveras deputy sheriff, who was behind the defendant. A third guard walked beside the prisoner, holding one of his elbows.

The prisoner was wearing an orange prison jumpsuit. The chain that encircled his waist also pinned his arms to his side. He shuffled as he walked, legs impeded by leg irons.

Clancy studied the defendant. Small, five-five, five-six. Chinese, perhaps somewhat Eurasian.

He's gained weight, she thought, since the last time I saw him. Thickened up a bit around the waist. One thing hadn't changed. The eyes. The black, lifeless eyes glaring out of a now puffy face. The eyes that reminded her of the shark she bumped into off Australia's Great Barrier Reef.

She'd been scuba diving with a friend. She'd felt a tap on her shoulder. She'd turned and stared into the death mask face of a great white shark. The huge shark had stared back at her, eyes pitch-black and emotionless, then turned and swam away.

Every time she related that story to colleagues, they all responded the same way, with a stale punch line from a lawyer joke: "Professional courtesy."

She'd quit telling the story, but she never forgot the eyes, those eyes that now had a twin reflection on the prisoner's face.

The bailiff called the court to order. An owlish, black-robed judge entered. She didn't recognize him. He had a jaunty air about him and an impish look unlike the stern-faced jurist Mewhinney, who had begun the whole case and had bored his audience for eight long years. She whispered to Matt, "Who's he?"

"Claude Perasso, a retired superior court judge from San Francisco. He'll be the trial judge."

Clancy wanted to ask more, but the judge shot a reproving look at both of them. She smiled and mouthed the word "Sorry."

The judge began, "All right. *People* versus *Ng.* The defendant is present. . . . We have a number of motions here, a bunch of which were filed this morning. The first one, which we should deal with, is the motion to continue the trial. . . ."

Naturally, Clancy thought. It's the first duty of the defense to delay as long as possible in a capital case. Webster conferred with his partner, his pencil mustache twitching. Marovich's long, clean-shaven face had a professorial cast. Though both were in vigorous middle age, they had the avuncular habit of peering over their glasses from time to time.

"The defense has never agreed," Webster argued at last, "to the trial date of January 13th. The date of January 13th was set on December 2nd of 1992 by Judge Airola. . . ."

For the next hour the lawyers argued over issues of "undiscovered discovery," and "inability to file 995 motion," and "change of venue motion," and "inability to have forensic examinations completed." Hedger dutifully scribbled in his notebook, searching for an angle for his story.

Finally, as the lunch break approached, Clancy observed to Matt that Webster and Marovich were caught in an unusual vise: the defendant had sued them for malpractice, yet they were forced to argue for their client, the defendant!

Judge Perasso, noted for his earthy practicality, summed it up: "I agree it is difficult to argue the issue of one's own incompetency, saying, 'Yes, I'm really pretty dumb.' " He went on to ask about Ephraim Margolin, who had argued "up to the California Supreme Court" to reinstate Ng's original attorneys. Surely here was a man who was familiar with the proceedings. The judge asked, "Does anybody know if he's prepared to deal with it?"

The judge looked across the room at the prosecution table, where district attorney John Martin sat with deputy attorney general Honnaka. Then a voice came from the defense table.

"Yes, your honor," Charles Ng said. "I believe I consulted Mr. Burt, and Mr. Margolin is prepared."

"Is he?" the judge asked.

"If he could be appointed by this court."

Clancy was stunned to hear the shackled prisoner speak up with such self-assurance. So he *had* studied law in his years in a Canadian prison. So he *was* determined to defend himself.

The judge nodded. "I'm satisfied Mr. Margolin is more than capable in handling the issue."

Marovich and Webster eagerly agreed. Margolin might be arguing that they be taken off the case, but at least Margolin was Ng's choice. Marovich had one last concern. "Judge, can you specify an hourly rate as part of your order?"

The deputy attorney general broke in: "The previous court order, I believe, was for seventy-five an hour."

Marovich insisted, "Judge, we would ask for one hundred dollars an hour. . . ."

Judge Perasso asked for a review of everybody's rates.

Marovich agreed that, in this case, it was "one hundred an hour" for him.

The state deputy attorney general said, "I believe my services are being billed out at ninety dollars an hour, your honor."

Judge Perasso smiled at the logic. "Well," he said, "we cannot pay Mr. Margolin less than the attorney general. He wouldn't speak to me again." Clancy also had to smile as the judge fixed the rates for the new attorney on the case at one hundred dollars an hour, to match Webster and Marovich.

But the fun wasn't over. Deputy Attorney General

Honnaka rose to ask that "one last thing" be put on the record in regard to Margolin. "I do recall," she said, "that he was quoted in the *Daily Journal* . . . and made some provocative comments with respect to the defense lawyers being up to their knees in money. . . ."

The judge thought, "That's not very deep—up to their knees, up to their hips, maybe."

"Maybe he said," Honnaka speculated, "up to their . . . he said up to their something. . . ."

"In the stench of money," the district attorney now remembered.

Judge Perasso rose to the occasion. "All right. Now he will be stenched to the same degree. . . . Anything further?"

The trial was set to begin on May 12, 1993. Margolin was to be notified that he could begin the process of arguing for reinstatement of Ng's original attorneys. The defense attorneys still protested that four months was not enough time. But the court had ruled.

Judge Perasso rose and swept out of the room. The orange-clad defendant was led out by his jailers. All five lawyers huddled by the bench. A slightly dazed Clancy followed Matt outside.

They stood under an overhang. The rain had started up again, a drizzle under a slate-gray sky. In the distance, the barren limbs of foothill oaks rustled from a gusting wind.

Clancy asked, "Another delay . . . when is this trial ever going to start?"

"They can't even make up their minds on representation. Eight years of nit-picking. Did you hear anyone mention venue?"

"I thought that was already decided. No change of venue."

"Want to bet? I live in Calaveras. This is a gigantic county, measured in land. But less than thirty thousand people live here. Do you think any of them hasn't heard about what happened eight years ago?"

"Just the preschoolers."

"Even they have older brothers and sisters, mothers and fathers."

"So the potential jury pool is tainted."

"This community, as much as it would like to, hasn't forgotten what happened. When that many people die or disappear in a rural place like this, almost everyone is likely to have known someone involved. Either Lake, the defendant, or a deceased."

"Then why wasn't a change of venue requested?"

"By who? They can't even figure out who's going to defend, let alone where."

Whatever happened, Clancy thought, to the terrible swift sword of justice?

She walked to her car, turned and watched a white van drive by, led by an unmarked Department of Corrections lead vehicle. A similar car followed closely.

The caravan was taking the prisoner back to New Folsom Prison, back to administrative segregation, back to maximum security, back to a solitary cell.

Guilty? Innocent? Fiend or dupe?

She noticed the lawyers leaving the courthouse. They hurried through the soft falling rain to their various cars. None of them appeared concerned by what had just occurred.

Clancy slipped into her car. She thought for a moment, then opened her notebook. She quickly wrote a reminder to herself to follow up on.

She penned: *Maybe I covered the wrong story—the brutality of the crimes.*

But what about the judiciary system? she thought. What was happening didn't seem to be justice. And if it was, then it was tortured justice.

She thought about the events of the past eight years: the recent preliminary hearing, the years of long battle between the Canadians and the Americans—lawyer to lawyer—State Department to State Department—President Bush to Prime Minister Mulroney.

She remembered the manhunt, the killing field, the police, the coroners, the anthropologists, the forensics experts.

The trail wound its way back in her mind from 1993 to 1985, back from lawyers politely dissecting the fine points of law, back to a lumberyard, to an observant customer in a lumberyard. And the whole despicably malignant evil had burst in the public eye over nothing but a seventy-five-dollar workbench vise.

Part One

The Fantasy

Chapter One

SUNDAY, JUNE 2, 1985, NOON.

THE SOUTH SAN FRANCISCO LUMBER YARD IS a fixture of the industrial and bedroom community that separates the City from the posher neighbors farther to the south. "South City" for short, the town once had a reputation for "anything goes," but in the 1980s it had become a no-nonsense kind of place, with legalized poker parlors and discount stores. On this warm summer day it was business as usual at the lumberyard.

John Kallas entered the store. He was with a friend named Glen. John wandered down an aisle, then noticed an Asian customer wearing a parka.

A parka?

The weather was too warm for winter clothing.

John picked up unusual signals: the head swiveling around the store, instead of on the shelf in front of him, the nonchalant browsing, as if he were in the stacks of a library.

The loiterer reached the skill saws, rows of Black & Deckers and Makitas.

He finally settled into his approach pattern: bench vises. He's groping at the seventy- to eighty-dollar stuff, high-end, John thought.

In a fish-eye mirror in a rear corner of the store, John saw a workbench vise suddenly disappear into the folds of the parka.

He grabbed Glen and said, "Tell the store clerk." John then followed the Asian man out of the store.

A phone call to the South City police station traveled at the speed of electrons, not light, but it was fast enough. Radio waves went from the dispatcher to a police car at near the max, so that, depending on the agility of the dispatcher, and the location of the roving patrol car, a cop could be in the yard in sixty seconds.

John watched the Asian toss the vise into the rear of a Honda Prelude, then slam the trunk. The Asian stared over the top of the car, directly at John, then turned and hurriedly walked away.

Glen walked out and said, "Police are on the way."

John nodded and walked over to the Honda Prelude. Both men peered inside the car's rear window. On the rear seat were some clothing, a cardboard box, and a wrench set. In the front, on the passenger's seat, was a work jacket.

Kallas said, "Wonder what he did with the vise?"

"He put the vise in the trunk." Glen pointed at the key still in the trunk's lock. He lifted the lid.

"There's the vise," John said. "Price tag's still on it."

Inside the store, a man approached the store clerk. He had a heavy, scruffy beard and was balding. He demanded, "What's going on? I just heard you call the cops."

"Shoplifting." The store clerk pointed out the window.

"You mean the Chinese guy?" He pulled a wallet from his hip pocket and started to dig. "Look, he's a friend of mine from work. The poor guy don't know any better."

"You came in together?"

"I'll pay for whatever he took."

Officer Daniel Wright of the South San Francisco Police Department knew he was a good peace officer. That's what they used to call them, he thought, people who brought peace to people's lives. His beat was clean: a few drug busts, rare homicides or rapes, mainly drunks.

Wright's radio sputtered static and cleared. "Crime in

progress at South City Lumber; shoplifting. Asian, wearing a parka."

Be prepared, he told himself. Even a lowly shoplifting bust could turn ugly. With the rise in drug use had come the proliferation of weapons and the willingness to use them. Everybody seemed to be packing Uzis these days.

Wright's pulse jumped to 120.

Calm down, calm down, he instructed himself. Remember the three P's: professional, polite, prepared.

He focused straight ahead and visualized the Enter gate to the lumberyard. He'd approach it from the right to maximize the chance of blocking the guy leaving the lot with a right-hand turn.

"Calm down," he whispered audibly; it was part of his training. He could lower his pulse from 170 to 80 by getting the tension out of his throat and back down into his belly. *Calm down. Focus on him.*

His Christmas-tree blue and red lights went on as he pulled into the lot. Wright swung his car in front of the 1980 Honda Prelude and got out.

John said, "There's the stolen vise."

Officer Wright looked into the trunk. He saw the vise, a bag with Ace Hardware printed on it, and two green tote bags. He asked, "Who opened the trunk?"

"We did. An Asian-looking guy, about twenty to twenty-five, put it in there, then saw me and took off."

Probable cause, Wright thought, no problem. The store provided the first cause, the call about the stolen vise. *He* didn't open the trunk, two civilians did—so no problem there.

He could see the vise, but he could also see the outline of a gun in one of the tote bags.

First he searched the Ace Hardware bag for a receipt to the vise. Then, using his radio, he read the car's license plate numbers to headquarters: 838WFQ.

He noticed a couple of black-and-white slides. He could make out a man and a woman on one and a child on the other. As he waited for a reply on the DMV check, he saw a bearded man walk briskly out of the store and across the parking lot toward him. He's about forty, the policeman thought. Medium build, balding in front, with wild, tangled, full beard and mustache. His hair is brown. His eyes are animated, hard, dangerous.

Something's wrong.

The bearded man held out both hands, a universal sign of peace. "Look, sir, here's the receipt. I paid for the vise my friend took, sir. There's no need for the police."

Officer Wright was familiar with the two-man shoplifting routine. He feigned interest in the receipt, while waiting for the car's license-plate report.

Wright positioned himself slightly to the right of the man. This gave him the advantage against an attempt to swing a punch or draw a weapon.

The bearded man tried to work his way to Wright's left. The policeman kept shifting his position.

Wright asked, "Who's the car belong to?"

"Lonnie Bond."

"Where's Bond at?"

"Up north."

The squad car radio blared out, "The car's license plate is issued to a Buick, not a Honda. The Buick's license plates are registered to a Lonnie Bond."

"Let me see your ID," Wright ordered.

The bearded man shrugged. "Sir, I was just trying to help out a friend, sir."

Wright thought: too friendly, too polite. He'd discovered in the past that the overuse of the word "sir" usually meant previous prison training, or an attempt to ingratiate oneself with the police officer.

He examined the man. No physical evidence to indicate anything. The shoes weren't manufactured in a prison. Neither was the belt, or the ring on his finger. He was wearing a long-sleeve shirt, on a hot June day. Maybe the shirt was to cover needle marks—a telltale sign of drug use.

"What's in the tote bags?"

The bearded man shrugged. "It's not my car, sir."

I have enough probable cause now to search the car,

Wright thought. The DMV check came back registered to a Buick—that was more than probable cause that this was a stolen car. But it would be better if the suspect consented and opened the tote bag; less hassle later on in court. He asked again, "What are you afraid I might find?"

"Nothing."

"Then you can't possibly mind if I have a look?"

The bearded man shrugged. "The vise is paid for, what's the big deal?"

Wright ran through what he knew. The man had a sales slip for the vise. The store wasn't going after him. The only evidence he had was the switch in the car's license plates. That was a crime. But was this man Lonnie Bond? That's who the license plate was registered to. Or was this man just a friend who had borrowed the car?

I can see the shape of the gun, Wright thought. I want to search that tote bag.

He repeated, "What's in the tote bag?"

"How should I know?"

"Let's find out. Why don't you open it up?"

"It's not mine."

"Is it your friend's?"

The bearded man shrugged.

"I think you're hiding something."

The bearded man shrugged again.

"If you're not hiding anything, why are you afraid to open the tote bag?"

"I'm not hiding anything."

Officer Wright smiled and pointed at the vague outline of the weapon pressing against the tote bag. "I'm a cop. I love weapons. I know that's a gun. You know it's a gun. I just want to look at it."

The bearded man opened the tote bag. Inside was a light green-gray, zippered pistol case. Inside that was a Ruger .22 pistol.

Officer Wright jotted down the serial number: 1270329. In the tote bag he saw a long metal tube, six inches long. One end was threaded. A silencer, he realized.

Wright thought, Why a silencer? How many reasons were there for a silencer? You didn't go hunting rabbit with a silencer. Twenty-two automatics with silencers were the classic hit pieces.

Wright thought, Do I have enough for an arrest? My probable cause to initially interrogate was the call from the lumberyard about the stolen vise, but that trail led to the Asian. That trail also led to the initial DMV check.

Officer Wright had been burned more than once in court—arrests that he thought impeccably done were suddenly scrutinized, a tiny flaw found: dismissed.

The policeman smiled. "Nice weapon, I have one at home."

The bearded man looked relieved. He returned the smile.

Wright said, "I don't go hunting much, just shooting beer cans off the fence."

"I love hunting."

"Do you use this weapon?" Wright held his breath and grinned as widely and warmly as he could. *Say yes, say yes.*

"Yes."

Wright asked, "May I see some identification?"

The bearded man now gave off extreme signs of agitation. He held out a California driver's license. The name on it was Robin S. Stapley. The birth date made him twenty-six. The photo was smudged.

Twenty-six? Wright thought. This guy looked at least forty. Returning to his squad car, he called in the serial number on the .22. It was registered to Robin Scott Stapley.

Officer Wright pushed the bearded man against the car. "Hands on top of the roof. You're under arrest."

"What the hell for?"

"Owning an illegally altered weapon."

"Bullshit!"

"No, I'm afraid not."

The bearded man put his arms out and said, "Take me away."

"Spread 'em." Using his nightstick, Wright forced the

man's legs back until his body was at a forty-five-degree angle from the car. He searched the right side of the suspect first, placing his right leg in front of the man. All the leverage, position, and balance were on the police officer's side.

The police officer searched quickly for a weapon, found none, then applied the handcuffs.

Wright read the bearded man his rights and stuffed him in the backseat of the squad car. He called in an all-points bulletin to the station: Asian male, slight build, about twenty-five, last seen wearing parka and blue jeans.

Wright leaned over the backseat. "What did you say his name was?"

"Fuck you."

"Your friend's name, what is it?"

"These cuffs are killing me."

Wright didn't answer.

"They're cutting my wrists, asshole!"

Wright pulled out of the lumberyard's parking lot. He called the station and requested that the Honda Prelude be towed to the South City impound yard. The police station was only a few blocks away. He repeated as conversationally as he could, "What's your friend's name?"

"I was talking about the goddamn cuffs."

Wright asked himself what he had: a shoplifting scam, a gun with an illegal silencer, some homemade family pictures, a license plate registered to a different vehicle and belonging to a Lonnie Bond, not Robin Stapley.

He pulled the squad car into the station. He turned off the engine. "Before I book you, it'll help if you play ball."

"All right, I know the Chinaman."

Wright led the man into an interrogation room. He had the bearded man empty his pockets.

He took out a number of keys and a receipt from Golden Crest Travel made out to Charles Gunnar.

Who's Charles Gunnar? Wright wondered. He said, "We can end this now, if you'll tell me what's going on."

Another officer signaled to him from the door. He said in a low voice, "We ran a VIN." He glanced at his notebook. "The vehicle identification number on the engine block of the Honda Prelude was SNF, 2023947."

"Registered to Lonnie Bond? Robin Stapley? Charles Gunnar?"

"Nope. Paul Cosner, of 1918 Filbert Street, San Francisco. I called S.F. He's been missing since last November."

Officer Wright tried to will his blood pressure to stop soaring. Calm down, calm down. Impossible. This was shaping up very ominously. He asked, "Did you report this to S.F.'s Missing Persons Unit?"

"The desk sergeant's contacting them now. Plus homicide inspector Detective Hopper has been contacted."

"Do they want me to continue interrogating?"

"Didn't say."

Wright sat across the table from the suspect. "The car's identification number doesn't match the phony plate. The car is registered to a Paul Cosner, a San Franciscan reported missing last November."

The bearded man's body suddenly went limp. Officer Wright saw the defiance go out of his eyes.

The suspect asked, "Please, take these cuffs off."

"Are you really Robin Stapley?"

The bearded man snorted, a mean, guttural sound that came from another place in his psyche. He slumped in his chair and closed his eyes. A hoarse voice whispered, "Get me a pen, paper, and a glass of water."

"No telephone call?"

"Just a piece of paper and something to write with."

"Want to write a confession?"

"A note to my wife."

Harmless request, Wright decided. He filled a plastic cup with cold water and placed it on the table. He ripped a sheet of blank paper from his notebook and placed it and his pen by the cup of water.

The man held up the handcuffs and said, "I can't write with these on."

Another officer stood by the interrogation room's door while the handcuffs were taken off.

The bearded man quickly scribbled something on the paper and put the note into his shirt pocket.

Wright offered, "I can have that delivered for you."

The bearded man said, "Who would have thought that a lousy workbench vise would bring me to this?"

"I beg your pardon?"

"My partner's name is Charlie Chitat Ng. Chitat, pronounced Cheetah, and Ng, pronounced Ing."

Officer Wright scribbled this information into his notebook.

The bearded man said, "You want to know who I really am?"

"Yes."

He paused, then raised his head and stared into the police officer's eyes. "I'm Leonard Lake, fugitive from the Feds." He grabbed something from the lapel of his shirt and sucked it into his mouth. He gulped the water and repeated hoarsely, "Lake."

His throat and chest convulsed.

Wright yelled for a medic. He had seen this before: it could be a nerve pill, it could be cyanide. The symptoms were the same. Oxygen is suddenly cut off from the brain, and the body's cells can no longer breathe.

Wright took the man's pulse; feeble but still there. He said softly to himself, "Good God, you don't kill yourself over a stolen car."

The officer called Kaiser Permanente Emergency and asked for an ambulance.

After Lake was given CPR and taken away, Officer Wright went to the impound yard behind the station, with Inspector Hopper, Homicide.

They carefully searched the Honda Prelude. There was a dark maroon stain on the front passenger's seat. Under the front seat they found a First Interstate Bank card in the name of Randy Jacobson and an assortment of cards from AAA, National Enterprises Medical, California First Bank, Saks Fifth Avenue, and GEMCO Department Stores and Supermarkets—all in the name of

R. Scott Stapley, 4755 Felton, Apartment Number 4, San Diego.

Officer Wright entered the station and turned this evidence over to his desk sergeant along with his notes.

The sergeant said, "I reached S.F.'s Missing Persons Unit. They're contacting the officers involved in Paul Cosner's case."

"Who's handling it?"

"Irene Brunn and Tom Eisenmann."

"Eisenmann? I've heard of him, but he's not in Missing Persons."

"What's he in?"

"Child abuse and kiddie porn."

Chapter Two

SUNDAY, JUNE 2, 1985, 2:00 P.M.

SERGEANT TOM EISENMANN SWERVED ONTO the shoulder of U.S. 101 to avoid the Sunday traffic suddenly telescoping in front of him. Sure enough, there was an accident. A tank truck had caught the soft shoulder and rolled on its side.

Figures, he thought. He had to be in San Francisco in an hour. He would inevitably be late working his way through traffic across the Golden Gate Bridge into the Cow Hollow–Marina District, where the Missing Persons Unit of the San Francisco Police Department was quaintly located. Though he was not with that detail, his work often involved missing persons and he kept an office in the same building.

He was a tall, well-built man, with thinning black hair. At forty-seven, he was in trim shape. He ran five miles three times a week, watched his diet, drank infrequently.

He thought about a book he'd just finished reading, *The Abused Child*, by Serapio Zalba. The author had gone into great detail about the five signals of an abusive parent: mental illness, aimless life, unspecified disturbance leading to battering, harsh discipline, misplaced conflicts.

Eisenmann tried to concentrate on what he'd read about the complex subject of the psychotic parent, but his mind kept drifting back to the compulsive disciplinarian.

Two days before, he had arrested a father. The man

was under the delusion that his two sons, seven and nine, were never going to learn the multiplication tables unless he helped them along. He had accomplished this, when they answered wrong, by jamming the hot coal of a cigar into each small palm.

The father is in jail, Eisenmann thought, but what about the boys? What mental scars will haunt them until they die? What psychological terror will be triggered, at some point in their lives, just at the sight of someone smoking?

He parked behind the Missing Persons building. The two-story brick office was built in 1915 specifically as a police station to handle the crowds expected for the Panama Pacific Exposition. The farmlands and sloughs just inside the Golden Gate had been filled in and "the greatest fair the world has ever seen" was announced. The only buildings remaining from this extravaganza were the Palace of Fine Arts and the old police station, including its stable.

Eisenmann went into the building. He was greeted by the dispatcher with, "You're late. Where the hell have you been?"

"You work for the Missing Persons detail, you tell me."

The dispatcher ignored the familiar joke. "We got a lead on Cosner."

"Finally."

Once a month Tom Eisenmann pulled weekend duty in Missing Persons. The Cosner case had come up on his watch.

Eisenmann had followed the case for months. Paul Cosner had worked as a car salesman at a Marin dealership. By all accounts, he was a good citizen. Why would he want to drop everything and disappear?

Or who would want to kill him? Eisenmann knew that when a man is gone without a trace for months, the odds aren't good at ever seeing him again. There are only a few reasons people disappear: homicide, suicide, simulated suicide, amnesia, psychosis, abandonment.

Missing Persons cases were unlike most police work. The detail was often aimless and frustratingly slow—waiting for something to happen. Something had happened at last.

The teletype from the South San Francisco police was cryptic, but exciting. Cosner's 1980 Honda Prelude had been picked up by an alert cop in the parking lot of the South City Lumber and Supply Company.

Eisenmann called South City. "I have to locate my partner, but I'll be there within the hour."

His partner on this case was Policewoman Irene Brunn. Her title put her in historical perspective. She was one of only twelve San Francisco female officers who went by the old handle—police*woman.*

Irene Brunn was a grandmother, but hardly looked it. She had close-cropped, dark brunette hair, an athletic figure, and unwrinkled Latino skin. Depending on the situation, she alternated between the cold, analytical approach required of an investigative officer and the hot-blooded intensity of her ancestry.

She was in her Russian Hill apartment when Eisenmann called. He told her about Cosner's car turning up in South City.

"Don't wait for me. I'll meet you there ASAP."

Within minutes they both pulled into the South City police station. They were told by the arresting officer, Daniel Wright, that the suspect taken into custody, Leonard Lake, had tried to kill himself and was now at Kaiser Permanente Hospital.

"Let's interrogate him at the hospital," Eisenmann suggested.

Officer Wright shook his head. "No chance. He was in a coma when the ambulance got here. He had two cyanide pills taped to the underside of his lapel." He handed them a note. "You'll find this interesting. Lake wrote this just before he popped the pills."

Eisenmann read: *Please forgive me.*

Irene said, "I've never come across a suspect with cyanide on him."

"That's World War Two stuff."

"But why? Not over a stolen car."

"This guy had to be into something far more serious," Eisenmann said. "Where's the Honda?"

"We had it towed," Wright answered. "It's here, behind the station. Except for the slides, the gun, and Robin Stapley's driver's license and various cards, it's exactly like I found it."

"Where's that evidence?" Irene asked.

"Evidence locker room."

"If you agree, I'd like to have Cosner's car moved up to the impound yard in San Francisco."

"I have to check with my superior," Wright answered, "but I don't see any problem. A missing person means more than shoplifting. Besides, once you look in the car, I think you'll agree this is a lot more serious than even a missing person."

Homicide, Eisenmann thought, what else? Lake didn't swallow death because of car theft.

In a few minutes Eisenmann had received permission to move the car. He told Brunn, "You take the gun and the license, I'll have the Honda towed to our impound yard."

After signing a receipt for the car, Eisenmann scanned the interior of the five-year-old vehicle. Through the opened window he could see a dark maroon stain on the front passenger's seat. There was another hole in the inside of the door on the passenger's side. There was a bullet hole where the passenger's sun visor should be.

Eisenmann thought sadly, Paul Cosner's dead.

In the South City Police Station's evidence room, Policewoman Irene Brunn studied the driver's license: Robin Stapley, San Diego. She called the San Diego police. Robin Stapley, she was told, was one of the founders of the Guardian Angels in San Diego. The Guardians were a paramilitary national organization, started in New York City, to "assist" the police in urban areas.

She learned Robin Stapley had been missing since April.

MONDAY, JUNE 3, 1985, 9:00 A.M.

Eisenmann drove into the San Francisco Police Department's impound yard. He checked with Inspector Hopper, Homicide, who had made a preliminary inspection the night before, then began to search the Honda himself. In the glove compartment he found some old repair bills, all in the name of Cosner. Scraps of paper and receipts littered the passenger side of the car. There were two spent shell casings under the front seat.

He spotted a Pacific Gas & Electric bill.

The bill was made out to Claralyn Balazs, with a post office box address in Wilseyville, California. The town didn't ring a bell to Eisenmann.

He continued the search, but the PG&E bill was the only item that potentially pointed somewhere.

Who was Balazs? he wondered. Was she another missing person? There couldn't be too many women with a name like Balazs in the whole state.

Where was Wilseyville? And more importantly, what was the address of the property? A P.O. box didn't help.

Eisenmann called the business office of the Pacific Gas and Electric Company and ran a quick computer check on Balazs. Within minutes her name came up on older PG&E bills in Philo, California. Then a skyrocket went off—the older bills showed another name on the account as jointly responsible. The name was Leonard Lake.

Inspector Hopper called telephone information and learned that a Balazs was no longer listed in Philo. Another check was run—this time with the Department of Motor Vehicles in Sacramento. Claralyn Balazs showed a San Bruno address, on Cabrillo Street, just a few miles from the lumberyard.

Two hours later Tom Eisenmann met Brunn at the Missing Persons station. He told Irene what he'd discovered from his check on Balazs. "I have Claralyn's current address." He held up a slip of paper. "Let's pay her a visit."

"Inspector Hopper has already called me," she said. "We have an appointment with Claralyn at noon."

Eisenmann, Brunn, and Hopper arrived at the Balazs residence promptly one hour later. Waiting for them were Claralyn Balazs; Gloria Eberling, Lake's mother; and two of Lake's sisters.

Irene Brunn explained the events of the previous day, then asked Balazs, "You are married to Leonard Lake?"

Claralyn said, "Was married to Lake. We broke up over two years ago."

"Why's your name on a P G and E bill in a car he was driving—a car we now know is registered to a missing person?"

"When we lived in Philo we were married."

"Philo? The bill has an address in Wilseyville."

"Wilseyville's off Route 88, above San Andreas. There's a cabin there my father owns."

Brunn asked, "When did you see Leonard last?"

"I haven't seen Leonard in months. I don't see what this has to do—"

"We have a link between Paul Cosner, who has been missing for months, and your ex. That's why we're talking to you."

"I can't—"

"The front seat of Cosner's car is covered with blood. Two shell casings were found in the car. This could be a murder case. We want to see this cabin. What's the address?"

"It's difficult to find."

"Then we want *you* to show us," he insisted.

"Now? I want to visit Leonard. He's in a coma. Can we do it tomorrow morning?"

Eisenmann motioned to Hopper and Brunn and they went outside. He said, "Let's get her to agree on first thing in the morning. Besides, we have to get clearance from the Calaveras Sheriff's Department. It's their jurisdiction. I doubt it will come through today anyway."

They rejoined the two women. Claralyn agreed to meet them the following day. "Ten o'clock is fine," she said. "There's a grocery store just outside of West Point, at the intersection of Blue Mountain Road. Can't miss it."

Claud Ballard had been the sheriff of Calaveras County for years. His imposing figure was well known in San Andreas, the county seat, but he had few occasions to deal with other jurisdictions. The phone call from Eisenmann Monday afternoon took him by surprise.

He agreed to let San Franciscan law enforcement agents enter his jurisdiction, adding that he wanted two of his officers present. He also agreed to have his police cruisers make passing calls made on the Blue Mountain Road property.

"Passing calls?" Eisenmann said. "We think this is potentially big. Could you send someone to secure the property, just for the night?"

"I only have a roster of thirty-two full-time personnel. Can't afford to lose even one for guard duty on an empty house. Sorry, but it will have to be passing calls."

TUESDAY, JUNE 4, 1985, 9:00 A.M.

After an early morning drive from San Francisco, Eisenmann and Brunn arrived promptly at the Calaveras County Sheriff's Office. They met the two deputy sheriffs assigned by Ballard to go with them: Detectives Norman Varain and Steve Mathews.

Detective Mathews, a narcotics officer, was a well-built man with a firm jaw and a finely trimmed mustache. Sheriff Ballard had sent him because Eisenmann had found a file on Lake in another county: suspicion of growing marijuana. Strangely, the county was Humboldt—on the Northern California coast some three hundred miles away.

The four officers drove to the grocery store. They swapped war stories while they waited for Claralyn.

Eisenmann mentioned one they all knew, the Collins case.

Kevin Collins had become a symbol both to the police and to the terrified parents of missing kids; his disappearance a year before was still a frustrating mystery. The Collins boy's face on milk cartons was the first of many.

Deputy Varain said, "That case was big news here. I handed out flyers for a long time, until the milk companies got involved."

"I know," Irene said. "That was my job, to contact the various law enforcement agencies."

Claralyn entered the grocery store a few minutes after ten. With her was Lake's mother, Gloria Eberling. Claralyn apologized, "We went to the cabin first. There were things there that—"

Eisenmann interrupted. "Mrs. Lake, I want you to step outside."

Detective Mathews said, "I'll accompany you."

Eisenmann tried to control his anger as he eyed Claralyn. "You're saying you came up before us?"

"Why do you want her outside?"

Standard procedure, Eisenmann thought—separate everyone when you think something's going on, and I think something's going on. Instead of answering her, he asked, "What did you do at the cabin?"

"There were some things there that are personal, and have nothing to do with this."

"I warn you," Eisenmann said immediately, "you may have obstructed justice." He was furious at himself—and at the system. Maybe he had let evidence get away. He should never have let Balazs come up alone. *Damn! The old problem of getting permission from every jurisdiction before entering.* He saw that Brunn was equally dismayed.

"If I told you what I took," Claralyn said, "you'd just laugh. But I don't want this in the press."

"Make us laugh," Varain said.

"Leonard liked to take pictures of me nude," she answered.

"What about the pictures?" Irene asked. "What else was in them?"

"They weren't really pictures, they were videos. I would be embarrassed if you found them."

Varain asked, *"Did* you find the videos?"

"Yes."

"What else did you take out of the cabin?" Eisenmann demanded.

"Nothing."

"Did you destroy anything?" Eisenmann asked.

"No. I don't have to put up with—"

"Let's find out what's in the cabin," Irene suggested.

The two police cars followed Claralyn's to the house. They turned left off Blue Mountain Road, went through a gate, then down a road for fifty yards. They made a hard left and went up a driveway. There was a cinder-block structure on their right. The house was straight ahead. There was a new growth of pines and foothill oak around the property.

The ranch-style cabin was built on a platform that kept it above the occasional runoffs after heavy winters or flash floods from summer storms. The attached carport was vacant. Parked nearby were an old Plymouth sedan and an even older, gray Chevrolet pickup truck with personalized license plates that read: AHOYMTY. There was obvious damage on the driver's side of the truck.

The house's high-pitched roof created a second-story bedroom, but the roof line was barely visible from Blue Mountain Road.

Irene said to Claralyn, "This is remote, but not that remote. Given proper directions, I could have found this place."

Claralyn fumbled for a key without answering, opened the front door of the house and stepped back. She held Gloria Eberling's arm protectively.

Detective Varain suggested, "Irene and I can search inside the house. Steve, why don't you stay here—with Gloria and Claralyn?"

Eisenmann nodded. "I'll check the grounds."

Irene glanced at her watch: ten-twenty. She made a mental note of the time as she and Varain entered the front room.

Irene was in her element in a search like this. "A woman's touch," went the common wisdom in the Missing Persons locker room, but it was simply the eye of a detective, looking among the commonplace for cause and effect.

It was a two-bedroom, one-bath cabin. There were dried spots of dark maroon on the Sheetrocked living room ceiling. An Olympia typewriter sat on a desk in the corner. Next to it was a turntable. By the desk was a guitar and a guitar case.

One wall was covered with a painting of a forest going through the colorful changes of autumn. There was a bullet hole in the center of the scene.

On the left side of the mural were a lamp and a cabinet.

The kitchen was ordinary, except for wallpaper displaying a full-sized depiction of Buffalo Bill. A bullet hole gaped in the linoleum floor.

The spare bedroom was painted purple. The bed had a multicolored bedspread. There were a nightstand and a lamp on the left side. There were two oak-framed mirrors hanging on the wall.

The master bedroom was painted light green, the carpet and drapes dark green. An empty gun rack decorated a wall. Tied to each of the corners of the four-poster bed were electric cords. Fastened to the wall behind the bed was an outdoor light, 250 watts. Eyebolts were anchored into the floor, one at each corner of the bed.

Cause and effect, Irene thought, feeling slightly sick. I don't have to be Sherlock Holmes to imagine what went on here.

She opened the top dresser drawer. It was filled with women's lingerie. They were in a variety of sizes, some torn, some with dark maroon stains on them.

She went back into the front room. Varain was writing

down the identification numbers on the twenty-five-inch television set. He turned the VCR on. It flickered to life. It was a tape of *Hill Street Blues.* Larue was attending an AA meeting with Captain Furillo. He turned it off.

Irene went back into the master bedroom. The bed had a colorful quilt on top. She grabbed one end and lifted. Underneath was a mattress covered with a dark, maroon stain.

She returned to the front room. She spotted two pieces of video equipment on a book shelf. She went over, put her reading glasses on, and studied the Sony cassette player and a Hybrid 8 generator—a professional-quality piece of equipment for mixing tapes.

A Hybrid 8 generator? she thought, bells going off in her mind. The Dubs case flooded back. A year earlier, on June 25, 1984, Harvey Dubs, his wife Deborah, and their sixteen-month-old son Sean had disappeared from their residence. It was a shocker—second only to the disappearance of the young boy, Kevin Collins.

During the course of the investigation, a list of property stolen from the Dubs residence had been compiled. Among the items missing were a Sony cassette player and a Hybrid 8 generator.

Irene copied the serial number of the cassette player. The serial number on the generator had been filed off.

Using the radio in her car, she called the Calaveras Sheriff's Department and was forwarded to the San Francisco Missing Persons Unit. She got Inspector Glen Pamoloff, her regular partner, on the line, and read the serial number of the Sony to him.

Pamoloff pulled the Dubs file, thumbed through it and quickly came back. "Verified. The serial number is the same."

Irene disconnected. Verified, she thought. Two pieces of video equipment missing from the Dubs residence on Yukon Street in San Francisco had found their way to a bookshelf in a remote cabin in Calaveras County.

The Dubses are dead.

She told Deputy Varain what she had discovered.

"Seize the property," he ordered.

The property was secured. Eisenmann and Mathews stayed with Claralyn and Gloria Eberling. Brunn and Varain drove back to San Andreas and went to the District Attorney's Office. They spoke with Assistant D.A. John Martin, laying out the evidence they had discovered so far.

He agreed that there was enough to request a search warrant. They found Judge Douglas Mewhinney in his chambers. They presented the evidence unearthed so far. Mewhinney was a scholarly, even grim-faced jurist who took his time with everything. This time he immediately signed a search warrant for the house on Blue Mountain Road.

Varain and Brunn returned to the remote property.

"I want to talk to Claralyn," Irene said. She saw Lake's ex-wife sitting on the front porch and went straight to her. She asked, "You said you came here to get videos?"

"Of me and Leonard."

"Mrs. Eberling, is that correct?"

Gloria Eberling sat, her chin on her chest, and twisted the strap of her purse into a tight knot.

"Mrs. Eberling?" Irene repeated.

Claralyn said, "Leave her alone."

Irene noticed the clouded look of anger on Claralyn's face. She's mad, Irene thought, but so am I. Calm down, calm down, you get nothing from a witness when you're angry. She wanted to keep questioning Claralyn. But was it an interview, or an interrogation? Did she suspect her personally of doing anything criminal? If she did, Irene knew, she had to read her her rights.

I don't have evidence to suspect her yet, so I can keep questioning her. This is still an interview.

She said, "Claralyn, when did you buy this house?"

"I never bought it," Claralyn answered, "my parents did."

"Your parents?"

"They bought it from the fat guy."

"The fat guy?"

"I haven't seen the fat guy in ages," Claralyn said.

Irene thought, I'm blowing it, the interview is wandering all over the place. I'm emotionally upset at what I suspect. First Cosner's car, now the Dubses' video equipment. Two families, totally unrelated, linked to this house.

She knew the Latin side of her nature was overrunning the professional side.

She thought, I need help. She walked to the driveway and approached Eisenmann. "I need—"

"Look at this," he interrupted. He pointed at a bumper sticker on the rear of a beat-up Plymouth. It read: IF YOU LOVE SOMETHING, SET IT FREE. IF IT DOESN'T COME BACK, HUNT IT DOWN AND KILL IT.

Irene said, "That's chilling, unless it's a joke."

"Then what I'm going to show you next is really unfunny."

Eisenmann led her to an incinerator. It was squat, built of stone, with a blackened pipe rising from the top.

Using a branch, Eisenmann flipped the latch on the metal door. He pointed inside with the stick.

"What?" Irene asked.

"This thing's a kiln." He tapped the inside wall with his stick. "That's high-end fire brick. Capable of withstanding three thousand degrees."

She reached out toward the white powder covering the hearth.

"Hold it!" Eisenmann ordered.

"Why?"

"We can't touch this until the lab looks at it. Look at the fire walls inside this—you don't need three thousand degrees to burn trash. This thing is built like . . ."

"A crematorium."

Chapter Three

TUESDAY, JUNE 4, 1985, 10:30 A.M.

THE NURSE OPENED THE HOSPITAL ROOM door and went to the foot of the bed. She made an entry—patient still alive.

Pretty amazing, she thought, after the amount of cyanide he had ingested. She went to the side of the bed and leaned over. The man's eyelids were closed. Nothing suggested life except a steady noise from the respirator.

The nurse studied the equipment beside the bed. Various screens showed the steady heartbeat, the flat line of brain waves, the erratic pulse. The nurse shook her head and thought—this guy's brain dead.

Lake saw the nurse through the twin slits of his eyes. Help me! he screamed. Nothing came out. Then the blackness returned.

Deep in the blackness was a point of orange-red light, which buzzed like an electrical transformer. Inexorably the burning point came toward him, growing into a pulsating fireball. The pain filled his head to the point that he thought his cranium would explode. Then came a snap as feral as the breaking of a chicken bone, and he was plunged again into blackness.

The point of orange-red light started again in its endless cycle of pain.

* * *

The nurses monitoring the life-support systems for Leonard Lake were seeing minimal brain-wave activity. Yet his pulse was normal, even elevated. Still, liver functioning was poor, and pumping more drugs into the soon-to-be carcass would only overload the lungs.

The intravenous feeding of antibiotics and a saline solution were not going to reverse the massive brain damage of the cyanide. The tissues had already swollen; the cerebral cortex now pressed against the entire dome of his head. The visual centers were overwhelmed. The eyelids quivered from time to time, but no light entered. And yet, deep in the brain stem, where dreams are, there was a glowing coal.

"Who is this guy?" the physician asked, miffed. He had a way of cutting through the niceties about the "sanctity of life."

"Leonard Lake, Doctor."

The physician said, "This guy's taken pills to void his life, and yet here we are, working around the clock to make sure he doesn't die too soon. What irony."

"We emptied his gut," the young nurse volunteered. "The lab said there was no question about it being cyanide."

"But a coma, induced by cyanide, shouldn't take this long to—"

"My question too. Everybody's different, is all the lab would tell me. And we've flooded him with charcoal."

The physician felt the man's pulse and listened briefly to his irregular breathing. "You've checked his eyes?"

"No reaction."

"You've notified the nearest relative?"

"His mother was here yesterday afternoon—after the police."

"Is she going to pull the plug?"

"She hasn't made up her mind yet."

TUESDAY, JUNE 4, 1985, 11:00 A.M.

"Unfortunately," Eisenmann said, "our search warrant doesn't cover that structure." He pointed at the concrete-block, windowless bunker. For an out-building, it was large, perhaps four hundred square feet. The rear of the building butted up to an embankment. He said, "That's too big to be a wine cellar."

Irene said, "It's not underground, so it's not a bomb shelter. And if it were a workshop, it would have windows."

"A photography dark room?"

"That big? Maybe for a metropolitan newspaper, but here?"

Irene stared at the foreboding building. All about it the dried spring grass lay in brown, dead clumps. There was evidence of garbage and burn pits. "Let's try to get Claralyn to sign a waiver."

They walked back to the porch, where Balazs and Mrs. Eberling were sitting on a rough bench. He took out a note pad and said, "Ms. Balazs, I want to thank you for your cooperation, so far."

He watched the look of gratitude flash across Claralyn's face. He continued gently, "You do want to cooperate completely in this investigation, don't you?"

She nodded.

"I'd like you to sign a waiver and consent form so we can search that concrete bunker."

"I don't own this property."

"You pay the utility bills."

"I still don't own it."

"You have a key to the house."

"Yes."

"Do you have a key to the bunker?"

"Leonard called it his fallout shelter."

"Do you have a key to the fallout shelter?"

"No."

"Who has?"

"Leonard."

"Not on him. I saw the personal effects taken after his arrest: wallet, cash, coins, some keys, but no key to a padlock."

"I don't have a key."

"We don't need a key," Eisenmann said, "just permission to enter."

"I think you should ask my father, he's the owner."

Change tactics, Eisenmann thought, then come back to the bunker. "What do you know about a man named Charles Chitat Ng?"

Claralyn said, "Ing. That's the way his name is pronounced. It's spelled N–g."

"What about him? Who is he? Why haven't you mentioned him before?"

"You never asked. He was a friend of Leonard's. Charlie Chitat Ng."

"Cheetah?"

"That's how his middle name's pronounced. It's spelled C–h–i–t–a–t."

TUESDAY, JUNE 4, 1985, 11:00 A.M., CENTRAL STANDARD TIME.

Charlie Chitat Ng was on the run. He knew it had gone bad in the lumberyard parking lot.

They'd pulled that "he's my friend, he doesn't understand" scam. Charlie shoplifted, Leonard was the backup. The plan was if something happened, Leonard would jump in and pay for the item with apologies and cash.

After the nosy customer followed him out of the store, Charlie decided to split. He'd crossed the street and waited behind some bushes.

He'd watched the squad car arrive; watched the conversation between Leonard and the policeman; watched the policeman hold the gun with silencer aloft; watched Leonard get arrested.

Leonard was always a fatalist. Even when laughing his eyes looked sad. I'm not. I'm a survivor.

Ng took off at a jog. Once safely away from the South

City lumberyard, he paused to plan. He knew where he wanted to go. He could board a bus, or flag a cab. But that would leave him vulnerable. He decided to run.

South from the lumberyard he headed to Old Bayshore, then over to El Camino. Soon he was walking down familiar streets to Claralyn's home. She was someone who had helped him before.

She was surprised to see him. She asked where Leonard was. The story spilled out. Ng went to her phone and called his attorney, Garrick Lew, in San Francisco. Then he called his landlady and asked if his paycheck, from the Dennis Moving Company where he worked part time, had arrived. She told him it had.

Then the call from Inspector Hopper came. He told Claralyn that her ex-husband, Leonard Lake, had tried to kill himself.

Ng asked Claralyn to drive him to his apartment. She agreed. When they got to Lennox Street, in the West Portal District of San Francisco, he made sure there were no police cars in the vicinity.

Charlie entered his basement apartment and got his other Ruger .22 and some shells. He packed the items and some clothes in a suitcase and dumped them in the car. He picked up a California driver's license and a Social Security card, both in the name of Mike Kimoto. He grabbed an envelope with several thousand dollars in cash.

Ng remembered what Lake had said: "If anything ever comes down, I'm not running."

"I am."

"Do your own thing."

"Where should I run to?"

Leonard had said, "I know the perfect place."

TUESDAY, JUNE 4, 1985, NOON.

On the porch of the rustic Wilseyville house, Tom Eisenmann opened a notebook. He made an entry and thought, *records and details. Each entry, done properly, means a clear, unassailable delivery on the witness stand.* Suspects changed their testimony, but so did witnesses at just as surprising a rate. People forgot things, twisted them in their minds, remembered things that hadn't happened, forgot things that had.

Eisenmann hated interviews in the field. An interrogation room offered so many advantages, like closed circuit TV, Dolby sound, serenity, soundproofing, seclusion.

He looked around. There was a squirrel chattering on a tree stump. Birds chirped on a nearby ponderosa pine. The wind was spreading the scent of spring: cut grass, new life.

This will have to do, he thought, and led Claralyn and Irene to some lawn chairs. He moved his chair next to the one Claralyn sat in, making sure that he had the high ground.

Tom asked himself, what do I know? We have a missing person, Paul Cosner, and his stolen car containing possible blood stains and two empty .22 shells. We have a .22 with a silencer, and a man using a driver's license issued to the Guardian Angel Robin Stapley, of San Diego. We have a suspect trying to kill himself with cyanide, and a woman who dashes up here with her ex-mother-in-law to look for nude videos of herself. We have a Sony and a Hybrid 8 generator known to belong to three missing persons: the Dubses. We have a house with a blood-soaked mattress, two bullet holes in the kitchen floor, a bullet hole in the front room wall, and a master bedroom with enough light to be a film studio.

Snuff flicks?

Dear God, Eisenmann thought, I pray not.

He wondered, what approach should I use? Indirect? Direct? Subterfuge? Emotional? And all the other subtle choices: unsympathetic or consoling, blunt or repetitive, lies or truth?

I'm still not sure what happened at that cabin, he thought, just enormously suspicious, so I'll use indirect.

Plus, what do I really know about Claralyn? She was cooperative on Sunday at her mother-in-law's house.

She's been cooperative since we met her today, showing us the way here, not interfering in our initial search.

The only blip I have in my head is her coming up last night.

Investigative detectives have to have good imaginations, visualizing possible scenarios. Eisenmann thought, I think of two possibilities off the top of my head. One, she was involved somehow in whatever went on here, and came up early to remove evidence; or, two, she's exactly what she appears to be—a distraught woman who realized that the police would find embarrassing videotapes involving her and Lake.

I don't have anything near enough in evidence to suspect her of anything. Which means this is an interview and not an interrogation, and I don't have to read her her rights.

I'll request information. Maybe I'll find a discrepancy. Plus, I'll use sympathy. It usually works. Especially as this woman has someone who was once close to her dying in the hospital.

Eisenmann had learned from many a gruesome case how sex or dominance or delusions can make people do strange things. He said to Claralyn in a gentle voice, "I heard this morning that Leonard is still hanging on at the hospital."

"Yes."

"It must have been difficult being married to him."

"Sometimes it was happy. Sometimes it was sad."

"I know about marital sadness. I got divorced a few years ago. It was not a very harmonious breakup."

"You're not the only one," Claralyn said.

Irene thought, Tom likes to use the "hot and cold" interrogator or interviewer method; from friend to antagonist, then back to friend. That tactic was very disconcerting to people, disorienting them.

Tom said, "Not the only one what?"

Claralyn said, "That's dealt with a divorce."

"Are you comparing your ex-husband to my ex-wife?"

Cold, Irene thought, definitely chilly.

"No, no, no," stammered Claralyn.
"Oh," Tom said, "sorry."
"Sorry?" Claralyn said.
Getting tepid, Irene thought.
"Very sorry," repeated Tom, "for comparing your very unfortunate marriage to mine. It must have been hell being married to Leonard."
Claralyn said, "Not always."
"Why don't you start at the beginning?"
"I met Leonard at the Renaissance Faire in Marin County. He was a good-looking man, clean-shaven except for his mustache. I remember he had one of those serf hats that peasants wore in the Dark Ages. I had on a white dress, with a garland of flowers in my hair. He worked a booth where he charged people to have their pictures taken with his pet goat."
"Pet goat?"
"Leonard had rigged the goat up to look like a miniature unicorn."
"Unicorn?"
"Named Sir Lancelot. The goat had a phony horn in the center of its forehead. It was done surgically." Claralyn began to relax. She was on comfortable ground now. "Lennie asked for a date. We courted for a while, then he asked me to marry him."
"Marry him?"
Irene smiled faintly. Tom was using the interrogation tactic of repeating the last thing the suspect said. It had a marvelous effect of goading the person into continuing to talk. And it kept Mrs. Eberling out of the conversation.

Eisenmann noticed Claralyn's hands; they were fidgeting. A poet once wrote that the eyes are the mirror to the soul, he thought, but I don't believe it: the hands are.
She said, "We found a small church in South San Francisco. That's when Lake introduced me to a roly-poly buddy, his best man."
"What about the roly-poly buddy?"
"The fat man, I call him, paid for the champagne and

food at the wedding. He was five foot eight and weighed three-fifty to four hundred pounds."

Eisenmann watched her rub her stomach with both hands. Her mid-section was tiny, firm, yet her hands waved away from herself, creating the image of a bulbous body.

"What was his name?"

"Charlie Gunnar."

"Where is he?"

"I haven't seen him in years."

"Where did he used to live?"

"Morgan Hill."

"After you married, what happened?"

"We moved to Philo, in Mendocino. Leonard managed a motel there. I was a teacher's aide at Anderson Valley Elementary School."

Eisenmann was familiar with Anderson Valley. He and his wife had spent a long weekend there recently. The valley was off the beaten track of the touristy Northern California wine centers: Napa Valley, Sonoma and the Valley of the Moon.

"I've been there," he said, and watched her fingers drum in a languid rhythm on her thighs.

She said dreamily, "Our neighbors were organic farmers and dairy ranchers. The whole thing seemed like a honeymoon that could go on forever."

"Then you started having problems?"

"The break came not quite a year after our wedding. That's when Charlie Ng arrived at the ranch and moved in with us. Leonard told me that Charlie, like him, had been a Marine."

Eisenmann watched her hands move about like snakes, twin cobras doing a hypnotic dance.

She continued, "We got along pretty good for five months."

"What happened?"

"One morning I saw an Army truck pull up. A SWAT team of FBI men got out. Leonard and Charlie were taken to jail."

"What charge?"

"Stealing weapons from a Hawaiian military base. That's what the Army told me, anyway. They found the stuff in our woodshed. Bail was set at thirty thousand dollars each. My husband phoned Gunnar and he raised it. Leonard was released. His trial was set for early August eighty-two. Charlie couldn't raise bail."

Eisenmann asked, "Is that when you split with Leonard?"

"Yes." Her hands fluffed her hair, played with her earrings, fiddled with the strap of her purse.

Eisenmann thought, I've got the background, time to dig into the meat. He asked gruffly, "Did you buy this house for your ex-husband?"

"I already told you. My parents bought it. They're going to use it as a retirement home."

Eisenmann studied her hands. They brushed nervously back and forth over each other. "Where's Ng?"

"How should I know?"

"When did you last see him?"

Claralyn's demeanor suddenly changed. Her jaw set.

Eisenmann saw it. She changed when I mentioned Ng. Does she know anything? Do I push, or wait?

He spotted the concrete bunker and thought, what I really want is to get into that. He said, "Will you give us permission to enter that concrete building?"

"I can't. It's not my property."

Eisenmann watched Claralyn and Mrs. Eberling get into the Pinto and drive it down the gravel road toward Route 88. He had no authority to hold them. All he could do now was prepare the papers for the Calaveras District Attorney's Office that would allow them to get an additional search warrant for the bunker.

Blast, Eisenmann thought. He should be in the pen for two more years, till 1987. Did Leonard Lake lie when he said the Asian with him was Ng?

"Ng was released last year, May 'eighty-four."

Eisenmann thought, Bingo! Back on track. He called

his captain and asked him to get someone to check out Charles Gunnar. He waited ten minutes, then called S.F.'s Missing Persons. He asked the captain if anyone had checked up on Charlie Gunnar.

"Yeah, me. We're so short-handed around here I had to do it myself. Always underbudgeted and understaffed. When are you guys coming back?"

"A lot later than I thought. What about Gunnar?"

"I talked to Victoria, his estranged wife. She says she reported him missing to the Morgan Hill police two years ago. Also, Officer Wright phoned—the San Diego police told him Robin Stapley has been missing since April seventeen, this year."

Eisenmann's pulse began to pound. *Good God! I have hard evidence connecting Lake to four independent missing-persons cases: Cosner and his Honda Accord, the Dubs family and the camcorder and Hybrid 8 generator, Stapley and his gun and driver's license, and now Charles Gunnar, the missing best man. I've got bullet holes in a car and in a house. I've got a mattress that looks like a cow was butchered on it. Plus Lake tries to commit suicide immediately following arrest. If all this doesn't point to homicide, then nothing does.* He asked, "How's Lake doing?"

"Still in a coma."

"Ah."

"You sound disappointed he isn't dead."

"I'm disappointed he isn't conscious. I'm aching to interrogate him. Captain, we need to hit this place with everything we've got. We need a task force."

Chapter Four

TUESDAY, JUNE 4, 1985, 1:00 P.M.

EISENMANN'S REQUEST WENT IMMEDIATELY to the top. Police Chief Cornelius Murphy interrupted his lunch to put together a twelve-man task force of San Francisco police headed by Joseph Lordan, Deputy Chief of Inspectors. Murphy then called Claud Ballard, Calaveras County Sheriff, who also formed a special unit. It was agreed that Joe Lordon would lead the San Francisco team and Calaveras Sheriff's Lieutenant Bob Bunning would head the sheriff's unit. Claud Ballard would supervise both, when possible: otherwise Bunning would be in charge, with Detectives Steve Mathews and Larry Copland directly under him.

TUESDAY, JUNE 4, 1985, 1:30 P.M.

Inspector Richard D. Adkins picked up Dorice Murphy from her home on the end of Yukon Street. Sooner or later, she knew this day would come.

The spry old woman asked, "This has to do with the Dubses, doesn't it?"

"I can't really explain, Mrs. Murphy. I am merely to take you downtown so that you can look at some pictures."

She pointed at a house. "My neighbors have been missing for almost a year. This has to do with them."

The investigator said, "I'm not at liberty to discuss

this." He drove her to the Hall of Justice on Seventh and Bryant. There Mrs. Murphy was shown six photographs of Asian males.

She picked out the photo marked Number Four.

Inspector Adkins drove her home and then picked up Mrs. Murphy's neighbor, Barbara Speaker. She was a tenant who lived below the Dubs family. The ritual was repeated at the Hall of Justice.

Barbara Speaker also picked out the photo marked Number Four.

TUESDAY, JUNE 4, 1985, 2:30 P.M.

The police officers had finished cordoning off the Blue Mountain Road driveway and cabin with yellow tape, and had eaten lunch. They were now assembled at Ballard's command post. A space had been cleared in front of the cabin, under a large pine tree. Already a county truck had disgorged an array of furniture: two desks, a few dozen folding chairs, some garbage cans, and two large tables—one for the lab and one for the pathologist.

Sheriff Ballard was a substantial man, with big, beefy hands and a moon face. He turned to the group of assembled officers and said, "I'll be handing out assignments in a minute. But first, I want suggestions on how to break into that bunker."

Various ideas were fired off.

"Sledgehammer."

"Knock it in with a backhoe."

"Jackhammer."

"Locksmith."

"At last," Ballard said, "someone with a suggestion that will leave the clues intact. Get a locksmith."

Eisenmann reported to the sheriff on the preliminary inspection he and Brunn had done. "Next to the concrete bunker, the ground's been disturbed in a circle approximately ten feet in diameter. Also, there's a substance that strongly resembles lye."

"You suggesting a grave site?"

Eisenmann shrugged. "There's also clothing visible in the telephone trench that runs from here to the base of the hill."

"Start on that first," Ballard said. "Label it Site One." He turned to the dozen officers in front of him. "I want you men to begin a quadrant search of that trench, starting at the base of the road. I want each quadrant to be a five-by-five square, that's feet, not yards. I want Mathews and Copland doing the itemizing of whatever's found."

TUESDAY, JUNE 4, 1985, 3:30 P.M.

Steve Mathews sat at one of the large tables under the cluster of oak trees. At the next table the Calaveras Coroner, Terry Parker, who had just arrived, was setting up his equipment.

Mathews was in charge of cataloging the items brought in from the quadrant search. Thc men working the telephone trench would place any items found in a neat row a few feet away from their work area. Periodically, Deputy Sheriff Larry Copland made the rounds carrying a garbage bag.

Sandy-haired and tanned, Copland was a poster-perfect peace officer, the kind who was "going places." His boyish good looks had turned heads in the secretarial pool in the office. Few people knew the kind of work he handled daily. Now this.

Copland would note the location of each item found, date and sign the article, and place it in the bag. Then he would carry the bag back to Mathews.

Mathews entered thc latest delivery into a log book.

Quadrant twelve. Items: sixteen empty Budweiser cans, an empty pack of matches from the Gold Rush Cafe, a rusted Phillips screwdriver, and three sixteen-penny galvanized nails.

Eisenmann watched the process and thought, Why aren't we digging? He was annoyed with sifting through garbage. He went to Ballard's desk and asked, "Why haven't you brought in heavy equipment?"

"In time, in time."

"No one's even examined the incinerator." Eisenmann pointed angrily toward the squat outdoor furnace positioned a few feet from the bunker. "Can't we at least analyze what's in that thing?"

"Patience, Tom. Besides, the lab crew isn't here yet. We do the surface search, then we excavate."

"But—"

"Tom, the odds are astronomical that so many separate cases, all separately tied by different evidence, are coincidental."

"That's what I think."

Coroner Terry Parker turned from his table and added, "Me too."

"So," Sheriff Ballard said, "let's take our time and do it right."

Eisenmann asked, "Sheriff, are you going to have a surface search done on the whole property?"

"I'm thinking about using dogs for the general search."

The coroner chimed in, "Don't worry, Tom, we'll find bodies."

"You're sure?"

"I saw maggots, and in more than one location. They're not the kind that like to chomp on garbage. These maggots are carrion eaters."

Eisenmann brightened. He went back to the telephone line trench. He sifted through the dirty bottle caps and bits of paper. Then froze.

There was a bone! Thin, perhaps an inch long, snapped off at one end.

Maybe a finger bone. He picked the bone up with tweezers and carried it to the table where the coroner sat.

Terry Parker was doing a crossword puzzle, glasses perched on the end of his nose. He looked up. "Something?"

"You tell me." Eisenmann dropped the bone onto the white sheet of butcher paper covering the table.

Parker studied the bone. "Not human. Looks like a chicken wing."

TUESDAY, JUNE 4, 1985, 5:00 P.M.

Ballard ran down a list of conjectures he wanted to verify. *Is there direct evidence of Ng and Lake having lived at the cabin? Is there anything more than a Hybrid 8 generator to connect the Dubs family to the case? Is there any physical evidence linking Paul Cosner to this site? Or Charles Gunnar?*

He called a meeting of all personnel. There would still be hours of sunlight, in case anyone was thinking of home and family.

Fifty-one-year-old Deputy Chief Bunning had arrived with five more officers in the sheriff's department. They joined the San Francisco contingent, which had grown to twelve with the arrival of the extra personnel sent by Chief Con Murphy. The combined San Francisco and Calaveras force interrupted their tasks and assembled at the foot of the driveway. It had been a typically scorching summer day, approaching one hundred degrees, and had not cooled down much with the approach of evening.

The sheriff lumbered onto the hood of his jeep and said, "I want to make one point crystal clear: mistakes made in the gathering and protection of evidence at a crime scene can never be rectified."

The twenty officers shuffled nervously.

Brunn thought, Good, Ballard's a book man, despite his "Smokey and the Bandit" appearance. Do it by the manual.

Ballard asked, "Deputy Chief Lordan, do you want to add anything?"

Lordan was part of the long tradition of Irish policemen in San Francisco. He was quiet, scholarly. He thought for a minute. "I don't want any of you scribbling your notes on scraps of paper. I know all about that habit and the flights of fiction that follow at the office when you're trying to decipher your own notes. It always comes out at trial and taints your testimony. Use notebooks, make your entries when you discover something, make them legible, note the time, be precise."

"Are we going to do a sweep?" County Sheriff's Detective Larry Copland asked. Despite his all-American boyish looks, he was looked up to by his fellow officers. As a seasoned veteran, his usual duties involved narcotics investigations.

"Not yet," Ballard cautioned. "I want a lid on this, no comments in town, no asides to your spouses or bartenders. A lid! The longer we have to work in peace without the world press trampling over the evidence, the happier I'll be."

Lordan added, "This isn't the big city, where you can block access with a few squad cars at various intersections." He waved an arm at the surrounding ponderosa pine and Douglas fir. "We're in the wide open spaces. It will use up a lot of manpower to keep people out of here —once they get wind of this."

The sheriff called the milling police officers to attention. "I'll second that motion. Now I want you to set up protection for this entire area."

"We already protected the trench, the house, and the—"

"All the property."

"This place is huge, over two and a half acres," one officer complained.

"So? I want the entire property roped off. I want more yellow crime-scene tape. I want this driveway barricaded. If any of the press get in, I'll have someone's butt. Let them take long shots from behind the barricade. No posing for photographs, unless I okay it. And I don't want any of you clumping around the property either, until we do a quadrant search. Stay on the perimeter when hanging the tape."

"The property's not fenced."

"Then give me at least a two-football-field circle from the house. Make that three football fields; tape's cheap to come by, evidence hard."

Lordan agreed, then turned to Eisenmann. "You were one of the first officers on the scene, right?"

"Yes, with Sheriff Deputies Norman Varain, Steve Mathews, and my partner, Irene Brunn."

"The sheriff wants to talk to you four."

The law enforcement officers stood in front of the sheriff. He asked, "Where are your notes?"

Four notebooks appeared.

Ballard asked, "Who opened the cabin door?"

"Claralyn Balazs," Eisenmann answered.

"Was the door locked?"

"Yes."

"Who went in?"

"Varain and Brunn."

"Where were you, Tom?"

"Doing a preliminary search of the grounds. Balazs and Eberling were ordered to wait on the porch. Officer Mathews stayed with them to make sure they didn't compare stories."

"You weren't part of the house search?"

"No."

"How about the windows, the lights, the drapes?"

Irene looked at her notes and said, "Closed, off, and no drapes at all."

"Odors?"

"Stale, musty," Deputy Varain answered.

"What time did you enter?"

"Ten minutes after ten."

"You had waiver and consent?"

"Yes."

"You did the search?"

"With Varain," Irene said. "Very thorough. We kept an inventory list."

"I need a copy. Were firearms or weapons found?"

"Just kitchen utensils. A butcher knife and a few carving knives. We made sure to tag and put them in plastic bags."

"How did you handle them?"

"I used my revolver and slid them off the kitchen counter into the plastic bags."

"I assume no one smoked, used bathroom towels, or the toilet?"

"No."

"Was anyone here when you arrived?"

"No."

Ballard glanced at his watch. "Where's that locksmith?"

Irene said, "I contacted one in San Andreas. He can't get here until tomorrow, mid-morning."

Ballard asked Irene to begin drawing a detailed sketch of the property, the cabin, the bunker, and the approximate location of the various trees. He finished with, "Include the next-door neighbor's house, the one up there on the hill."

Irene left.

Ballard told Varain and Mathews, "Start on an organizational chart. I think this thing's going to start escalating on a life of its own, and if we don't start right now, we're going to be overwhelmed."

The sheriff glanced at the lengthening shadows, then at his watch. He thought, The coroner from San Francisco should be here in half an hour. He tried to use the radio in his squad car. Too much interference.

Give me a phone that works, he pleaded. He went inside the house. The house phone hadn't been dusted for prints. It was off limits.

He saw that Irene Brunn was back already and drawing a crime-scene sketch. He pointed at the next-door neighbor's house up the hill and asked, "Contact the people who own that." It was a nice-looking home, painted green and partially screened by foothill oak. "Ask the owner if we can tie into his phone line." He pointed at his jeep. "The radio in that thing's worthless, too much static."

Edgy, Ballard looked outside the cabin for a trash pile. He found one in the telephone line trench. He thought, I know there's a live phone line eighteen inches under the ground. I'd love to tap into it. The trench was a hundred feet long and a couple of feet wide. It was littered with garbage.

He thought, It's surprising what evidence can come out of what people throw away.

Using a thin branch, he began to shift through the debris. Occasionally he would unearth something: an empty bottle, beer cans, soup cans, bones that were easily identifiable as the remains of T-bone steaks.

The two deputy sheriffs began making an organizational chart of the authorities on the scene. The S.F. crew now consisted of three detectives from headquarters, the two officers from Missing Persons, a three-man team of dog handlers, a forensic specialist, two patrolmen, and Deputy Chief of Inspectors Lordan. Even for a major case, this was a lot of personnel a hundred and fifty miles from home. And there were eight deputies on duty from Calaveras County.

A ninth deputy drove up and gave Sheriff Ballard a manila envelope. It was from San Francisco Police Chief Con Murphy. The file was on Leonard Lake.

Ballard read: *Lake joined the Marines on Jan. 27, 1964. He served seven years, two tours of duty in Vietnam, the first at Da Nang, the second for only one month.*

Lake was returned to El Toro Marine Base in Orange County. Reason: unspecified medical problems.

Lake received the Vietnam Service Medal, two Good Conduct medals, and a Vietnam Campaign Medal.

Ballard thought, No Combat Action Ribbon. That meant he hadn't seen action, he was stationed behind the lines.

He continued to read: *After getting a medical discharge, Lake lived in San Jose, California, for five years. He married Claralyn Balazs, nicknamed Cricket. In 1981, they moved to Philo.*

Ballard thought, Not much. But Lake's still alive. He might live to be questioned.

Irene came back from the neighboring house. "I called the owner of the property." She flipped open her notebook. "His name is Bo Carter. He lives in Burlingame. He has agreed to allow you to tap into his phone line."

"Great," Ballard said, "great."

"I called the telephone company—they'll have you hooked up in less than an hour."

"Fantastic."

"Mr. Carter also told me that his tenants—a man named Lonnie Bond, his common-law wife, Brenda O'Connor, and their infant, Lonnie Bond Jr.—didn't pay their rent when it was due on the fourteenth, last month. He called his real estate agent, who drove here."

"And?"

"And a man from this cabin came over and ID'd himself to the real estate agent as Charlie Gunnar."

"Gunnar?" The sheriff opened a file. "I thought so. That's the same man we identified from a Golden Crest Travel receipt in Lake's pocket. It was made out to Charles Gunnar." He flipped through the file. "And Lake's ex, Claralyn, told Eisenmann that Gunnar was Lake's best man at their wedding. Eisenmann ran a check on him. The Morgan Hill police said Gunnar's been missing for two years."

Irene said, "The man IDing himself next door as Gunnar said the tenants had been gone ten days—that they'd skipped out on the rent."

"Three more people missing? And one an infant?"

"There's more. The real estate agent said that another man was living here with the young couple. His name was Robin Stapley. Stapley was the name on the driver's license Lake gave Officer Wright."

"Another missing person?" Ballard said in disbelief.

"There's more," Irene went on relentlessly. "The real estate agent said he noticed that freshly turned soil has been layered on an eroded bank where his property meets this property."

"Fresh dirt," Ballard said, and thought, Four more. How many does that make? Cosner, the three Dubses, Gunnar, and these four, that makes nine. "I'll get someone on it immediately."

Irene said, "Bo Carter drove up here last Friday to check out his property. A man showed up, said he was

Charles Gunnar, and followed him around while he inspected the house. Carter said he found some items were missing, bedding and appliances. When he mentioned it, the man became agitated and kept saying that he didn't know anything about where the things went."

"Did Carter get a description?"

"Better. Carter told me that he recognized the man, who called himself Gunnar, on the San Francisco Channel Four news. After Lake took cyanide, they ran a local interest spot about crime and punishment on Sunday night showing his photo. The news spot, obviously, only speculated on why Lake killed himself. None of what's happening here is public yet. I didn't fill Bo Carter in on why I was calling. But that's how Carter learned the man's name was really Leonard Lake."

"Was there anything in the house that suggested foul play?"

"Just this. There is a tiny back room in that house. The only access to it is through a sliding panel."

"A hidden room?"

"Not really, just hard to find. Carter went into the room and found two suitcases filled with female and infant clothes."

"So?"

"Nobody skips out and leaves clothes behind."

Chapter Five

WEDNESDAY, JUNE 5, 1985, 9:00 A.M., CENTRAL STANDARD TIME.

CHARLIE CHITAT NG LAY ON THE BED IN HIS hotel room at the Chateau Hotel, in Chicago. He'd registered as Mike Kimoto.

He reread the entire *Chicago Tribune.*

Not a word.

No mention of Lake taking cyanide.

No mention of the cabin in the woods.

Maybe Lake died fast, he thought.

Maybe he died and didn't say anything.

Maybe the police didn't see him take the pills.

Maybe the police put it down as a heart attack.

He relaxed.

He began watching a movie on TV, *Winter Kill,* with Andy Griffith, Sheree North, and John Calvin. It was a fictitious story about a small town in a remote mountainous region where people were being mysteriously murdered.

An hour later a bellboy rang his hotel room and gave him Tuesday's *Sacramento Bee.* Charlie read the paper. Nothing: no mention of Lake's trying to kill himself, no mention of the bunker, nothing.

Charlie wondered, What's going on?

Was Leonard alive or dead?

WEDNESDAY, JUNE 5, 1985, 9:30 A.M.

The point of orange-red light began to fade, and from the blackness emerged gray shapes.

A finger twitched.

The alpha wave needle began to gyrate. REM sleep had begun, in which the muscular system was paralyzed—allowing the mind to postulate all sorts of fears without the slightest ability to move the muscles of speech.

He began to come out of the coma, feeling the plastic hose in his nostrils. He couldn't tell where his breath was coming from. Once again the orange-red light became a fireball and exploded in his head. His lips quivered as he tried to whisper. No sound came as he formed the plea "Morphine."

WEDNESDAY, JUNE 5, 1985, 10:00 A.M.

The second day of thc investigation of the Wilseyville crime scene began under another sweltering sun. The locksmith arrived. Sheriff Ballard made sure the additional search warrant, covering the block house, had arrived from the D.A.'s office. He ordered the locksmith to go ahead. The man knelt by the steel door to the bunker for a few minutes, then the door swung open.

Eisenmann and ten other officers tried to peer inside.

"Everybody," Ballard yelled, "line up."

The officers sheepishly formed a line.

"I want all of you, with the exception of Irene and Eisenmann, to join the quadrant search."

Eisenmann looked inside the bunker. Pitch-black. The light outside shone in only a few feet. He turned on his flashlight.

What the hell is this? he thought.

The beams of light flickered eerily over dim shapes.

Irene stood behind Ballard and Eisenmann in the doorway of the bunker. They had been joined by Jim Stenquist, a Calaveras County information officer.

Irene could smell an unidentifiable odor, faint, yet still pungent. The inside of the bunker was warm and dry.

"Don't touch anything," Ballard ordered.

Irene looked around. The room was about twelve by twenty. It was obviously a workshop. One wall had various tools hanging from nails on a four-by-eight sheet of plywood. There was a hacksaw, pliers, heavy duty chain cutters, a hand saw, a drill, and two circular saw blades. There was a workbench.

"There's something wrong with the dimensions of this room," Irene said. She went outside and paced, then returned. "Outside is twenty-one by twelve, inside sixteen by twelve."

They searched. They found a latch on the edge of the four-by-eight sheet of plywood. The tool rack swung open, revealing an interior room.

Inside was a double bed, with a wooden end table covered with books and a reading lamp. Irene snapped on the light and turned off her flashlight. Military equipment was scattered about: boots, fatigues, canteens, bayonets, gun belts, and a Coleman lantern.

There was also an array of armament: rifles, shotguns, assault weapons, machine guns.

There were two surgical gloves, a hairbrush, two cases of Coca-Cola, and mouthwash.

There was a crude wooden plaque on the wall. Written in red ink above it was: *Operation Miranda.*

She read the words chiseled into the plaque: *The Warrior's Code—For those . . . who even at the risk of defeat, will enter the arena. . . .*

Ballard said, "I want this stuff itemized—and analyzed."

Irene started writing.

Meanwhile, Eisenmann found a shirt on the floor. Above the pocket were the words *Dennis Moving Service.* A baseball hat with the same company's name on it was picked up in another corner of the room.

Numerous envelopes, with the return address to the Philo Motel, were found on a desk.

The rear wall contained a bookcase. On the shelves were a first-aid kit, a book on explosives, another on chemicals, and magazines on guns. There were manacles, handcuffs, and three knives, all long, all sharp.

A small window around which the bookcase was built was sandwiched between the novel *The Collector* and a copy of *Principles of War.* The window's dimensions were a foot by eighteen inches, and it looked out at nothing.

Irene thought, No windows on the outside of the structure. Why is there a window inside?

On a shelf was a Starlight Scope on a tripod. The scope amplified moonlight or starlight reflecting off an object, magnifying the light fifty thousand times. At that degree of enhancement, a votive candle a half mile away looked like the sun.

Thumbtacked to the left-hand wall were twenty-one photographs of women. They were all young, mostly teenagers, some even adolescent.

Where were these taken? No telling. Not enough clues.

The background in nineteen of the photos was outdoors. The remaining two had an unusual background: wallpaper depicting scenes from nursery tales: Little Bo Peep, Jack and Jill, Billy Goat Gruff.

Irene thought, Could it be? She explained to Eisenmann, "I think I know where those were taken."

"Call it in to S.F. and have someone check it out."

Irene said, "Would you do it for me, Tom? I want to check something else out."

She felt a stab in her stomach. *Possibly twenty-one more.*

She again paced the outside of the bunker. Then she paced the inside.

Eisenmann returned and said, "I called your idea in to Missing Persons."

Irene interrupted him. "There's still something wrong with the size of this bunker. I paced the outside dimensions. There's still three feet missing."

"There's definitely no inside door?"

"No."

The missing feet were behind the area of the interior

window. But Eisenmann and Brunn could see nothing in the pitch-blackness of the window. Their flashlights reflected the eerie glare of the pane.

"Look at the window caulking," Irene said. "I know that stuff, it's soundproofing." She tapped the windowpane. "Hear that? That's not single-pane glass, and I don't think it's double-paned either. At least triple-paned. If you were on the other side of this window, you couldn't hear a five-K generator roaring in here."

Irene went outside. The lab crew from San Francisco was unpacking their equipment from a van. She asked permission to find a way into the hidden room in the bunker.

Lordan decided, "This mystery will have to wait until the lab does their stuff on all the property. That won't be until tomorrow." Brunn knew the routine.

Sheriff Ballard introduced the San Francisco lab crew, which was made up of two men and a woman, to his own staff. He made it clear whose neck was on the line. "I want an impeccable chain of custody on anything discovered. I want intense protection of evidence, no alterations or the possibility of alterations. There will be no negligence or accidents on this crime scene."

The combined lab crews shuffled nervously.

Ballard said, "One of you take full responsibility for transporting what's found from here to my desk. You all know what we suspect happened here. Fingerprints could be vital in establishing identifications."

The lab crew went to work on the bunker first.

The technician put on plastic gloves. He found a fingerprint on the window. Using a brush, he dusted the surface lightly and stepped back.

Irene photographed the print. She took out the photo, signed the back, dated it, marked the location of where the shot was made, and put it in a manila envelope.

She took it to Ballard.

Ballard sat at his outdoor desk and peered through a microscope at the first print taken. "Looks like an adult's," he said. "The ridges are too far apart to be a child's. I'd guess, left hand, forefinger."

Lt. Bob Bunning volunteered, "I'll call the Marines at El Toro and have them send up a copy of both Lake's and Ng's fingerprints." Bunning was a good foil for his sheriff: smoothly professional, low-profile, not likely to run for office.

"Have them send on Ng's file. We don't know much about him."

"Will do. Is that print any good?"

"This is a full, clear print," Ballard said. "There should be no trouble getting the mandatory ten points that's required by California law."

Another fingerprint was found in the bunker. The lab technician used cellophane tape to remove this one. The tape went through the same procedure: photographed, dated, signed, then sent to Ballard's desk.

Other prints were found on the window glass. They were in patterns indicating that two hands had leaned up against the window. Even palm prints were visible.

These samples made their way to Ballard's desk. He ordered Irene Brunn to get fingerprints from as many of the suspected missing persons files as she could. "And get another table set up, a big one. Every law enforcement agency in California is going to be sending us their missing persons files."

WEDNESDAY, JUNE 5, 1985, 2:00 P.M.

As the second day of the fieldwork wore on, word of the investigation in Calaveras had yet to hit the news media. But if a police reporter had been tracking the in and out slips at the San Francisco Hall of Justice, a pattern would have been obvious.

San Francisco Detective Ed Erdelatz entered the FBI offices on the seventh floor of the Federal Building in San Francisco. He was wearing rumpled slacks and a cashmere sweater. Several agents gathered around him. They were wearing three-piece suits. Their hair had been cut within the last week: their sideburns were carefully trimmed above mid-ear.

Erdelatz rubbed a hand over his two-day stubble of beard. His was a well-known name in the City, and his own career in high-profile cases had brought him to the Feds many times before.

The conference room of the FBI soon began filling with investigators.

Erdelatz spread his papers on the lectern and immediately began to address the group. "Pardon my appearance, but I drove back from Calaveras this morning. We have a fugitive from a capital case. Our fugitive has been overseas."

Agent Karen Alexander added, "His name is Charles Chitat Ng. We've already notified Interpol, but we think we have him confined to the States."

Erdelatz went to a chalkboard. He drew six small circles on it in a horizontal row, labeling them meticulously: Hong Kong, Hawaii, Yorkshire, Calgary, Chicago, and Toronto.

He tapped the chalk on the board. "Ng's father lives in Hong Kong, he's a wealthy businessman. Ng has ex-Marine friends in Hawaii. He has an uncle in Yorkshire. He has sisters in Toronto and Calgary. Yet he ran to Chicago. We've kept a good lid on this. So far, the papers are out of it. Ng may think we're doing nothing."

"When was Ng in England?"

"Ng went to prep school there in the seventies."

"I'll touch base with Scotland Yard," said a middle-aged agent in the rear of the room.

"Who are you?"

"I do psychological profiles for the Bureau."

Erdelatz nodded. "I'll provide you with any information we have. Ng's father trades with all the Commonwealth countries. This is going to be a worldwide search."

WEDNESDAY, JUNE 5, 1985, 2:00 P.M.

The midday heat was dizzying in Wilseyville. Every hour loomed larger as the evidence began to mount on the examination tables.

Next to the driveway, what appeared to be two bones were found. They were taken to Terry Parker. The coroner puffed on his pipe as he examined them. "I think one is a vertebra and the other comes from a leg, but I can't be entirely sure."

"What do you need?" Ballard asked.

"I don't have the equipment here to make a positive identification. Get someone to run these down to the Department of Justice crime lab in Stockton."

WEDNESDAY, JUNE 5, 1985, 2:30 P.M.

Free-lance reporter Tomasina Boyd Clancy was in Davis, California, a small farm town in the Sacramento Valley, famous as the home of one of the largest campuses of the University of California. But she wasn't here to interview a Nobel laureate or to report on the partying habits of the college generation. She had hoped to get an exclusive interview on the biggest espionage case of the decade.

She clicked off her radio. Nothing had gone national yet. And she had the first account of the arrest, in Davis, of Jerry Alfred Whitworth. Whitworth had been implicated with the accused traitors, the Walker family, and had just been charged with conspiracy to commit espionage.

Clancy had a network of "moles" throughout all major U.S. cities—reporters or civilian clerks who worked in the accounting offices of metropolitan police forces. They were all men. They were all rather plain-looking. Clancy's red hair matched her personality: dazzling.

Besides making her contacts' hearts beat faster every time she met with them, Clancy paid a five percent finder's fee on any lead that ended in a sale to a magazine or a newspaper.

Five percent wasn't shabby; Clancy made a lot of money.

She drove through downtown Davis, past the university campus. Using a cellular phone, she called her home in Chicago. She picked up her calls from her answering machine. She had three calls—from her contacts in Atlanta, Philly, and San Francisco.

In a minute she had a San Francisco reporter who covered the police department on the line. "Twelve officers were—"

"Give me the background," Clancy ordered, and pulled onto Interstate 80. She headed toward San Francisco at sixty-five miles an hour.

"Two patrolmen, one policewoman, one deputy chief, three lab crew, one pathologist, three dog handlers, and a specialist."

"What's the specialist do?"

"He's Tom Eisenmann, the top authority on child abuse and child pornography."

Clancy's speedometer edged toward seventy. She said, "What else?"

Her mole continued, "Wednesday morning none were at their regular stations."

"Anything else?"

"Everyone's talking about San Andreas, in Calaveras County, California."

Clancy pulled off the freeway, took out a map, and found her target. Back on Interstate 80 to Sacramento, southeast on 99 to Lodi, straight up 16, dead south on 49. An hour, an hour and a half, tops.

She pulled into San Andreas and parked around the corner from the Black Bart Hotel one hour and twenty-eight minutes later, at precisely four in the afternoon. She walked down the quaint, narrow street, flanked with 1850s brick buildings. She went into the hotel's dimly lit bar. Hanging behind the bar was a huge picture of the dapper, distinguished stagecoach robber, Black Bart.

Clancy ordered a Bloody Mary, with Beefeater. A group of four people entered and sat at the end of the bar. A few minutes later another three came in and sat at the other end.

Locals, Clancy thought, from the look of the 49er caps, Levi's, denim work shirts. The only woman was dressed in an immaculate white blouse and a knee-length white skirt.

Nurse, Clancy thought. She watched the woman down a shot of Wild Turkey and corrected, Beautician.

Clancy sat on her stool and kept her mouth shut. She said nothing, except the six times she closed off the attempts by the males in the bar to hit on her.

She listened. They talked about an up-and-coming quilt fair that was going to be held Saturday at the local Grange. They talked about last Friday night's softball game and how the team from Mark Twain St. Joseph Hospital waxed the pants off the bums from Pine Mountain Lake.

Every subject discussed was benign.

Twelve San Francisco police officers, Clancy thought, didn't just drop everything and head up here to attend a quilt fair.

She asked directions to the sheriff's office and left. At the sheriff's office she told the clerk that she was thinking of moving to the mountains.

The clerk began praising the attributes of Calaveras in general, and San Andreas in particular. "Friendly place," he said.

Clancy eyed the man. The clerk looked back at her lacy blouse.

She said, "I don't know, I've heard that crime—"

"No crime," the shocked clerk said, looking up for a moment and forgetting her blouse.

Clancy studied the large personnel status board on a far wall. It showed the whereabouts of the county's officers.

Eight were checked out to BMR.

What was a BMR? she wondered. And more importantly, why did it need eight officers? She pointed at the board and said, "If there's no crime, why are eight officers checked out to BMR? And what's a BMR anyway?" She fluttered her eyebrows.

The clerk frowned. "I can't tell you that."

"I thought there was no crime in this town."

She watched the officer. All flirting was gone from his face.

This is big, she thought as she left the sheriff's office. Definitely big.

WEDNESDAY, JUNE 5, 1985, 5:00 P.M.

The second day of the investigation at the cabin was winding down. The results on the two bones that had been discovered were disappointing. The Department of Justice in Stockton had not been able to make a conclusive finding on what had appeared to be a vertebra and a portion of a leg.

Lordan suggested using Dr. Boyd Stephens, the San Francisco Chief Medical Examiner and Coroner. He was called immediately, and said he could make it the next day. He would make arrangements for any bones found to be transported back to the Bay Area, and San Francisco's more sophisticated equipment.

At first the lab crew in the bunker didn't have any better luck than the Department of Justice. There was a momentary round of excitement when they discovered a rust-covered spot, but after performing tests microscopically, microchemically, and running a spectrographic analysis, they learned that it was just that—a rust spot.

Damn, Sheriff Ballard thought.

The lab crew discovered a bullet hole in a wall of the main bedroom. They pulled out a .22 slug and sent it to the lab table.

Then, in the same room, they found the diary.

The small, spiral-bound book was tied to the springs under the double bed. After the lab crew lifted prints and photographed it, Ballard took the diary to his command post and began to read.

A few minutes later he put the diary down. It had been

written by Leonard Lake. Ballard was nauseated. *Unbelievable. This explains the bedroom scene in the house. The bastard has been hunting, raping, and killing people.*

He decided to read the diary later. Right now he had to push for more evidence. He looked out at his battlefield. The officers were working their way up the telephone line trench.

The sheriff wandered over. Steve Mathews said to him, "We just found a camera in Site One."

The sheriff said, "Tag it and have the film sent down for development. Make copies of the film and send them on to Ed Erdelatz in the City."

Norm Varain held up a metal logo—it read Suzuki.

"Tag it," Ballard said. He watched the D.A.'s investigator, Crawford, pick up a small photo. He was aiding the law enforcement agents in collection, packaging, sorting, transportation, and identification. His main job was liaison on the progress of the case with Calaveras County Assistant D.A. John Martin.

Ballard asked, "What have you got?"

"It appears to be a photo of a small white baby." Crawford flipped the photo over. "It's very deteriorated, but I can make out some writing on the back: Stephanie Jennie Carr, three and a half months, 7–81."

The sheriff wondered, How many are buried here?

Years earlier his county had been a sleepy retreat for rural people and retirees.

He thought, Has it been turned into a graveyard?

Eisenmann, Brunn, and Stenquist stood at the open doorway of the bunker. The lab crew had finished its work.

Brunn pointed at the interior window and said, "There's got to be a way in there. It'll be simple when we find it."

Eisenmann said, "There are no trick doors outside. The exterior is solid concrete cinder block." As he talked, he led them into the now-lighted room. He said, "In this room there are three walls made of concrete block and—"

"A floor-to-ceiling bookcase," Irene completed excitedly. "The same bookcase that has the interior window facing the missing space."

They looked along the edges of the bookcase. A spring release catch was found behind the first-aid kit. Eisenmann pulled the lever; the bookcase swung out.

There was a door behind the bookcase. It had two hinges and two throw bolts; both were secured. He peered at the two hinges. "These appear to have been bent, then pounded back into shape."

The bolts were thrown, the door swung open.

Eisenmann squeezed in and began measuring. The room was three feet three inches wide, seven feet six inches long, and six feet high.

Eisenmann studied the tiny room. There was a roll of toilet paper on one wall, a single shelf with a one gallon plastic water container, a dirty towel, a can of air freshener, and a can of ant repellent. There was a narrow wooden bed, no pillow, no sheets.

The back of the door was painted the same gray color as the other three walls. There were tiny air holes punched out in a row along the top, six feet high. There was blocking on the other side of the air holes, a clever system that allowed air to flow, but damped out any light coming from the larger room. When the door and the bookcase were shut, one got the feeling one was entombed. No light—no sound—no air movement.

The floor was concrete. There were no outlets for electricity. Eisenmann ran his hands along the walls. The texture of the concrete block was the same, even on the backside of the door. The only break to the monotony of the walls was a small mirror on the wall.

This is two-way glass, he realized; on the reverse side is the interior window. He stepped out of the tiny enclosure. With the bookcase open, letting some light in, one could see through the window into the small enclosure.

He asked Irene and Stenquist to go into the small room. They crammed in.

Eisenmann swung the bookcase shut. He noticed a small button, partially hidden under the window frame.

He pushed it and heard Stenquist say, "Look at this. On the wall. Someone's written: 'Cliff, P.O. Box 349.' "

Eisenmann thought, Without those flashlights in there, I wouldn't be seeing anything. So what's the purpose of this two-way window?

He thought for a moment, then took the Starlight Scope off the bookshelf. He opened the bookcase and asked Irene and Stenquist to shut off their flashlights. He closed the bookcase.

Looking through the interior window with the Starlight Scope, he saw the eerie, purplish-pink shapes of Irene and Stenquist. They both looked edgy.

How long could a person stand being locked up in that room? Eisenmann wondered.

He'd read articles on sensory deprivation. No sound and no light quickly brought a person to the brink of insanity.

How long were people kept in there? This was worse than solitary confinement, where at least you had light, air, noise.

How long could I last?

A day? A week? A month?

Then would I be willing to do anything, anything at all, to get out? What sort of depravity went on here?

He swung open the bookcase and asked, "Now can we get some heavy equipment in and start digging?"

Chapter Six

WEDNESDAY, JUNE 5, 1985, 6:00 P.M.

THE PARKING LOT OF THE CALAVERAS County Government Center was empty, except for a few police vehicles. At closing time there was a mass exodus. Now Tomasina Boyd Clancy waited across the street from the sheriff's office. There was a park, complete with baseball diamond, at the top of a hill. It afforded a view of the valley and all the relatively modern government buildings.

She sat on the grass and looked through her binoculars. She hoped a bus or a truck would have shown up carrying the missing eight county police officers. None did.

Too bad, she thought. If they were being taken by bus back and forth to wherever they were going, they were working late.

There's other ways to skin a cat, she thought, and drove back into old-town San Andreas.

She went back to the Black Bart Hotel's bar. There was a crowd of men bunched at the end near the door, all of whom simultaneously gave off low, husky wolf whistles. They were all wearing cowboy hats. There were two groups of tourists sitting at tables, and three couples at the far end.

Clancy took a stool in the center. She ordered a martini and asked the bartender to tell the galoots at the end of the bar to buzz off. But she knew it was only a "boys will be boys" scene.

A woman in her mid- to late thirties took the bar stool next to her. She had long, red hair, just like Clancy's, except that it was done up in a ponytail and slung over one shoulder.

Clancy introduced herself and learned the woman was Shanda McGrew. She lived in nearby Mokelumne Hill. The woman appeared very upset.

T.B. asked, "Are you all right?"

"No, not really. My mother is dying of cancer. I just found out she's getting worse."

What can I say? Clancy thought. Her dad died of cancer. Her mother of a stroke. She remembered the feeble words, the rote sympathy, the standard mumbling of compassion.

Despite herself, Clancy said, "I'm sorry for your trouble."

"Are you Irish?"

"Why?"

"That's an Irish expression."

"Half Irish."

"You don't live here."

"No, Chicago. Have you ever heard of a BMR?"

"A BMR? No, I can't say I have."

If this woman knows anything about what is going on, Clancy thought, she sure isn't letting on. She asked the bartender for a telephone book.

According to the listing, the county coroner was named Terry Parker. He was also listed as Public Administrator and Public Guardian. She looked up his address in the phone book. She unfolded a local map and found his street.

She thought, If the coroner's not involved in this, then I'm not interested anyway.

WEDNESDAY, JUNE 5, 1985, 7:00 P.M.

The sun was going down fast over the valley beyond San Andreas. Sheriff Ballard returned to his office at the Calaveras Government Center. He sat behind his desk and took out a legal-sized piece of paper.

Organization, he thought, I need organization. Lines of help—each department utilized for what it could best provide.

He penciled in *Office of Emergency Services.* Underneath he wrote: *Need mobile van with its work stations.*

Next he wrote: *C.A.R.D.A.—California Rescue Dogs Association.*

He reached in his desk and pulled out a standard form from the FBI. For this type of case there were several possible areas of help listed:

1. Branch assistance
2. Develop Federal Fugitive Warrant
3. Coordinate and supervise international search
4. Performance of ballistics tests
5. Conduct out-of-state and International interviews
6. Behavioral Science psychological profile

Who else can I tap for help? Ballard wondered. He carefully wrote:

California Department of Justice (DOJ)
1. Latent prints
2. Criminalistic Lab
3. Missing Persons Unit
4. Personnel
5. Facilities for processing evidence
6. Forensic Lab
7. BOCI Homicide analysis unit

What else? More manpower, I need manpower. And money—lots of money. This thing was going to cost a bundle, and no way could Calaveras County, with its fewer than thirty thousand citizens, afford to pay it all.

He added a dollar sign to his list and put it away for the night. It was time to get home, to rest for what was coming tomorrow.

THURSDAY, JUNE 6, 1985, 5:00 A.M.

Clancy was up before dawn after her first frustrating day in San Andreas. She drove to a rustic area east of town. She parked her car down the street from coroner Terry Parker's house. The street was lined with Victorian houses, each clean, each painted an array of colors.

Half an hour later a man left the Parker residence, hurried to a 4 × 4 Jeep parked at the curb, and drove off. The jeep had the Calaveras County logo on the side.

Keeping a good hundred yards behind, Clancy followed him out of town and up Mountain Ranch Road.

She thought, Mountain Ranch Road, MRR, not BMR. BMR was the checkout code on the sheriff's status board signifying where the eight deputies had gone.

She followed Parker down a winding road that meandered through the forest. Thick pines flanked the road, an occasional meadow appearing in the distance. Seven miles out of town, Parker turned left onto Railroad Flat Road.

Railroad Flat Road. RFR.

She followed Parker for another six miles, through the same kind of primeval landscape. She passed a sign pointing the way to a rubbish dump, went by the few houses that constituted Wilseyville, and turned onto Blue Mountain Road.

Blue Mountain Road, she thought. This is it!

THURSDAY, JUNE 6, 1985, 6:00 A.M.

Ballard had arrived at his office early and continued to work on his hit list of necessities. It was the third day in the trenches, literally.

He decided, if the need called for it, to tap into the

California Department of Forestry. The CDF could provide extra equipment, prison labor, and, maybe most important, reports of smoke or fire without a permit in the Wilseyville area during the past two years.

He didn't think the people burning an incinerator on Blue Mountain Road had bothered to take out a permit. Why would they? It might just call attention to them.

Then again, maybe they took out permits to avoid attracting attention to the smoke.

He had to check both ways.

He wrote in "California Conservation Corps"—for possible labor for evidence gathering. He glanced at his watch and left his office.

He arrived at the crime site and stood with his hands on his hips. A team from CARDA, California Rescue Dogs Association, had arrived. The three dog handlers and their German shepherds lined up in front of him. The men were yawning, the dogs barking.

The sheriff said, "I want the dogs on leashes at all times. I want the search methodical. The dogs' quadrants will be twenty yards by twenty yards."

An hour later the dog handlers reported to Ballard that there was nothing obvious being found—a few dead birds and a decayed fox carcass.

Ballard ordered the heavy digging to begin. A backhoe was ordered from the county Road Management Department.

Eisenmann was called to the command center. A detective from San Francisco was on the phone calling from the Hall of Justice.

Eisenmann asked, "How's Lake doing?"

"He's brain-dead."

"Damn, I'm sorry. I want to question him."

"You're not alone. I've learned some things. Nearly two years ago, Donald Lake, Leonard's brother, went off on a gambling trip to Reno. He never returned."

"No one's seen him for two years?"

"His mother said he always wrote her."

"Did he ever write his older brother?" Eisenmann asked.

"When Leonard was in Vietnam."

"Leonard skipped bail about the same time Donald disappeared. Did he ever push Donald for money?"

"Still working on it."

THURSDAY, JUNE 6, 1985, 10:30 A.M.

The morning shift was leaving the hospital in San Bruno. The nurses who had to clean up the charcoal enema from the cyanide patient did not take kindly to the news that the bearded man's mother hadn't pulled the plug yet.

As the blood began to drain from his head, the nurses could see the signs of the end: the skin whitening, the jaw protruding, the eyes deepening. His face began to resemble a skull. Oxygen sucked in from the respirator gurgled down his throat with phlegm. There were spasms of gagging, then great gasps of air. The nurses checked his fingers. They had turned yellow.

THURSDAY, JUNE 6, 1985, 11:00 A.M.

Tomasina Clancy took hours scouting the perimeter of the Blue Mountain Road property. She had parked a mile past the driveway where Terry Parker had pulled off the road. She changed into good hiking boots, jeans, and a Pendleton shirt. She stayed well away from the yellow crime-scene tape that had been draped from tree to tree.

This is big, she kept repeating. Take your time. Don't foul up. There isn't another reporter within miles.

After walking the perimeter, she chose her surveillance spot. The hill, a hundred yards behind a greenhouse that was obviously empty, was ideal.

Clancy toted her telescope up the hill first. She went down and lugged up her parabolic reflector mike. On the last trip she brought a Coleman ice chest and a tape recorder.

The telescope was a good-quality astronomical instrument; it had no problem with the six hundred yards that separated Clancy from Sheriff Claud Ballard.

His face filled the lens. Beads of perspiration trickled down his cheeks.

It is hot, Clancy thought, and it's not even noon yet. She opened the Coleman ice chest and popped the tab on a Miller's Genuine Draft, the can still glistening from the shards of ice clinging to it. She slugged off five ounces of beer.

She took her time. There were over twenty people working around a house and some sort of concrete-block building. She aimed her telescope at each worker. Some were sergeants, some detectives, some inspectors. She could pick out a lieutenant, a captain, and the sheriff.

She focused in on Captain Lordan and thought, That guy looks familiar. Was I on a story he worked once? What were the big S.F. stories? Zebra, Zodiac, Dan White?

Nothing rang a bell.

She set up her shotgun mike. Using the small telescopic sights on top of the state-of-the-art microphone, she aimed it at Lordan. She fiddled with a few dials and heard a male voice say, "We found something."

Clancy peered through her telescope and saw a man, obviously a dog handler, hand over something small to Lordan, who said, "It looks like a bone."

Now this, Clancy thought, is what freedom of the press is all about.

THURSDAY, JUNE 6, 1985, 1:00 P.M.

Attorney Ephraim Margolin put down the phone and stared out at the bustling scene in Union Square. It was tourist season, when people came from perfectly good places to inspect store windows in San Francisco and talk about the coldness of summer weather here. Secretaries still on their lunch break jammed the park benches alongside panhandlers.

He had just received a phone call from Garrick Lew.

Lew was a criminal defense attorney for many unpopular clients, but he had never before been threatened by a federal agency. In fact, Lew had spent his adult life defending people who had nowhere else to turn. And now the FBI was threatening Garrick with jail. Ephraim didn't know where to begin.

He pushed a stack of file folders to the side of his desk and tried to recall the people he knew in law enforcement—preferably someone at the top. He ran through his Rolodex. Then he remembered: a United States attorney at the local FBI office had been the Sheriff of Santa Clara County years ago. Now there was a man he could trust; he had worked scrupulously with Ephraim on a false arrest case. Ephraim called the San Francisco office of the FBI.

"Bill, please understand. I don't have any idea why the FBI is on this case. All I know is that they've put out bulletins that the man is armed and dangerous—extremely dangerous. The man then calls his attorney from God knows where, and says 'Hey, the FBI is going to kill me on sight.' He's scared—his attorney told me so."

Ephraim swiveled in his chair and listened patiently, nodding but not breaking in. Under his desk were cardboard file cases, and steel file cabinets stood sentry duty at both sides. Two chairs were wedged in front of his desk for an occasional visitor. It was a busy office, and hot.

"The point is this, Bill: the FBI must have picked up that phone call. They barged into the attorney's office and demanded to know where his client was calling from. The attorney is Garrick Lew, an old friend."

Ephraim had the shock of silver hair of a musician or a physicist—a Leonard Bernstein or an Albert Einstein. It was no secret to those who met him in a courtroom that he liked to borrow from music or even quantum mechanics to make a point.

"What do I want you to do? Please, can you explain the law to your men?"

Ephraim spelled out the details to the U.S. attorney. Lew had represented this client in a misdemeanor case several years ago. Shoplifting, something like that. The charges were dropped when he later joined the Marines. He was now claiming he was innocent and wasn't armed or dangerous. And Lew either didn't know where the call came from, or even if he did, he couldn't release that information.

"Has the FBI called you?" the U.S. attorney asked.

"No—they couldn't know my connection with Garrick. But for all I know, they're monitoring any calls between us."

There was silence on the line for a moment. Finally Margolin heard, "Doesn't sound right. Better give me the name of the fugitive, if you know it."

Margolin checked his notepad. "Capital N, small g. Pronounced *Ing.* Charles Ng."

"Common enough Chinese name. I presume they gave a description in the bulletin."

"That's another point. I think all they have is his name and nationality. And already they've put him on the Most Wanted list. He may be Number One."

There was another long silence. Ephraim felt the wheels turning. He could visualize the attorney pulling up names on his screen. "Bill, understand me—at this stage all I want is to get the FBI out of my client's office. Doesn't 'client privilege' mean anything anymore?"

"You're right, of course. Even if Mr. Lew knew the origin of the call, he could hardly be forced to divulge it. 'Harboring a fugitive' is a little strong."

Margolin drew some arrows on his scratch pad as he listened. I'm missing something here, he thought. Why was the FBI in Garrick's office in the first place? Could the investigation be so serious that Lew was discovered from that old misdemeanor case, then his phone tapped?

He said to the attorney at the FBI, "Sounds to me that Ng is already on the FBI blotter for something else."

The answer came back instantly. "Sure. Any federal offense, any time in a federal penitentiary. I'll check it all out and call you back."

Margolin called Garrick Lew and happily announced

the lucky break. What if he had been in court when Lew called? What if he had never known the former sheriff of Santa Clara County? And what if Bill had been on vacation when he called?

He asked Garrick for a few more details about his client. "I can't give you," the reply came, "as much as what's in this afternoon's *Examiner.*"

Margolin penciled the day and the hour on his calendar and thought, This is something that's likely to grow.

THURSDAY, JUNE 6, 1985, 2:00 P.M.

Dr. Boyd Stephens, Chief Medical Examiner and Coroner of San Francisco, arrived at the site on Blue Mountain Road at the height of the afternoon heat. He unloaded equipment, then examined the two bones found the day before. He pronounced the vertebra and leg bone as human.

An administrative decision was immediately made that the San Francisco Missing Persons case be turned over to the Calaveras County Sheriff's Office as a homicide case.

Eisenmann heard. He asked the sheriff, "Can I use your phone?"

"Surc."

Eisenmann called the South City Police Station and got Officer Daniel Wright on the phone. He told him what had happened, then said, "I want to thank you."

"For what?"

"For impeccable police work. Many officers would have done it the easy way and taken a hike once the store was paid for the workbench vise. Because of you, a major case is breaking, potentially involving a lot of bodies. Because of you, Lake's dying in a hospital bed and Ng's on the run. Because of you, the killing has stopped."

One of the dog handlers found a four-inch bone. He marked the spot with a stake. The stake had a white flag on it, not unlike a miniature-golf flag. The flag was marked with an assigned number.

The dog handler carefully wrapped the bone in plastic and carried it back to the command center.

"What quadrant?" Ballard asked.

"Thirty-three."

The coroner examined the bone.

"Human," Ballard asked, "or animal?"

"Human," Stephens answered after peering through his microscope. "And almost totally decomposed. This bone has been sawed off at both ends. There is some soft tissue present. I'll remove it for toxicological analysis. We're going to need an anthropologist. I recommend Dr. Heglar, he's a specialist in forensic odontology."

"I've met him. I'll phone him right away."

"I won't need him for a few days," the coroner said. "Those anthropologists like their bones bleached and clean."

"What *do* you need?"

"Get me a soil sample from where this bone was discovered. That'll give me a general idea of how long decomposition took."

Stephens continued to examine the bone. The upper half was a grayish-white, the lower half brownish-black. He said, "The different colors indicate that this was only partially buried. That's probably why the dog found it."

The coroner removed the rest of the tissue from the bone. He wrote down the location on the bone where he had gotten each piece of tissue, tagged it, and put it in a plastic container. When he was finished, he immersed the bone in a dilute aqueous solution of trisodium phosphate and household detergent.

The bone would be allowed to soak for two days. The solution would remove whatever remaining tissue still clung to it. Once clean, the bone would be odorless and left to bleach in the sun.

Deputy Sheriffs Steve Mathews, Norman Varain, Larry Copland, and Ron McFall were bearing the brunt of uncovering evidence in the telephone trench that afternoon.

Ron McFall was TV's image of a cop—square-jawed,

clean-shaven, tall, husky. He had started his career with the San Jose Police Department and moved to the mountains in 1979, leaving the city because of the escalating crime there. He moved because he'd been afraid for his wife and three sons. Now, sifting the dirt, he wasn't sure he'd made the right choice.

The deputies were facing each other in squatting positions. A long line of officers worked the telephone line trench for a few minutes at a time, checking their discoveries with McFall and Copland. Irene Brunn joined them.

Eisenmann walked over and told her, "I called the office. No one's had a chance to follow through on your idea regarding the photos found in the bunker."

"What did the captain say?"

"He said he had more personnel up here than in his station."

"Sounds like him."

Eisenmann left.

Larry Copland asked, "How long have you known Eisenmann?"

"Ten years," Irene answered.

"He's soft-spoken."

"He's seen a lot. You wouldn't know it, but he's the top authority on child abuse and child pornography in Northern California."

"That's tough duty."

"He handles it all, the snuff flicks, the multiple child molesters, the mothers who suffocate their babies to get them to stop crying, the fathers who lock their kids in the closet."

"How does he stand it?"

Irene watched Mathews pull a T-shirt out of the disturbed earth. He dusted it off. It had the words Guardian Angels on the back. Another shirt appeared out of the crumpled dirt. It had a National Medical Home Care patch on the shoulder. He pointed. Above the left pocket was stitched the name "Scott."

Copland repeated, "How does Eisenmann stand it?"

"He believes what he does is more important than any other type of police work."

Copland was surprised. "Even homicide?"

"Especially homicide, as Tom likes to say. The victim's relatives notwithstanding: for the victim, the crime is over. You're dead. Period. In all other cases, from petty burglary to wanton rape, the victims are still breathing, still hurting and suffering."

"I never thought of it that way."

"Most people don't. And who suffers the most? And potentially the longest? The little kids. The kids Tom Eisenmann has spent his life trying to protect."

"You like him a lot."

"I like the way he works, and I like his guts."

"Why's he working a missing persons case?"

"We all pull a general caseload weekend shift once a month. Cosner's case happened on Tom's watch."

Irene watched Mathews and McFall hold a window screen horizontally. A deputy shoveled dirt onto the screen. The two sheriff's deputies, like forty-niners searching for gold nuggets, shook the window screen; dirt fell through and what remained was examined: teeth, small bones, buttons, and an occasional buckle. The items were tagged, put in plastic bags, and, with a log of the chain of evidence, sent to the table, where they were catalogued.

A green plastic garbage bag was unearthed. In the bag was a receipt dated July 24, 1984 from Captain Video, a rental shop in San Francisco. The receipt was made out to Harvey Dubs for two movies. In the same garbage bag was a letter addressed to Charlie Ng.

"This is incredible," Copland said. "Usually, you're lucky to find a clue once a week. We're turning up dozens with each shovelful." He held up a pinstripe shirt. The name "Scott" appeared again—over the right pocket.

Irene thought, The clothes and bones filtering out of the dirt sifting through the screens aren't just objects to be scrutinized as clues, they belonged to someone.

Who? A man? A woman? A child?

In her original investigation involving the Dubs family, she had seen a family portrait. The wife, Deborah, long hair draped over a shoulder, eyes twinkling, mouth smiling, was cradling her son Sean. The husband, Harvey, wearing a Film Festival T-shirt, had his arm around her. His hair was tousled, his head bent close to his wife. He looked happy, content, in love.

Real people. A real family. Missing for months.

Were they here? Did the tooth that the deputy sheriff just tagged belong to one of the Dubs family?

Tomasina Boyd Clancy slumped back and rested against a tree. She had watched the trench scene for an hour. This place, she thought, belongs in the Mother Lode. What a gold mine! What a story!

The sun would be going down in a few hours, then she'd be off to a phone.

How much, she wondered, and who? Somebody big, like the *London Sun*—maybe the *National Enquirer.*

The sun moved through its endless cycle, dropping steadily toward the horizon. The light and shadows around Blue Mountain Road shifted and grew longer. As the angles changed, places that moments before were in shadows suddenly were hit with sunlight.

One ray cleared an overhanging branch and warmed the lens of a stargazer's telescope owned by a free-lance reporter. The light refracted downward to the command post below.

Sheriff Ballard blinked and squinted. *Where is that light coming from?* He shielded his eyes with both hands and studied the terrain uphill. He moved slowly to his left, then back to his right.

There it is again!

Something—or someone, was up there.

He thought, Probably just a reflection off a beer can.

He went back to work, but a dark thought kept nagging at him.

Mathews and Copland found a floor mat in the carport. It was for a Honda automobile. This was tagged, signed, dated, and sent to San Francisco.

The lab crew had finished its examination of the dungeon at the rear of the concrete bunker.

The armament found in the bunker on Wednesday morning was being itemized.

Lordan would examine a weapon, call out its stats and serial number. Eisenmann would methodically list it in his notebook.

Lordan had a collection of old pistols in his office in San Francisco. He liked to show visitors one in particular, an old frontier gun with a small cup for powder next to the flint. "This is what they mean when they say something is a flash in the pan," he would tell visitors. "The flash better hit the fire chamber, or there's no shot."

Lordan pointed at the growing inventory of lethal weapons. He said, "It's nice to be prepared."

"For what," Eisenmann said, "World War Three?"

Part Two

The Hunt

Chapter Seven

THURSDAY, JUNE 6, 1985, 4:30 P.M.

AN OFFICER STUMBLED DOWN THE HILLSIDE, his eyes wide. "Where's Ballard? We've found two bodies."

Two skeletal remains had been discovered in the telephone trench. A crowd quickly gathered, but everybody was ordered back to work by Sheriff Ballard. A stretcher was brought, the first skeleton tagged and sent to the table where the coroners were working.

The Calaveras County coroner, Terry Parker, studied the grisly remains. With him was San Francisco Coroner Stephens.

Parker said, "This body's been badly burned."

Stephens said, "We need the photographer."

The photographer arrived, took one look, and rushed to a nearby portable latrine. Once composed, the photographer went back to the table and grimly began taking photos.

THURSDAY, JUNE 6, 1985, 5:00 P.M.

The sun was slipping behind the trees. It will be dark very soon, Ballard thought. He carefully put one foot down, gently probed for anything among the fallen pine needles and cones that would make a sound, then shifted his weight and repeated the performance.

Whatever caused the reflection he'd seen had disappeared, but the nagging itch in his brain hadn't gone away. He'd thought about ordering someone to investigate, but had decided to do it himself.

He had been careful in his approach. It might only be a beer can, he thought as he touched the handle of his gun, but then again, maybe not.

He edged around an outcropping of rocks.

Fifteen feet in front of him was a woman, her back to the sheriff, facing down the hill. She had brilliant red hair and was seated on a tree stump. She drained a beer, crushed the can, and looked through a telescope. A small sound speaker rested on the stump next to her. Next to that was a tape recorder. A wire ran to a mike.

Ballard heard Mathew's voice come over the speaker, "Dark soon, time to call it a day."

"I agree," the redhead said.

"So do I," Ballard said.

The redhead spun around, almost falling off the stump. "Who are you?"

"Sheriff Claud Ballard, and you're under arrest."

"For what?"

"For . . . for . . ."

The redhead smirked.

"For trespassing."

"How do you know I don't own this place?"

"I've spoken with the owner."

"How do you know I don't have his permission?"

"Because we have his permission, even for the use of his phone."

Ballard led Clancy back down the hill. He asked, "Are you a reporter?"

Clancy said, "You're detaining me on false charges. I'll sue your butt off for false imprisonment."

"I haven't charged you with anything."

"I thought I heard trespassing."

"You did, but you explained that you had permission."

"In that case," Clancy said, "I'll be going."

" 'Fraid not," Ballard said. "I'm holding you as a material witness."

"What! For how long?"

"Just overnight, until I can contact a few reputable papers and get the press up here. Sorry, your scoop will be scooped."

THURSDAY, JUNE 6, 1985, 8:00 P.M.

In South San Francisco, at Kaiser Permanente Hospital, Mrs. Gloria Eberling signed the release form. That evening the life support system that had kept Leonard Lake's heart pumping was turned off by his physician.

The respirator and the intravenous tube swinging from the bedside stand were snapped from their holders by a nurse and dropped into plastic bags for disposal. The woman did not look at the body on the bed. When she finished turning off the instruments of survival, she walked quickly from the room and nodded to a policeman.

The officer entered the hospital room and gathered personal belongings from the table next to the bed, recorded the time, and copied a few lines from the physician's report on the patient's clipboard.

He removed a Polaroid camera from his briefcase, hovered over the lifeless face and pressed the button. The flash unit popped. The film developed slowly, revealing Leonard Lake's face, captured in color, three minutes after his death.

FRIDAY, JUNE 7, 1985, 6:00 A.M., GREENWICH TIME.

The early morning London train pulled into Birmingham, and the Scotland Yard inspector boarded the train bound for Leeds, Yorkshire. He was on his way to interview the headmaster.

Tea was ready when the headmaster received the policeman, who asked, "The Yard did call and bring you up on why I'm here?"

"Yes," the headmaster said cautiously. "I do not want the school's name mentioned. The tabloids would—"

"We're not looking for Ng here. Just leads. His sister attended school here also?"

"Yes."

"Do you have any idea where she went after graduating?"

"Why don't you ask her uncle?"

"Her uncle? And Ng's uncle?"

"Of course, he teaches here."

Dr. Rufus Good was summoned. The Scotland Yard Inspector asked, "You're Charlie Chitat Ng's uncle?"

"Yes."

"Your last name is Good."

"Ng's father married my sister. What's going on?" Dr. Good learned what was happening and said, "That's why I had Charlie expelled from here."

"You expelled him?"

"He was an embarrassment to the family."

"We know Charlie has two sisters living in Canada. His father has business interests in Quebec, Toronto, Vancouver, and Calgary. The Bureau told us they've run checks on all four cities. Many Ngs, none related to Charlie."

"Easily explained. Charlie's sisters have married. They no longer use their maiden names."

FRIDAY, JUNE 7, 1985, 7:30 A.M.

Sheriff Ballard began the day by handing out his permanent assignments. Deputy Sheriffs Mathews and Copland would run the crime scene. Mathews would process evidence from inside the residence, Copland do the same for the bunker. Both men would oversee the fire pits and trenches.

Dr. Stephens had forbidden the backhoe to be used on the telephone line trench, because of the charred bones and fine bone fragments located there.

The backhoe would be used instead to excavate the disturbed ground next to the bunker. When the cinderblock structure was built, the bank had been dug out. This dirt was back-filled against the concrete building.

In that pit, articles of clothing had already been discovered. Parts of cloth had been aboveground. Investigators merely had to tug on them and they came away intact.

FRIDAY, JUNE 7, 1985, 9:30 A.M.

Two hours later, Joe Lordan hung up the phone and muttered, "Incredible."

Eisenmann asked, "What is?"

"That was the S.F. Vice Squad. Captain Philpott remembered a case. A prostitute filed a complaint. She said a man hired her to be an escort. He took her out to dinner. Then he took her to a motel in Milpitas. She went to the bathroom and opened the door. A naked Chinese man was standing there holding a knife. He raped her while," Lordan peered at his notes, " 'all the time stabbing a knife into the mattress close to her head. The other man took photographs.' "

"Lake and Ng."

"Yes. Philpott had the prostitute rounded up this morning. Half the men in the photos were Caucasian, half Chinese. She had no problem pointing them out. Lake told her that he did this all the time, but usually killed the women afterward, but he liked her. He took her driver's license and said he knew where she lived, and if she told anyone, he was going to torture her to death."

No charges were ever filed.

FRIDAY, JUNE 7, 1985, 10:00 A.M.

The big break came by accident the next morning. A county road maintenance worker stood by the edge of the driveway leading to the cabin. He was supervising the movement of equipment, the backhoes and bulldozers, directing traffic, guiding the heavy machinery into a staging area.

Coroner Stephens wasn't letting the big stuff in yet, while the hands-on, meticulous search continued.

A D-5 bulldozer lumbered up the road. The county road worker stepped out of its way and the ground gave way slightly under his feet. He thought nothing of it, until he stepped on the same spot again, and the ground depressed again. He called Deputy Norman Varain and Inspector Tom Eisenmann over. "There's something buried right there."

"How do you know?"

The worker pressed his boot down on the spot, then lifted his boot. The ground flexed back. "Ground don't work that way. If you compact it, it stays compacted, it don't keep popping back up."

Using a small entrenching tool, Eisenmann and Varain carefully scraped away dirt. Three inches under the ground they uncovered a round, white, metal surface. Working painstakingly, they dug around the object and finally unearthed a white, five-gallon container with the lid sealed.

Eisenmann placed the can in a plastic bag and carried it to the command post. He could hear something rattling around inside.

Ballard was talking to the lab crew. "I want that incinerator examined next."

Eisenmann gave him the five-gallon bucket. Ballard had it photographed, then he pried the lid off. Inside were wallets, rings, bracelets, necklaces, credit cards, driver's licenses, and videotapes labeled "M. Ladies Kathy/Brenda."

Ballard pointed at the videotapes and said, "What the hell?"

A deputy sheriff said, "I have a VCR at my house."

"Get it, please, and a TV."

Ballard began itemizing the rest of the contents of the pail. There was a checkbook with the name Scott Stapley on the checks. The address was 4755 Felton, Apartment Number 4, San Diego. Inside the checkbook was a Food Mart card with Stapley's name on it. Also inside the pail was a still photo of a dark-haired woman.

The sheriff said, "Someone make copies of this. We're going to need them to attempt identification on this woman."

The deputy returned with the VCR and TV. He asked, "Do you want this set up in the house?"

"No, the lab hasn't had time to go over it yet. Put your stuff at Bo Carter's cabin next door."

The nineteen-inch TV and VCR were hooked up. As several officers gathered at the cabin, Ballard closed the drapes, then shooed everyone outside. He couldn't have increased the tension at the crime scene more if he had been Alfred Hitchcock.

Rumors and wild guesses flew from officer to officer. *What was on those tapes?*

County Sheriff Lt. Bob Bunning and Deputy Chief Joe Lordan watched with Ballard. The TV flickered to life with snowy black-and-white images, then a commercial started in vivid color. The ad abruptly changed. There was no lead-in. A woman appeared, pathetic in her unsexuality. She was chained to a chair. Her listlessness only accented her terror. Behind her was wallpaper.

Bunning said, "That wallpaper looks the same as that in the front room of Lake's house."

Ballard nodded.

On the screen a figure appeared, shadowy, vague. The shape moved to the woman's side. His back was to the camera.

The woman told the two men they were "crazy."

A man's voice granted that there was craziness all around them, but then accused the woman, whose name he gave as "Brenda," of being a "first-class asshole" during the time she had lived there.

The shadowy figure moved. His face appeared, dancing and flickering light from the lantern.

"Lake," Lordan said.

Ballard added, "The bastard."

Leonard Lake told the woman that they were going to allow her to atone for her bad behavior.

Another figure appeared. He tore the T-shirt off the woman.

Lake admonished the man—calling him "Charlie"—for ruining a T-shirt that he liked.

Charlie answered quietly that they should take a look at "what we're buying."

Ballard said, "That woman is the same as the one we found on the still photo in the bucket. He called her Brenda. Irene Brunn talked to the owner of the place next door. His tenants were," the sheriff flipped open his notebook, "Lonnie Bond, his common-law wife, Brenda O'Connor, and their child, Lonnie Bond Junior. Lonnie Bond's license plate, for a Buick, was on Cosner's Honda. Get someone on trying to ID the woman on this tape. Starting with Brenda O'Connor, whoever she is."

The police officers watched the rest of the tape in uneasy silence. It was more of the same, only cruder. When it was over, Bunning said, "The officers are going to be curious about what's on these tapes."

"I'll handle it," Lordan said.

Sheriff Ballard said, "No, I'll do it."

A somber Lordan and a serious Bunning left the cabin.

Eisenmann asked, "Anything significant on the tapes?"

As Lordan walked away slowly, he held up one of the videotapes and answered, "We have an eyewitness."

Chapter Eight

FRIDAY, JUNE 7, 1985, 1:00 P.M.

AFTER A HURRIED LUNCH, THE POLICE OFficers stood in a knot, speculating about the ashen looks on their leaders' faces after they left the neighbor's house. Curiosity about what was on the videotapes mounted; the work around the site was at a standstill.

Ballard called the entire task force together in front of Lake's cabin. He studied the mixed bag of uniforms, deputy sheriffs in green, the two S.F. patrolmen in black, a variety of investigators in jeans and work shirts, the dog handlers in fatigues, the pathologist in a suit.

The sheriff said, "I want the wasted energy and effort everyone is expending over the videotapes to stop."

"So let's see one."

"I am going to let you do just that."

Ballard led the task force up the hill to Carter's house. They were a suddenly subdued, expectant crowd. They formed a semicircle around the TV.

T. B. Clancy followed them in and hid in a corner. Ballard said, "I can see your red hair from here."

"Do I have to leave?"

"No," Ballard said, and held up a tape. He peered closely at it, then slid it into the VCR.

A dining room appeared on the screen. The people sat on one side of a long table. It was a scene like the Last Supper, allowing the camera to pick up everyone's face.

Clancy said, "I wonder which one's Judas?"

Eisenmann recognized Leonard Lake, seated in the middle. Claralyn was on Lake's left, his mother, Gloria Eberling, on his right. It was soon learned from the conversation that two of the others present were Claralyn's parents, Louis and Grace Balazs.

A large turkey was in the center of the table, flanked by a ham, yams, mashed potatoes, cranberry sauce, asparagus tips, and assorted white and red wines.

"What is this?" one of the puzzled police officers asked.

Putting a finger to his lips, Sheriff Ballard pointed at the TV.

The assembled officers watched Lake and his extended family eat Easter dinner. They talked about John Walker, retired Navy officer, his son Mike, and John's brother Art, also retired from the Navy. They had been arrested by the FBI for espionage.

Lake was talking heatedly, using the word "bastards" to describe the Walkers. They had sold out the country, he contended, giving away the country's best-kept secrets. The Soviet menace was real, and "we" were closer to nuclear war because of the traitors. Lake wished he could take care of the Walkers personally, with a form of capital punishment to fit the crime—slow and painful.

Claralyn's father, Louis Balazs, insisted there'd be no nuclear war. But Lake demanded to know what would happen if he were wrong.

"Speculation," Balazs persisted.

"I'll survive," came Lake's answer. He was prepared, he said, and if they knew what was good for them, they would know where to go when nuclear war came.

Again Mr. Balazs backed off. He would rather be at "ground zero," he said, if such a calamity occurred.

Leonard Lake brushed aside this mood of defeatism. He began to carve the turkey, all the while continuing to spell out his utopian plan to repopulate the earth after the war. "Someone" had to live to do it, he boasted.

Lake's mother sighed. On this holiday she wished that her son Donald could have been present.

A sudden change came over Leonard Lake. Moments before his face was glowing; now it turned dark. He snarled that Donald was "an asshole."

Mrs. Lake, almost in tears, whispered that Donald had never been away this long before.

The videotape ended abruptly, the screen turning into a gray void.

"That's it?"

"Not quite," Ballard answered and shoved another tape into the VCR.

Leonard Lake appeared again, sitting in a chair. He spoke like a talk show host, only now it was about his fantasies: to kidnap a female and enslave her. She would take care of all his needs.

He lamented that he was developing a pot belly, getting bald, no longer very attractive to women.

He explained the inevitable coming nuclear holocaust—the almost total destruction of the planet, and his future role as the new Adam. He told how he intended to build a series of bunkers, each to house an Eve, the mothers of the new world order.

The screen turned snowy again.

"That's it?" Ballard was asked again.

"That's it," the sheriff said. "Now will everyone get back to work? The real evidence is outside."

The officers filed out. Eisenmann dawdled behind. When he was alone with Lordan, he said, "I know why the sheriff showed the tape, but the tape didn't make you turn so serious."

"No, Tom," Lordan said, "that one didn't."

"Not snuff flicks?"

"No."

"Murder?"

"No murder is shown. But the tapes are degrading and vicious. Not even in your line of work have you encountered anything as debasing and mentally cruel."

* * *

The lab crew had begun work on the incinerator. The steel hatch was dusted for prints. The results were taken to Lordan.

Next the lab crew took samples of the fine powder in the bottom of the fire pit. The samples were put into glass jars, sealed, and sent on for microexamination at the sophisticated facilities in San Francisco. Samples were also forwarded to the FBI and the other law enforcement agencies involved.

Lordan asked, "Anything?"

The technician shrugged, "I doubt it. Whatever was burned in that thing was cooked at extremely high temperatures. But you never know, I'm looking at it with the naked eye, not a fifty-thousand-dollar microscope."

FRIDAY, JUNE 7, 1985, 1:30 P.M.

Meanwhile, having secured a search warrant for Charlie Ng's residence at 136 Lennox Way in San Francisco from the Honorable Phillip Moscone of the Municipal Court, Police Officer Jerome DeFillipo entered the premises. He began a careful search.

By the bed, in a letter rack on the floor, he found two street maps of San Francisco. On one he noticed that a red circle had been drawn around Yukon Street. He found a G.E. VCR connected to the TV. This was compared to the list containing the missing property from the Dubs residence. A G.E. videocassette recorder was listed as stolen.

He found a solitary book.

In the top center of a black desk located on the south wall of the apartment was an envelope containing a First Interstate Bank credit card issued to Lonnie Bond.

The envelope with the credit card in it was partially torn. It was addressed to a Mr. Abe and Ms. Marsha, "the cowardly Labradors." In the torn corner were the letters e-l-t-o-n, Number 4, and a zip code—92116.

He found another envelope. Inside was a check from the Dennis Moving Services, Suite 806, 16 California

Street, San Francisco. The check was made out to Charlie Ng.

Officer DeFillipo continued to search. He found a photo album. Inside were, among other things, pictures of a concrete building under construction. There were also photos of Leonard Lake.

The officer found a Cross pen and pencil set with the initials C.R.P. monogrammed on it.

Officer DeFillipo found a box under a desk. Inside were videotapes. Some were labeled: KQED, KSAN, McCartney interview 20/20, Roberto Duran versus Sugar Ray Leonard, and TV Guide, 25 years, 10/79.

Two more tapes were labeled "Taboo" and "Vice Squad." DeFillipo didn't have time or authority to play the tapes. He labeled them, signed the chain of evidence line on the manila envelope, and turned it into the San Francisco S Squad Exhibit Property Room.

Other investigators in San Francisco contacted Harvey Dubs's employer, Stan Pedrov. He said he had received a phone call from an unknown person explaining that Harvey was relocating to Washington.

"I can't understand it," Mr. Pedrov said. "Harvey was very punctual, very thorough. This is so unlike him to leave work, not to show up without a word."

FRIDAY, JUNE 7, 1985, 3:00 P.M., CENTRAL STANDARD TIME.

Charlie Chitat Ng lay on the king-sized bed of the Chateau Hotel in Chicago. He had paid for the room with cash. He ordered a lavish meal from room service.

He was cleaning his .22 Ruger semiautomatic pistol. He oiled the barrel, then the wooden handle.

Ng examined his weapon and thought, This thing's too puny, I need my Uzi. He glanced at his watch: after twelve on the coast, that's when he opened. He dialed a gun dealer in San Francisco.

Using the name Mike Kimoto he'd left when he

dropped the gun off to be repaired, Ng identified himself and asked, "Is it fixed?"

The gun dealer said, "Yes, I fixed it myself. You didn't come in. You said you were going to come in Monday to pick it up."

"I want you to send it to me. I'm in Chicago."

"I can't do that."

"It's my gun."

"I can't ship a weapon to anyone besides another gun dealer. It's the law."

"If I get a gun dealer here in Chicago to accept delivery, will you ship it?"

"Sure, just have him phone me."

Charlie disconnected. He opened the Friday newspapers: *Chicago Tribune, San Francisco Chronicle, Sacramento Bee.* Nothing about Lake on the front page. Nothing in the first section. Nothing in the whole paper.

What was happening? Could it be possible? Were the cops so stupid they missed what had happened? Did they really think that all Lake had done was steal a car?

FRIDAY, JUNE 7, 1985, 2:00 P.M.

Ballard sat at his makeshift desk outside the mountain house and pondered the tapes he had just seen. He thought, I haven't felt like having a drink this early in a long time.

Leonard Lake's diary was in front of him.

Ballard saw a couple of his deputy sheriffs nearby talking to Tomasina Clancy. She was waving her arms about, mouth wide, gleaming teeth flashing. The two officers were bent over with laughter.

That woman's a realist, Ballard thought. Once she knew I had her, there was no complaining. Just acceptance and a "wait till next time" attitude.

He'd put her up at a female deputy sheriff's house last night. He'd made sure Clancy was aware that the deputy sheriff was responsible for keeping an eye on her—and that she was not to leave.

I need a drink, he thought again as he opened Lake's diary.

He read that Lake planned to build a prison to keep women to fulfill his "sexual fantasies." It would also serve as a fallout shelter.

His ideal woman, he wrote in the diary, would be someone under his complete control. There would be no letdowns with this "totally submissive" woman, only "pleasure and contentment."

Ballard closed the diary. Maybe, he thought, I should read this after work while watching a mindless TV sitcom. . . .

Dr. Roger Heglar arrived. He was the biological and forensic anthropologist from San Francisco State University.

Sheriff Ballard ran over and shook hands.

Heglar waved toward the long line of officers who were sifting dirt and said, "This is bigger than some of the digs on the Gaza Strip."

"I wish the bones were as old."

"Let's get at it. I need large quantities of dirt from wherever bones are found."

"You got it."

"Don't put the samples in sealed containers, just open buckets. I want to see what kind of insect larvae and pupae are in this area. That will help when I get around to analyzing and dating the time of death from the bones."

Stephens said to Heglar, "You're early, the first bone's not even bleached yet."

"I've got prep work to perform before even looking at a bone. How many have you found?"

Ballard pointed to the table where Eisenmann was working. "Hundreds."

"The skeletons are disarticulated?"

"So far, most have been sawed into two- to four-inch pieces."

"Damn, that makes it rough. I'm going to have to

match up parts, very time-consuming. But not as bad as one we did years ago at the museum. You should try reassembling a Mesozoic Tyrannosaurus rex, whose bones have been snapped into tiny pieces by a saber-toothed tiger. I'm going to need a large area."

"Will do," Ballard said. The command post was beginning to look like a circus encampment. Huge tents had been erected with netting around them, necessitated by the mosquito problem.

In the telephone trench various items were being uncovered: magazines, soup cans, a suitcase, paper articles, clothing, burned ash, a vacuum cleaner, toys, children's coats, jewelry, hairbrushes.

A small sealed pail was found. Inside was an envelope with the return address of the Philo Motel. Inside was identification in the name of Kathy Allen. She worked for the Safeway store in Milpitas, California.

This information was relayed through the command post. Investigators on the San Francisco end would follow through on this new evidence.

A partial skull was found in the telephone trench. It was brought to the command center.

Stephens held it out, like Hamlet held Yorick's, and said, "The walls of the cranium are thin, might be a man's skull."

"Why?" Ballard asked.

"Because," Heglar said, before the coroner could explain, "against the belief that my wife has long suspected, men are not thick-headed. The walls of men's craniums are thinner than the walls of women's."

The coroner pointed at the roof of the cranium. "The ossification lines are saw-edged, very pronounced."

Heglar peered into the cranium and read the suture lines like a tree surgeon reading the age of a tree. "The lines, plus indications on parts of the interior wall lead me to say—thirty to forty years old."

Ballard thought, Charlie Gunnar was thirty-six, Lake's brother Donald, thirty-three, Harvey Dubs, twenty-nine,

Paul Cosner, thirty-nine. Was the cranium one of those missing persons? Or someone else's?

Heglar asked the coroner, "Are you going to do superimposing?"

"Sure. I have photographs of all the suspected missing persons connected to this site. I'll get on that tomorrow."

"And the teeth?"

"Of course the teeth. I've already requested dental records on the same people."

Heglar peered at the jaw of the skull. "The crowns are in pretty good shape. We should know who this joker is in a few days."

"That's a little irreverent," Ballard said.

Heglar looked surprised, then grinned sheepishly. "Sorry, I forgot what's going on here. In my line of work, the skulls usually belong to someone who died ten thousand years ago."

Chapter Nine

FRIDAY, JUNE 7, 1985, 4:00 P.M.

THAT AFTERNOON, THE FIRST REPORTER, A husky young man from the *Calaveras Enterprise,* arrived at the murder site. Ballard asked Clancy to leave the crime scene.

Damn, she thought, I was so close.

Within an hour there were a dozen reporters, from the *Sacramento Bee* and the *Sacramento Union,* from Fresno and Stockton, chatting among themselves behind the barricade at the foot of the driveway. A photo crew from Associated Press had just pulled up.

Clancy thought, These jerks are searching for quotes from each other. She looked around. Task force members were everywhere, and they had been warned about her.

She spotted a lanky, thin-faced man and thought, I heard one of the officers talking, that guy's a forensic specialist, Heglam, Heglas, something like that. The man walked down the road, went around the barricade and opened the side panel on a van.

Clancy went over, introduced herself, and asked, "Are you involved in the investigation?"

"Sure am, I'm Roger Heglar. I'm an anthropologist."

"Anthropologist?" Clancy said, feigning surprise and fishing for a quote. "Here? Why?"

"Did you hear about the big bone that was found?"

"No," Clancy said, trying to keep the excitement out of her voice.

Heglar's lips turned up slightly. "Yeah, they found a two-million-year-old dinosaur hipbone in the Petrified Forest National Park. They're shipping it from Arizona to the University of California, in Berkeley. I should be down there, analyzing something significant, instead of stuck up here, in the middle of nowhere."

Heglar's mouth now formed into an enormous grin. He touched a hand to the side of his head in a mock salute, got a black satchel out of his van and sauntered back up the road.

Clancy thought, What a jerk.

By mid-afternoon Sheriff Claud Ballard decided it was time to call in more help. He had Lordan call the California Conservation Corps headquarters in Sacramento. The director said that it would have to be voluntary—he couldn't order young people to help in a search like this.

Twenty minutes later he called back and said, "I have ten teenagers for you, they'll be up in a couple of hours."

Fine, Ballard thought. He was sitting at his desk. There was no air moving. The thermometer read 101. He tapped a finger on the diary in front of him.

Bits and pieces, he thought, that's all I can stand reading at a time.

He flipped open the journal and came across a reference to "PP1, PP2, PP3." Lake referred to these designations as "them," and wrote that he had "hired" them and had taken them to this location.

The next paragraph spelled out a grandiose survivalist plan. Strangely, it was titled "Operation Miranda." It would begin with a "network" of bunkers that would be supplied with guns and provisions. Each of these "fallout shelters" would house a woman, whose duty it would be to perform the normal servant duties. These would include "sexual services." No question, a nuclear war would come. And after this holocaust, the women in his camp would breed a new race—from "my loins." The future of mankind depended on Leonard Lake.

Ballard slammed the book shut. Dear God in Heaven,

he thought, I hope I won't need a psychiatrist when this is over.

What did PP one, two, and three mean? What did Operation Miranda mean? There was a place named Miranda on the Avenue of the Giants, north of Garberville on 101. And the Miranda decision, involving reading a person his rights.

Ballard thought, There's another Miranda, and linked to something I've seen since I've been here. He couldn't put his finger on it.

He tried to blank out his mind, so that wherever the information was stored could have a chance to rush to the surface. It'll come, he thought.

The lab crew, which had been working directly with the officers sifting dirt, was now finally ready to go over the house. Irene Brunn was assigned to help, as she was one of the first two officers to investigate the premises.

Kaiser Permanente Hospital had sent up a sample of Leonard Lake's blood. The Marines had given them Charlie Chitat Ng's blood type. The various Missing Persons Units involved—San Francisco, Calaveras, Humboldt, Mendocino, and San Diego—had sent up copies of their files; part of the information contained was each missing person's blood group and type.

The mattress in the master bedroom had already been examined. The bullet in the kitchen floor and the bullet in the living room wall were extracted. They were both .22 slugs. A section of the ceiling, dotted with small red stains, was removed.

After an hour, Irene took a break. I've got too vivid an imagination, she thought. This place is going to have ghosts for eternity.

She walked into the woods until she came to the cordon of yellow tape. She sat down and leaned against the trunk of a towering pine tree. There was a gentle breeze that cooled her skin and refreshed her mind.

A woman with flaming red hair came up on the other

side of the warning tape. She said, "I'm a reporter, what do you do?"

"Just about anything the task leader wants."

"Find anything?"

Irene knew that Ballard's gag order involving the press was over. Or almost over—there were still some sensitive areas to the case that he wanted withheld. She also knew this was the woman the sheriff had detained.

Irene thought, I'll answer as long as it's in a general nature only. She said, "Yes, we did. Do you know anything about blood?"

"I know it keeps me alive."

"I mean scientific?"

"O, A, B, and AB, positive and negative."

"Those are blood groups. There's also blood types—M, N, MN, and P. There's also eight Rh blood types. Using those separate combinations, there are 288 unique groups."

"Interesting," Clancy said, and turned on her tape recorder. "What did you find?"

"A mattress. The entire thing had been soaked with a maroon stain."

"Maroon?"

"We did preliminary field tests on it. A benzidine test was run—"

"Why test? You know it's blood."

"Yes, but human or animal? If tests weren't run, a good defense attorney would say his client just butchered his hog."

"On his bed?"

"Simpler to do it right, then there can be no shadows raised later. The benzidine test, combined with the Hemin crystal test, proved it was blood."

"Animal or human?"

"A precipitin test was run. Our lab has a guinea pig back in the City. That animal is injected with human blood and human serum, giving us an antihuman serum. A tiny cutting taken from the mattress was dissolved into a salt solution. The guinea pig's serum was added. A gray ring formed in fifteen minutes. We now know that the stain on the mattress was human blood."

"Whose?"

"Exactly, whose? We did groupings: agglutinogens and agglutinins. The first is found in all humans except those with type O."

"Was it O or the others?"

"We found samples of both. Next we ran tests on the lingerie found in the dresser. Sixty percent of the human race carry something known as secretors, the rest are nonsecretors. We found samples of—"

"Both," Clancy finished.

"Exactly."

"What else did you find?"

"There were stains on the living room rug. We did the same tests, same results. A part of the ceiling was removed, but we did nothing to it except protect the chain of evidence. It was sent to the City because it requires far more complex examination than we can do in the field."

The redhead's face became puckered.

Irene thought, Here comes a question I'm not going to answer. Feeding the reporter a lot of general information had been fun. But there wasn't a quote in her whole dissertation.

The redhead cleared her throat and said softly, "I heard that black bodies are being found."

Irene had been around long enough to know what a "No comment" response looked like in the morning papers. It had become tantamount to admitting a yes to the question. She said, "Bodies found?"

"Yes, remains. And belonging to blacks."

"Interesting, who'd you hear that from?"

The redhead frowned. "From some of your fellow officers."

What a fishing expedition, Irene thought, and said, "Which officers?"

The redhead's frown grew larger. "I didn't get their names."

No kidding, Irene thought.

"Their names," the reporter repeated. "That's why I asked you. For verification."

"Of what?" Irene asked, starting to enjoy herself for the first time since arriving in Calaveras County.

"Of some of the bodies being black."

"Black?"

"I heard a rumor that a body was found and IDed as black."

A body, Irene thought, she'd used the singular; the first time she used the plural, bodies. For a fishing expedition, this redhead was using a humungous drag net. First black —then bodies. "Sorry, but in my profession, it's dangerous to rely on rumors."

Irene was rewarded by a glint in the redhead's eyes and thought, She's just realized she's getting her chain pulled.

The reporter glanced around. A good-looking deputy walked by. Clancy nodded to Irene and took off after the man.

Irene thought, Off for greener pastures. Except, the aggressive female reporter wasn't going to find one. She could talk to every law enforcement officer on the crime scene and not get a quote. Not with the way Ballard, Bunning, and Lordan had laid down the law.

In the blinding sun and stifling heat of the afternoon, Ballard stood beside Terry Parker, the Calaveras coroner. The doctor was patiently examining one of the hundreds of small bones on the table.

Ballard asked, "Have you made an identification yet?"

"No, and if by some miracle I do, I'll tell you."

"Miracle?"

"Isn't it obvious, Sheriff? The bodies were systematically hacked up. The bones were sawed, some with a hacksaw, some with an electric skill saw. Look at this."

Ballard looked at the bone. The ends were smooth, like a log that'd been chain-sawed.

The coroner said, "It's almost impossible to get any information from a bone this size. And the people who did this must have known it, otherwise why go to all the trouble?"

Ballard went back to his desk. A courier gave him two manila envelopes. One was from the Marine base in El Toro, the other the San Francisco Police Department. Both contained Ng's background.

He opened the Marine file and read: *Born: December 24, 1961.*

Christmas Eve? Lordan thought, Christmas Eve! What a travesty, what a mockery. I'll never be able to celebrate Christ's birth again without thinking about this bastard. This case has taken the happiest day of the year from me.

He angrily continued to read Ng's file. *Enlisted in Marines, October 12, 1979.*

Ballard remembered something Eisenmann had told him. He opened the S.F. file and placed it beside the Marine file.

He read the S.F. file: *In Sept. 1979, Ng lived in San Leandro, Alameda County. He drove into a telephone pole and left the scene. He was arrested for hit-and-run. Charge dropped after Ng's enlistment in the Marines.*

Aha, Ballard thought, that's probably why he signed up. He continued reading: *Place of birth—Bloomington, Indiana.*

S.F. file: *Place of birth—Hong Kong.*

Marine file: *Family lives in Belmont, California.*

S.F. file: *Family scattered throughout Commonwealth.*

Marine file: *High School education in Yorkshire, England.*

What bullshit, Ballard thought.

S.F. file: *High School education in Yorkshire, England.*

A *fact,* Ballard thought, then added—maybe.

He jotted down notes as he read: *On October 13, 1981, Ng robbed the Marine station armory at the Marine Corps Air Station at Kaneohe, on Oahu. He and three others stole two machine guns, three grenade launchers, a night-sighting scope, and seven pistols. Value: $11,406.00.*

Nov. 11, 1981. Ng went AWOL after being questioned over robbery. One of his accomplices led military police to the top of a hill and showed them where Ng buried the weapons.

April 29, 1982. Ng arrested with Lake by an FBI SWAT team at Indian Creek Ranch Motel, in Philo, Mendocino County.

Aug. 15, 1982. Ng convicted, sent to Leavenworth. Released June 29, 1984.

Miranda! suddenly popped into Ballard's mind. He grappled with the elusive connection, but the link he knew was in his brain retreated into his subconscious.

Damn, he thought, I almost had it. He went back to reading the two files.

Oct. 16, 1984. Ng charged with petty theft by Daly City police for shoplifting a fifty-dollar waterbed sheet from a Mervyn's department store.

Oct. 17, 1984. Claralyn Balazs puts up $1,000.00 bail for Ng.

What? Ballard thought. Claralyn bails Ng out?

He shuffled through the growing mountain of paper on his desk. He compared various dates.

I knew it, he thought, October seventeenth was after she and Lake were divorced. On October seventeenth Lake had already skipped bail and was a fugitive living here in the mountains.

What the hell was going on?

Ballard was a good policeman, suspicious by nature.

He thought, How many people do I know who would post a thousand-dollar bail for me? And in only a few hours after being called? Most of my friends are cops, they're broke all the time.

He looked up to see the volunteers from the California Conservation Corps piling out of a truck. Renee Nolan came over and introduced herself as the trainees' leader.

Ballard directed her to Bob Bunning, who explained he wanted the crew to assist deputies in their inch by inch search of the property. They were going to crawl on their hands and knees, looking for bones.

FRIDAY, JUNE 7, 1985, 5:30 P.M., CENTRAL STANDARD TIME.

Charlie Chitat Ng left the gun store just before closing time. The dealer had phoned San Francisco; his Uzi would be delivered Air Express, arriving tomorrow afternoon. He could pick it up any time after four in the afternoon.

He returned to the Chateau Hotel. He flopped on the bed and listened to Madonna sing "Angel" on the radio.

"Angel" was number seven on the charts. That song should be number one, he thought. He scanned the pages of the *Chicago Tribune* again. No news. Nothing.

Today was Friday. Lake got busted last Sunday. Almost a week—and nothing.

The music on the radio changed to "Everybody Wants to Rule the World" by the Tears and Fears.

Tears and fears, Charlie thought. Lake and I saw a lot of that.

He pictured Leonard's face and remembered Philo. *Those were the days. Like belonging to a family: Claralyn would cook and clean, Leonard and I would grow the food and hunt animals.*

"This is real life," Lake would say, then scowl. "Except it will all be gone after the next war. Just charred earth and slow death. Those fucking commies are going to start throwing nukes, I know it. And look at us, standing in a field, planting corn and lettuce, naked from the waist up, waiting to get fried from the blast."

Charlie had looked out at the peaceful valley, the green trees, the bunched clouds.

Lake had said, "Blackened earth and poisoned air. We need a safe place to be when it happens, and this fucking wide-open valley isn't it. If it happened right now, we'd end up two pieces of burnt toast, or just shadows on the ground. That's what I heard happened when we nailed those fucking Japs. Some of them just disappeared, only their shadows left, painted right into the ground."

Charlie had looked at the rich loam beneath his feet.

Lake rambled on, "Not for me, no way. Be prepared, like in the Marines. I've got to get out of this valley and somewhere where it's safe."

He did, Charlie thought. After skipping bail on that bust, he was a fugitive. He went to the mountains. Once there, Leonard couldn't wait to build the bunker.

He'd said, "This place is remote enough and we have protection from nuclear blast waves, unless we took a direct hit, but there's too many trees. Think of the fire storm. I've fought fires before, I know. This whole mountain range will turn into one gigantic ball of flame. We need a fallout shelter."

Charlie remembered. Lake hired some kid, at first, to help, but then got mad because it was taking so long.

He'd say, "This isn't something you can wait on. When the time comes, it has to be finished."

The music on the radio turned to Madonna's "Crazy For You."

Charlie listened and thought, That song should be number one.

FRIDAY, JUNE 7, 1985, 4:00 P.M.

It was not yet Happy Hour, yet the Black Bart Hotel's bar was jammed. T. B. Clancy entered.

She'd given up on getting anything fresh out of Blue Mountain Road. The law enforcement agents out there were as tight-mouthed as any she'd met. Every officer she'd talked to had stonewalled her, or directed her to the information officer.

She spotted Dr. Heglar. He'd stiffed her the last time she'd tried to get a quote out of him. She had to get a story tonight, to peddle to the foreign press, or the trip would be washed over by the wire services.

She decided to challenge Heglar on the forensics.

She squeezed through the mob and confronted him. "Are we really going to solve this by looking at bones?"

"We're not looking for a solution, we're looking for evidence."

"That's why you were hired?"

"That's why I was sent here."

"So you can tell whose bones are whose?"

"Did you read this morning's paper? They're digging up Josef Mengele today in Sao Paulo."

"That's a forty-year-old story. This, here, is real."

"Do you think forty, or a thousand years, make bones less real?"

"How can you tell from a bunch of bones who they belong to?"

"Looking for a quote, aren't you?"

Clancy took a pencil and a notebook from her purse.

Heglar said, "Why not? If you're right-handed, the bones on your right side are longer. Bones model themselves after your life experiences, your strengths, your illnesses. The only thing that doesn't shape itself to the body is your teeth. You can grind them, or chip them, but they're constants."

"You test all your evidence in the field?"

"No, I'll be making trips back to the Bay Area every few days. I just pieced together a femur. Under a microscope I'll be able to see thc concentric layers of bone, and the little blood-carrying canals in the cortex of that bone. Then I can tell the age of the bone."

"How about DNA?"

"You need flesh for that."

"How can you get an identification from a bone?"

"You can't, only negative IDs."

"And to get a positive?"

"I recreate a picture from the skull."

Clancy thought, Just information. I have to salvage something from this, I need a salable quote.

She worked her way through the bar crowd.

A man, face filled with lines created from smiling, grinned at her. She sized him up. Obviously a workman—not a law enforcement agent—unless he was working undercover for narcotics.

He said, "How on earth did Lake miss you?"

"I beg your pardon?"

"If I was going to set up a female prison, I would at least be selective on who I put there."

"Who are you?"

"Louie."

"Louie?"

"The town's maintenance man."

"Did you know Lake or Ng?"

"No way, they were never arrested for DUI."

Clancy pushed him aside. The good-looking law enforcement agent had moved. He was now standing by the popcorn machine. She batted her eyelashes at him as seductively as possible. "How do you feel about what's happening here?"

"We're not supposed to talk about it."

"I don't care about what's going on, only how you feel about it," Clancy said in her most provocative voice. "I mean, they're making a big deal out of nothing. I covered the Manson case. Now *that* was scary."

"You think the Manson family was scary?"

I need a good, catchy word, Clancy thought, noticing how provoked the man had become with one barb. She said, "I think Manson was a monster."

"You think Manson was a monster?"

"I suppose you're going to tell me Manson was like someone who organized Sunday school picnics compared to this?"

"Compared to this, yes."

The next day, Saturday, papers in California carried a page-one headline—from a reliable source inside the police investigation: "You think the Manson family was scary? You think Manson was a monster? Wait till we get this together. Manson is going to look like someone who organized Sunday school picnics."

In the *San Francisco Chronicle*, Police Chief Con Murphy was quoted: "This may be a case of mass murder or a cult situation. Right now we don't know. A cult case is a possibility we're not going to exclude at this time."

Grace Balazs, Lake's ex-mother-in-law, was quoted in

disbelief: "I don't believe Lennie did anything. What kind of fool would someone have to be to burn bodies where you live?"

When asked about Ng, Grace said, "He just showed up one day to see Leonard. Lennie said he never met Ng before that day. I don't believe Lennie killed anybody. He wasn't that kind of person. . . . He loved animals. He was good to children."

The *Calaveras Enterprise* asked Sheriff Claud Ballard about the videos. He was quoted as saying, "It's worse than a horror film, vicious, vicious, vicious." The sheriff added that the diary found was very detailed, except that several pages were missing.

SATURDAY, JUNE 8, 1985, 10:00 A.M., CENTRAL STANDARD TIME.

Charlie Chitat Ng had slept in late. He didn't hear the news until he flipped on the TV.

He saw a black-and-white photo of Lake. The announcer said, "Lake died from cyanide poisoning Thursday night, at Kaiser Hospital.

"San Francisco Police Chief Con Murphy said this morning that, and I quote, 'There is still a lot of work to be done. A great deal of investigating remains. We still have a lot of sites to be looked into and lots of other property to be searched. This case will never be fully resolved until Ng is captured'."

The announcer continued, "Still at large is Charlie Chitat Ng." The TV screen filled with a black-and-white image of Ng. "Because of his military background and his knowledge of martial arts, ammunition, and explosives, he is considered extremely dangerous. The Federal Bureau of Investigation has declared Ng the most wanted man in America. Agents are hot on the trail."

I'm alone now, Ng thought. Lake's last few days must have been spent flat on his back with tubes running up his nose and into his arms. Now he's dead.

Lake was weak, Charlie thought, he took the easy way out. I am a survivor.

I am not killing myself.

I am not going to get gunned down.

He threw his horn-rimmed glasses onto the hotel bed and inserted his contact lenses.

The only defeat is in death, staying alive is victory.

I don't need Lake, Charlie thought, and mentally repeated, I am a warrior. He felt the weight of the .22 semiautomatic tucked into his belt at the small of his back.

It was time to move. It was time to go where Leonard said it would be safe.

He went into the bathroom and shaved off his sideburns. He thinned his eyebrows.

He felt his adrenaline pumping. The rush came, that pleasurable punch of excitement. Except this time he wasn't the hunter, he was the hunted.

Chapter Ten

SATURDAY, JUNE 8, 1985, 11 A.M., CENTRAL STANDARD TIME.

THE SPECIAL AGENT IN CHARGE OF THE FBI task force on the Ng case arrived in Chicago late in the morning and went to the Bureau's downtown headquarters. He opened the door to the office and faced twenty agents wearing bullet-proof vests and armed with machine guns and sniper rifles.

"Come on, you can be in on the kill," one said. "We know where Ng is."

The SAC rode in the FBI SWAT van. Agent Karen Alexander said to him, "We've been circulating Ng's photo all over the country."

"Airports?"

"Yes, bus stops, all the usual. A porter at O'Hare remembered Ng. Wouldn't let him help with the luggage, plus was rude."

"We hit all the hotels in Chicago. Just got a phone call. Ng's registered at the Chateau Hotel under the name of Kimoto. The manager told us he hasn't checked out, he's still in his room."

The hotel was surrounded. Snipers took up firing positions on adjacent buildings. The manager of the hotel told them what room Ng was in, and was escorted from the building.

The SAC joined Alexander on the roof of a building facing the hotel. They had a good view of the fourth floor window where Ng was staying.

"See anything?" Karen asked the FBI sniper.

"Nope. The drapes are open, I got a beautiful line of sight on the room. Ng's probably in the bathroom."

The SAC raised his binoculars. He focused the lens. The room came into view. There was a pair of glasses on the rumpled bed.

He said, "I read in the FBI background report that Ng's myopic."

"He is."

"Then he's over there! No one nearsighted would leave his glasses."

The front door of the room crashed open, SWAT team members poured through, aiming weapons in every direction. The bathroom door was smashed in.

An agent flipped up the visor on his bullet-proof helmet, came to the window, raised a fist, then gave the thumbs-down signal.

Charlie Chitat Ng had left the hotel room thirty minutes before without checking out, slipping out of the rear service entrance.

Eight blocks south of the hotel he started to hitchhike. He waited for someone Asian to stop, saying to others, "Sorry, changed my mind."

Three Chinese stopped. Each was going somewhere in the city. The fourth was headed for Gary, Indiana.

Ng got into the backseat and said in Chinese, "I'm really tired, do you mind if I lie down and nap?"

The old man nodded.

Charlie thought, With their computers, their communications, their manpower, they must have learned about my phony ID in the name of Kimoto.

When they do, they'll find the hotel. But they'll be converging on nothing.

He felt pride in his escape, in his cunning.

SATURDAY, JUNE 8, 1985, 1:00 P.M.

By midday the crime lab in San Francisco had viewed most of the tapes seized from Ng's residence on Lennox.

The tapes marked KQED, KSAN, had been watched: normal commercial TV programs. The Roberto Duran versus Sugar Ray Leonard was just that—a copy of the fight.

The next video was inserted—"Taboo." This time both police officers were alert, waiting. A brief flash of amateurish image came on before the commercial X-rated film started.

The half-second image showed a heavy-duty, construction-type bluish wheelbarrow.

The projectionist said softly, "That sure looks like a body in that wheelbarrow."

"In rigor."

"Full rigor, it's laying straight across the barrow. Full extension. It looks like it's wrapped in something."

"Yeah, some sort of plastic."

"Is that a second body next to the wheelbarrow?"

On the ground to the right of the wheelbarrow was a second form, definitely shaped like a human being. It also was covered in plastic.

In San Francisco, Detective Gary Hopper, having obtained a picture of Charlie Ng, showed Mr. John Kallas a photo lineup. The observant customer from the South San Francisco Lumber Yard pointed at Ng's picture and said, "That's the man who I saw shoplifting the vise."

Kallas signed the photo identification form with the number of the photo he picked.

SATURDAY, JUNE 8, 1985, 1:30 P.M.

In Calaveras County, the ten trainees from the California Conservation Corps were assigned to search a large slope covered with Mountain Misery. Mountain Misery is a small weed that flourishes throughout the Mother Lode. The plant has tiny, fernlike leaves and is quite attractive.

It gets its name because of its ability to spread like a wild fire, not because of its looks.

Sheriff Ballard studied the group of CCC volunteers in front of him and said kindly, "This is going to be a difficult task. Young people have active enough imaginations, without this sort of thing. I want you to try and think that what you're searching for is evidence, not just bones. And that the evidence may help identify a missing person."

One of the teenagers said, "Why would anyone really want to know for sure a loved one is dead?"

"They do, believe me. The torture comes from not knowing. The dead can never be mentally laid to rest until one knows for sure. That's where the ancient ritual of a wake and an open casket comes from."

"Why are we searching here?"

Dr. Heglar, the anthropologist, noticed something. "This whole slope has been recently fertilized. Now who would fertilize a plant like Mountain Misery? We believe the reason was to cover something up."

A CCC trainee said, "They should call this whole place Mountain Misery."

Eisenmann put the phone down and grinned. Irene had been right about the photographs. He went over to where she was sifting dirt and said, "The captain just called. He finally got the time to drive over. The wallpaper at the South City Juvenile Hall matches exactly that in the background of two of the twenty-one photos found in the bunker."

Irene smiled a tired smile.

"Plus, he found out that Claralyn works there as a teacher's assistant."

Irene's smile wasn't tired-looking anymore. She said, "Is she here yet?"

"Not yet, she's being driven up this morning."

"Is Sheriff Ballard doing the—"

"Yes, he's doing the interrogation."

"This news should help."

Eisenmann went back to work. He added another entry

to the long list of bones being brought from the area where the CCC workers were combing.

Lordan said, "Want to take a break?"

Eisenmann stretched. "Do I ever."

"Not really a break. There's a mother and her teenager down at the barricade. She wants to make a statement."

Eisenmann walked down the road, learned it wasn't the mother who wanted to make a statement, but her child, Scott Mosher. He led them both to an area that had been set aside for just this purpose. A few comfortable chairs and a coffee table were under a stand of trees. Mosquito netting protected the area.

Scott Mosher was a good-looking fifteen-year-old. He said, "I answered an ad and—"

Eisenmann asked, "When?" He knew interviewing teenagers was tough. They had a tendency to spurt out everything as fast as they could, no matter how incoherent the statement sounded.

"Last January," Scott said. "I knew the man who ran the ad, he was called Charlie Gunnar. I saw his picture in the paper this morning, he's really Leonard Lake."

"What did he want?"

"He hired me to help him and his friend build a toolshed." Scott pointed at the fallout shelter. "I saw a carton in the house. It was marked 'one-way glass.' "

The teenager paused. Eisenmann watched his hands wring together, almost in violent prayer.

Scott continued, "One day it rained. Lake said that instead of working we could watch a video. The tape was of women undressing. There were also nude men. I asked, 'Can I go home now?' After I got home I cried. That really shook me up."

Eisenmann was angry. Another of Lake's victims. This one wasn't scattered bones in a ditch, this one was breathing, having nightmares, his mind filled with fear when it should be filled with wonder.

Scott said, "He asked me once if I'd bring my sister Angie along. I asked why? He said he just wanted to take a few family pictures."

Diane Mosher, Scott's mother, said, "He gave me the creeps. I'm so relieved my children are both all right."

"So am I," Eisenmann said, "so am I."

Ballard paced around the autopsy table. He watched the doctor take samples from a large, bloated corpse.

Stephens said to the photographer, "Taking initial shots of bones is all that's usually required, but this is a full-fledged corpse. I need you taking photos of what I do. Normally we'd do the postmortem at the hospital. There I have cameras to record what I do, but this is fieldwork. I have a camcorder in my vehicle. Get it, please, so I can get on with it."

The photographer got the camcorder, set it on a tripod, and focused on the corpse resting on the butcher paper on the table. Eisenmann and Brunn walked up and watched.

Coroner Parker said, "Chief, I finally have something to work with. Even though this body has been burned, I think I'll have our first identification very soon."

Parker removed a tape recorder from his briefcase, turned it on, and asked Sheriff Ballard, "Where do you want to start?"

"Was the victim alive in the fire?"

"Right. I think, because of what's going on here, we can rule out alcoholic intoxication, sedatives, poisonous drugs—"

Ballard interrupted, "Don't rule out anything."

"Then let's start with a surface-body search. There doesn't appear to be any antemortem burns, only postmortem. Antemortem trauma is destroyed if the fire continues for any length of time. If this body was burned in that incinerator beside the bunker, then—"

Eisenmann said, "If that corpse was burned in that incinerator you'd have only white powder and small fragmented bones left."

Parker pointed at the blackened hulk of the burned corpse. "Look, that's edema and erythema. Doesn't that prove circulation? You can't have blood pumping in a corpse. Except, look at the vesicles. They're different than those formed by a live body."

Ballard said, "I saw a body that looked like this once. It had been burned on a funeral pyre."

"Like a Viking?"

"Exactly. The part of the body on the flame cooks differently than the part facing away."

Eisenmann said, "So what's the answer? Was this body burned before, or after, it was dead?"

An exasperated Lordan barked, "Exactly, give us something concrete."

"Concrete?" the doctor said.

"Evidence."

"Come back in a few hours. These things take time."

Two hours later Ballard returned. Irene Brunn had just walked up too.

The sheriff asked the doctor what he had learned.

Parker said, "There's no thermal damage in the pharynx, or the epiglottis and the larynx. Which means he was dead when burned."

Ballard pounced with, "He?"

"Yes, and also, I'm fairly certain, black."

"What? There's been no indication whatever that any blacks were—"

"Look, Sheriff," Parker said and pointed. "See the lower border of the nasal passage? We're not saying we're positive this is a black man, but at the very least of mixed origin."

Irene said, "What!" She saw the surprised looks on those around the autopsy table. She said, "Sorry. I just remembered. That redheaded reporter took a stab in the dark when she interviewed me. She tried to use the old tactic of saying something so outrageous that it gets an involuntary response."

"What did she say?"

"She said she heard some bodies had been identified as black. The thought just struck me, what an incredible blind shot."

Sheriff Ballard thought, That's all this case needs: racial overtones.

Claralyn Balazs arrived at the property. She had been driven there by two detectives with the San Francisco Police Department.

Ballard didn't waste time with any formalities. He knew what tack he wanted to take: right in her face. He said, "What was on the twenty tapes you took from here?"

"I didn't take twenty."

I know, Ballard thought, I read in Eisenmann's report, your ex-mother-in-law said ten or twelve. He said, "How many did you take?"

"Twelve."

"You want us to believe that all twelve are of just you cavorting with Lake?"

"Yes, that's what's on them."

"Why did you drive up before us?"

"I told you, I wanted—"

"Why didn't you wait and come with us? You could have explained about the tapes. We could have had a woman, like Irene Brunn, view them. Your privacy would have been protected."

"I didn't think of that. But why are you treating me this way? You act like I did something."

"Did you?"

"I've been deeply troubled. This thing is killing me."

"Why, did you do something?"

"No, I keep telling you—"

"We matched the background in two of the twenty-one photos we found in the bunker. Those shots were taken at the South City Juvenile Center. That's where you work."

"I want my lawyer."

"My lawyer? You've hired a lawyer?"

"Yes."

"Why?"

"I want immunity."

"From what? You said you didn't do anything."

"I'm not saying another word. I want to be taken back to San Francisco." She crossed her arms and stared at the ground.

After she left, Ballard said, "Damn, I blew it."

"No you didn't," Eisenmann said.

"No? Now she wants immunity."

"You tried the ramrod approach and it didn't work, but at least it saved time. I don't think any other interrogation tactic would have."

"Thanks," the sheriff said, "I'll have to think about it when I write my—Miranda!"

Eisenmann saw the pleased look on Ballard's face. He asked, "Miranda?"

"I know why Lake called this place Operation Miranda. It's nothing to do with Miranda rights. It just clicked. I saw John Fowles's book, *The Collector,* on the bookcase the first time I went into the bunker. I thought nothing of it then."

"What's it mean?"

"You're not familiar with the novel?"

"No."

"It's the story of a butterfly collector, Ferdinand Clegg, who kidnaps a woman. He keeps her in the cellar. The entrance to the cellar is behind a false bookcase."

"So the woman's name was—"

"After two years she dies of pneumonia. Her name was Miranda Grey."

Eisenmann smiled. "Nice bit of deduction, except it doesn't do us much good."

"It does me some good, trying to remember has been driving me crazy."

SATURDAY, JUNE 8, 1985, 5:00 P.M., CENTRAL STANDARD TIME.

Once well away from the hotel, Charlie Chitat Ng asked the driver to stop. He needed to make a call before a store closed, he said.

He spotted a pay phone and called the gun dealer. He remembered the place stayed open until midnight on weekends.

His Uzi hadn't arrived yet. Charlie said, "Give me another one."

"I can't do that."

"You know mine's being sent, you spoke to the guy in San Francisco."

"I still can't do it."

"I'll take one that's not as good. Mine's just been overhauled, that's why it was in the shop."

"Why don't you just wait? It might be in any minute, or it might have been misrouted. It should be here no later than tomorrow."

Tomorrow? Charlie thought. That isn't any good. I need that Uzi *now!* He said, "I'll buy one off of you."

"There's a waiting period."

He slammed down the phone. It was time to move on. He had been in one federal pen and hated the thought of returning to that awful life. He rode with the old Chinese man until they got to Gary, Indiana.

He rented a car in Gary.

He took his time, driving carefully. He used Highway 94, passing towns like Porter and Waterford.

He remembered what Lake had said. "If you fly straight into Detroit, they'll know where you're headed, they know about the ferries. Don't use the ferries. Fly to Chicago, then use the back roads to get to Detroit. Don't speed, don't break the law."

Charlie checked the speedometer: fifty-five. He glanced at the map in his lap. He'd been studying it since Sunday night.

He moved north into Michigan on 94, past Sawyer and Bridgman.

Lake had said he could go the other way on 94 if he wanted. Only then he'd be crossing Minnesota, instead of Michigan. Lake had told him Minnesota was called the Gopher State. Leonard had laughed. "The Gopher State, Charlie, get it? That's where you go for it."

The base of Lake Michigan was on his left. He wasn't interested in Lake Michigan—the lake he was interested in was Lake Saint Clair.

He drove through Kalamazoo and Marshall. He entered Detroit, still on Interstate 94. He cruised down the Edsel Ford Freeway, turned onto the Fisher Freeway, passed Tiger Stadium, and came to the Ambassador Bridge.

Lake had said, "If you go east, use the bridge, not the Detroit-Windsor Tunnel."

"Why?"

"Because if they catch you in a tunnel, you're screwed, nowhere to run. If you think you're spotted on the bridge, you can always jump off and commit suicide."

I'm not killing myself, Charlie thought. He felt the Ruger .22 against the small of his back. If they try to arrest me, I will die like a warrior, not like Lake, not like a vegetable.

He crossed the bridge. The guard in the glass booth only gave him a cursory glance, then waved him on.

He drove down Wyandotte Street, turned right on Walker Road, then left on Tecumseh Road. After a few minutes beautiful Lake Saint Clair spread out, glistening in the sun.

He was safe.

He was in Windsor, Canada.

Canada, a country that didn't allow extradition to another country—if that country intended to bring the death penalty.

Saturday's heat was finally waning. The sun had slipped behind the tall trees, a faint breeze was carrying a cooling touch. Tomasina Boyd Clancy had returned to the crime scene. She was talking to Coroner Terry Parker. She glanced around. This place was turning into a bust. Too many reporters. She asked, "What did you find out about the bodies that turned up?"

"It's all in the press release Stenquist handed out."

Clancy thought, I'd starve to death if I had to live on press releases. "Where'd the bodies go?"

"San Fran, they have better equipment, we should know something in a few days."

A few days? She glanced around and saw Sheriff Ballard stuffing papers into his briefcase. She went over and said, "I'm thinking about bagging out."

"Not enough news for you?"

"Not enough original news for me. Friends?" She stuck out a delicate hand.

"Sure," Ballard said. "I'm glad you see it my way. If I let reporters get away with the kind of surveillance you use, we'd never—"

"I think you owe me a quid pro quo."

"Owe you?"

"As a friendly gesture. I was a good sport."

"What do you want?" Ballard asked suspiciously.

"A lead. I know you got the file on Ng. The FBI is following the trail in Chicago. I kind of like to let the beaters drive the quarry to me. You've read the reports, where do you think Ng's running to?"

"This is a quid pro quo?"

"Who's it going to hurt?"

"All right," Ballard said, shaking his head. "Ng has sisters in both Toronto and Calgary. My guess is, he's headed for family."

Clancy left.

She thought, Toronto or Calgary, which one would I run to? Ng flew from San Francisco to Chicago, almost a dead line to Toronto.

Would he do that if that was his destination?

If it was me, I'd aim at Toronto, leave a hot trail, then double back to Calgary.

She was smiling as she drove down Blue Mountain Road.

SUNDAY, JUNE 9, 1985, 6:00 A.M.

Irene slipped into the rear pew of the Saint Joseph's Catholic Church for the early mass. She had been raised in a strict Hispanic household. She noticed a considerable number of other officers, both from San Francisco and Calaveras, shotgunned throughout the church.

The priest started mass.

Irene had been working twelve-hour shifts since Tuesday. She faced another one today, Sunday. *It didn't seem right, going to that terrible place on the sabbath.*

The priest read the gospel. Then he said, "I know many of you here think that this should be a Requiem Mass, but I am saying the Mass of Resurrection."

Resurrection? Irene thought. From what?

The priest said, "The shocking depravity that has hit our small community has brought us all to our knees. We are faced with the very essence of evil. But we are a community, and together we must work and pray to heal these terrible wounds." He paused and gathered his breath. "And the Christian message is a fierce one. We must even pray for sadists. We must even pray for murderers."

Chapter Eleven

SUNDAY, JUNE 9, 1985, 8:00 A.M.

LIZ HODGSON AND IAN MARKHAM-SMITH stood by the barricade at the foot of the road. They asked to see whoever was in charge.

Irene walked up, introduced herself and said, "Sheriff Ballard's not here right now. Lieutenant Bunning is in charge, but I'm not sure where he is."

Liz said, "I represent the *News of the World,* which is England's largest national publication."

"England?"

"We Brits love this sort of thing. Ian works for *Mail on Sunday,* a London paper."

"London?" Irene said vacantly.

"Yes," Liz said. "We are partners in Newslink International, based in Beverly Hills."

"Beverly Hills?" Irene started shaking her head slowly in amazement.

"We heard about this tantalizing story," Liz said, "and flew up immediately."

Ian waved a well-manicured hand over the panorama. "The Wild West."

Liz agreed. "This is an old gold-mining area, so our readers will think of every cowboy movie they've ever seen."

"Cowboy movies?"

"Of course, we have a lot of homegrown murder stories, but this one has a combination of murder and sex which the English simply relish. I guess it goes back to Jack the Ripper."

"Jack the Ripper?"

"It's a shrinking world," Liz said, "what with television and satellite news. You don't see as many of the foreign bureaus as in the past."

Ian said, "Rather than wait for a plum posting, we started Newslink."

"On the whole," Liz said, "it's been jolly good."

"Jolly good," Irene repeated and walked away. She ignored the frantic pleas of the two correspondents to come back. I'm not the information officer, she thought, let Jim Stenquist put up with this junk.

Even Tomasina Clancy was preferable to these two.

Tomasina Clancy was on a plane to Nicaragua. The Ng case would have to wait. President Daniel Ortega, an old friend of hers, had lifted a self-imposed moratorium on arms imports.

He had said on the news, "Nicaragua is almost the only country in Central America that does not have the ability to defend itself rapidly by air."

Clancy thought, If I know Daniel, he'll start by demanding jet war planes, then let the U.S. beat him down into accepting interceptor aircraft, which is what he really wants in the first place, for his fight with the Contras.

Daniel will slip me any lead stories twenty-four hours before they happen. Calgary can wait.

She had read the morning newspapers. One report from Calaveras stated: an unidentified source, deep inside the investigation, was quoted as saying: "This place reminds me of Connell's short story, 'The Most Dangerous Game.'

Clancy thought, I wish I'd thought of that.

Investigators from San Francisco had contacted the Safeway store in Milpitas. That lead had come from the envelope with the Philo Motel return address found in the telephone trench. Inside were items with Kathy Allen's name on them.

The investigators talked to Andrea Medrano, a fellow employee at the Safeway.

She said, "The last time I saw Kathy was on April fourteenth. She told me she had received a phone call that her boyfriend had been shot."

"Who's her boyfriend?"

"Mike Carroll. Kathy said she had to go up to Lake Tahoe because of this."

The investigators talked to James Baio, a friend of Kathy Allen's. He also said that the last time he saw or talked to her was April 14. "She said she was going to Tahoe, that Mike was in trouble. I asked her to call me when she got there. She never called."

Investigators interviewed Monique Mavraedis, another coworker of Kathy's. She stated, "On the evening of the fourteenth, 1985, at about seven-thirty, Kathy Allen left with a man in a copperish-looking Honda automobile. The man had been waiting for her since about five-thirty or six."

Investigators talked to a John Gouveia, the foster brother of Mike Carroll. He told them that he had received a letter from Kathy Allen, Mike's girlfriend, stating that some people would be by to pick up Mike's property.

The investigators next checked with the phone company. Phone records for the Wilseyville residence indicated that on April 14, 1985, just after one in the afternoon, a phone call was placed from that house to the Safeway store in Milpitas, California.

Phone records also revealed three phone calls made to San Francisco: on April 14, at 4:19 in the afternoon; on April 15, at 7:42 in the evening; and again on April 15, at 7:57 in the evening. The first number was discovered to be the residence of Dennis Goza. The investigators learned that Mr. Goza was the owner of the Dennis Moving Service company. The second two numbers were Mr. Goza's business phone.

The investigators interviewed Dennis Goza. Charlie Ng was an employee. Employment records revealed that Ng did not work on April 14, 15, or 16, 1985.

SUNDAY, JUNE 9, 1985, NOON.

There was no respite for the workers on the quiet sabbath afternoon. A second intact body was unearthed in the telephone line trench. Fifteen minutes later they found a third one. Ten minutes later, a fourth one. One minute later the corpse of a small child was discovered.

Coroner Terry Parker asked Ballard for more tables.

After a cursory inspection of the corpses, Ballard asked, "Anything?"

"I'm sorry to tell you, Sheriff, but one is another black male. Two are women, the last a child."

Another black male? Ballard thought.

Did this involve some kind of racial mania? There weren't many blacks in the county.

He went back to his desk. Ng's court-martial transcripts had arrived from Hawaii. He opened the fat file and begin making notes. A picture of Ng's life was emerging.

He read: *Statement of Ng to the Navy investigator, "While I was living with Lake, he and I shared an interest in weapons. He bought me a semiautomatic pistol. With my knowledge of weapons, I filed . . . to make it an automatic weapon. I also made a silencer from ordering parts from various catalogues.*

"I asked Lake to get me an AR-15, which I wanted to convert into an M-16, and he did."

The Navy investigator asked, "Did Lake know you were a fugitive?"

"I told Lake that I had embarrassed the government in a big way, but nothing more."

Ballard flipped through the pages, scanning the text. He read: *A psychiatric evaluation of Ng was done during the court-martial—he was pronounced sane.*

A naval attorney said that Ng told him, "I consider myself a good liar. They never know who you are: Your best friend is your best enemy. If you want to kill someone, make him think you like him, then it will be easy."

The Navy lawyer said Ng told him he put potassium cyanide in the salt shakers in the Marine mess hall, but no one got sick, and Ng couldn't figure out why not.

Semper Fidelis, Ballard thought.

He read: *The attorney stated that Ng tried to kill a staff sergeant. He used a grenade launcher but it failed to detonate. Ng claimed to have blown up two cars, and said he enjoyed military operations, as long as he planned them.*

The Navy investigator asked Ng about his school days. He answered, "People harass me, I keep the feeling to myself most of the time and see how much I can take."

"Why did you steal the weapons?"

"I feel I am a born fighter, and I like to plan tactics and try to perform clandestine operations and stuff like that, so I was thinking I could be a good elite soldier. I was basically in charge of the execution. My main feeling is just to prove that I can do something like that nobody did before."

Near the end of the fat folder, Ballard found a quote by Ng about his life with Claralyn and Leonard in Mendocino.

"I found a family that really treat me as part of the unit. Back then, my friends treated me like their own son."

Ballard looked at his watch and thought, it's only one o'clock—what else can happen today to make me feel even more ill?

At the autopsy table, the coroners were working on the four new cadavers. They stopped for lunch. Irene, who had been pitching in as a substitute photographer, snapped one more picture of the wound that Heglar had pointed out. Then she went in search of Eisenmann.

She couldn't wait to ask him a question that had been nagging her all morning. She found him and asked, "Do we have any basis for arresting Claralyn yesterday?"

"For what?"

"Look at the evidence," Irene said hotly. "She came

here before us and took God knows what. She admits to having spent time with Ng and Lake all last year. What else do you need?"

"You forgot the credit cards."

"What credit cards?"

"Lordan told me this morning. Before driving Claralyn up here yesterday, she was interrogated in San Francisco. The fraud detail did a trace on all credit card charges on cards owned by missing persons. Claralyn's signature matches on two bills, both for meals at restaurants. She admitted to treating Ng and Leonard, but said Lake gave her the cards."

"For the love of God, all this isn't enough for suspicion?"

"No. We're police officers, not speculators, we deal in fact. She turned over the videotapes. She told the truth. They were homemade pornography of her and Lake."

"Is there anything to charge her with?"

"What did you want me to arrest her for—aiding and abetting in pornography?"

Eisenmann went to Lordan, spoke for a minute, was handed a file, then returned. "Ng may have killed a gay San Francisco disc jockey named Don Giulletti.

"According to this file, Giulletti's roommate said Giulletti had been killed by an Asian matching Ng's description."

"What about the roommate?"

Eisenmann glanced at the file. "Supposedly, Ng shot him also, but the man didn't die. He recovered."

"An eyewitness?"

"An eyewitness. Lake also told Robin Stapley's friend Doolin, that he and Ng had discovered their neighbors, Robin Stapley, Lonnie Bond, his common-law wife Brenda O'Connor, and their child, Lonnie Bond Junior, shot to death in the cabin next door. Lake claims they were cooking amphetamines over there and someone bumped them off for the cash and the drugs. Lake said he and Charlie . . ." Eisenmann paused, held the file up to the light, then read, "'. . . disposed of the bodies by burning them Indian-style on top of some wooden, built-up thing and then they had buried them. Leonard said he got rid of the bodies because he didn't want the police snooping around.' "

Irene said, her voice quivering, "I feel so goddamn helpless."

Sheriff Ballard was beginning to feel the same way. he watched a clean-cut man in a business suit walk up the driveway. How could he stand the heat in that getup? The man flipped open a wallet. Ballard looked at the FBI agent's credentials and asked what he could do for him.

The agent, mid-thirties, with the inevitable Bureau haircut, asked, "So where are the videotapes?"

Ballard trudged up the hill to Bo Carter's house. He opened a portable safe where Bunning was keeping the videos locked and took them out. He closed the drapes in the front room, turned on the VCR and TV, and, heart souring inside his chest, slipped the first tape in.

The agent watched Lake, friends, and family eat Easter dinner with growing agitation. He finally said, "What is this?"

"The Balazs family's Easter dinner."

"You know what I mean."

Ballard looked into the bright, sparkling blue eyes of the agent and said softly, "I know exactly what you mean."

The screen turned snowy. Then Lake appeared. He stared at the camera and announced his full name. He then launched into a deadpan soliloquy of the world according to Lake. He talked about the coming nuclear holocaust and his inevitable role in rebuilding civilization.

The TV turned snowy once again. Then the screen filled with Leonard and a woman chained to a bed and sobbing for her baby. The scene abruptly changed. A different woman was chained to a chair.

Ballard said, "The wallpaper in the background matches that in the house."

"Thank you," the FBI agent said, and wrote this information down in his notebook.

Leonard Lake's voice came over the TV speaker: he would make sure they were "busy" while they were confined on the property. They would perform all the usual household chores. "Us," "us," "us," came through loud and clear. Especially, they would "fuck" for us.

The woman, eyes filled with tears, face taut with terror, kept nodding her head and mumbling.

Lake walked behind her. He ran the forefinger of his right hand across her face. It wasn't much of a choice, he told her, but there it was in brief. But there was always the chance that she had a "death wish."

The young woman sobbed, "No, I—"

Lake smirked. Really, he said, he had a fondness for her.

Using the remote control, the agent hit the pause button. The screen froze, the woman's mouth open, eyes wide, her moment of terror locked on a single frame of film.

The agent asked, "Kathy who?"

"Kathy Allen. Investigators in San Francisco have shown her picture to fellow employees at the Safeway store in Milpitas. Positive ID."

"Has her body been found?"

"Not that we know of."

The agent pushed the play button. Lake was still holding forth about what he expected Kathy to do for him and his partner. It wasn't fair, of course, he conceded. But "we" didn't operate on principles of goodness or fairness —just self-interest. "Selfish bastards," he called himself and his partner. Then he laughed that perhaps Kathy would find better names to describe them for what they would do "in the next four weeks." But it was a tough life: they had worked hard the whole day and had been "nervous" and strung out. They needed some release from that tension. Lake suggested that Kathy might be able to "do something" about their problem.

Ballard opened the door of the cabin. The sun was

filtering through the surrounding trees. A faint breeze had picked up, rustling leaves and branches.

He went to the deck's railing and looked down. The area below teemed with working people. The CCC trainees had covered almost half the slope filled with Mountain Misery. He could see the coroner bent over a small corpse. Roger Heglar was holding a vial up toward the sun and staring at it. Dozens of officers were digging in the telephone line trench.

This place looks like Dachau, Ballard thought.

Again his ruminations were interrupted by some ominous news. Investigators had traced the Ruger found in the bunker to the Accuracy Gun Shop located at 3651 University Avenue, San Diego, California. The owner stated that on March 30, 1985, Robin Scott Stapley, 4755 Felton, Apartment 4, San Diego, purchased a used Ruger .22 caliber semiautomatic pistol, serial number 12-70329.

Cost: $146.10.

In San Francisco, ballistics expert Richard Grzybowski examined Paul Cosner's car. He retrieved spent bullets from thc hcadliner above the passenger seat and from the passenger door. Both were .22 caliber.

The sun visor found at the Wilseyville property had been forwarded to San Francisco. Grzybowski took the sun visor and placed it in its proper position in the Honda Prelude. The bullet hole in the sun visor and the bullet hole in the headliner matched up. The trajectory appeared to be the same.

Down the San Francisco peninsula, investigators spoke to a George Blank. They had tracked him down through the Wilseyville phone logs. Mr. Blank said, "On April fourteenth, I received a phone call from Leonard Lake."

"Did you know Lake?"

"Yes, I did. Leonard asked me to pick up and repair a car. He said that a man named Charlie would be delivering the keys. Two days later, on April sixteenth, my two children, Deborah and Ryan, met an Asian man in his early twenties named Charlie at the bus station in San Jose. He gave my kids instructions on where to find the car and the keys. I went to the parking lot of the Safeway store in Milpitas, California, and picked up a 1974 Mercury Capri."

"Do you know who the owner was?"

"The pink slip was registered to a Mike Carroll."

Sheriff's Deputy Steve Mathews was giving a tour to a group of reporters. He led them to the hill where the CCC trainees were working. "We're raking each section as thoroughly as we can." He randomly reached down into a thick clump of Mountain Misery and dug. He opened his hand and revealed a half-dozen bone fragments. "Whoever did this did a real good job of destroying the evidence. It's as if they cut the bodies into tiny pieces, threw them into a bucket, and then just chucked them all down this hill. This place is a boneyard."

Chapter Twelve

MONDAY, JUNE 10, 1985, 9:00 A.M., EASTERN STANDARD TIME.

THE FBI SPECIAL AGENT IN CHARGE GOT OFF the plane in Toronto. With the agent was a member of the Toronto Metropolitan Police and a Royal Canadian Mountie. The Mountie took pride in his city, and pointed out the waterfront development as they drove into town. Nearby was one of the three Asian sections of town. They went directly to their target.

Ng's sister, Vanessa Marlow, wasn't home, but her daughter gave them her work address—her father's import-export business.

They drove into the downtown area. They were shown into Mrs. Marlow's office and introduced themselves.

She looked more Eurasian than Chinese. High cheek bones accented her placid face.

"Mrs. Marlow, your brother is in very serious trouble. There is an international manhunt going on. Ng is now number one on the FBI's Most Wanted list. I think it is in your best interest to cooperate. And in Charlie's also."

"Charlie's also?"

"He has been listed as 'armed and dangerous'. If we could capture him by surprise, we could arrest him without harming him. No one wants him dead. If he is cornered and resists, then he will probably be killed."

"I do not know where he is."

The law enforcement agents left the office.

MONDAY, JUNE 10, 1985, 9:30 A.M.

At the same moment in San Francisco, Dr. Heglar was examining anatomical remains in the basement of the coroner's office. Dr. Stephens and D.A. Investigator Crawford were with him. Crawford had just brought down another batch of evidence.

There were two long tables covered in brown butcher paper. Pieces of bone and charred remnants of personal items were spread out.

Crawford asked, "How's it going?"

"We're computerizing everything," Heglar answered. "First we segregate the evidence into recognizable groups, identifying, when possible, as to sex, age, and race, then enter it into the computer. Then, say you run a program and it showed how many left or right kneecaps you had—say four—then you know you have at least that many disarticulated bodies."

MONDAY, JUNE 10, 1985, 10:00 A.M.

Eisenmann and Brunn said good-byes to each other. Irene was going back that morning to San Francisco to interrogate Claralyn Balazs later that day.

A deputy sheriff approached and told Eisenmann, "There's a private dick that wants to talk."

Eisenmann went to the barricade, met private detective Henry Meister, and led him to the chairs under the clump of trees.

Meister showed his P.I. license. "For almost a year I've been searching for a Jeffrey Askren, of Sunnyvale. His parents live in Indiana. They're the ones who hired me. Jeffrey was an electronics engineer."

"What makes you believe that he's part of—"

"Let me finish. Fourteen months ago Jeffrey told friends he was going on a photography excursion. He said he was first going to West Point, take some pictures, then stay at the Sutter Creek Hotel."

"He never arrived?"

"No, but he did make reservations. The Sheriff's Department found his locked car seven miles from where we're now sitting. It was on a logging road. The cops think his car got stuck in a snow bank. Remember, this was at the end of March, of 'eighty-four. They think he tried to walk out. One of them said that it happens once in a while, and the bodies always turn up when the snow melts."

"And Jeffrey didn't turn up when the snow melted?"

"No, he's never turned up. It may have gotten dark and he lost his way. He was not a camper, not woodwise."

"Was he married?"

"I thought of that," Meister said. "Sometimes people just drop out. I talked to the people he worked with in Santa Clara, and I couldn't find a reason why this guy would drop out."

"You think he's here?"

Meister opened a briefcase and gave Eisenmann a file. "This has Jeffrey's dental records, pictures, medical history, photographs, last—"

"Thank you," Eisenmann said, "I'll let you know immediately if we learn anything." He carried the file back to Lordan's desk and added it to the growing number of missing person files that were coming in from all over the country.

TUESDAY, JUNE 11, 1985, NOON.

Ballard had the flu. He asked Eisenmann to fill in for him at the lunchtime press conference.

He assembled the four dozen reporters in front of the cabin and said, "As different evidence is uncovered, we bring in different specialists. Calaveras County has a fourteen-person force on the case. San Francisco has a three-man homicide team, a ten-man tactical investigation unit, two missing persons officers, a handwriting expert, and a link analyst."

"What's a link analyst?" a reporter asked.

"He links the victims to the suspects. We also have five

special agents from the Department of Justice here. We have fingerprint experts, crime lab experts, forensic—"

"Why did you wait so long to inform the press?"

Eisenmann thought, Here comes the old First Amendment rights. "We didn't want to give away too much."

A stout reporter, with a full beard not unlike Leonard Lake's, interrupted with, "Maybe if we had run Ng's photo on the front page of the papers, he'd be in custody now."

"You ran his photo on the front page of your papers Saturday and he's not in custody."

A female reporter shouted, "This case is being carried out with the speed of a snail."

Another reporter added, "A snail with a bowling ball tied to his tail."

Eisenmann had been through this before. He flipped open his notebook. "You want an official opinion on that? Glen Craig, director of the Department of Justice's law enforcement division, said this about the handling of this case. And I quote: 'There has been some criticism about slow movement, but you basically know who the suspects are. And there's no point in trying to move so fast that you make mistakes that would damage any potential prosecution. It takes time to make a strategic plan. And I don't know of any evidence that's been destroyed or lost'."

A black reporter asked, "We have reports coming out of Mendocino County that Ng hated blacks and Hispanics. Even other Orientals."

"You'll have to ask the Mendocino Sheriff's Department about that."

WEDNESDAY, JUNE 12, 1985, 1:00 P.M.

The next day, in Nicaragua, Clancy was boarding a direct flight to Los Angeles. She hadn't decided where to go next. Bhopal's legal situation looked interesting: Melvin Belli had just volunteered to represent all of the thousands of Indians who had inhaled vaporized cyanide.

Besides, Clancy thought, I haven't been to India in ages. She dialed Chicago and got her secretary on the phone. One of her "moles" in the New Zealand government had called—urgent. Clancy asked, "What did he want?"

"He said it was so confidential he would only tell you."

Clancy clicked off her cellular phone. She flipped open her black book and dialed Wellington, New Zealand. She said, "What's all the hush-hush about?"

A male voice whispered, "Prime Minister Lange is furious."

Clancy thought, This guy sounds like Deep Throat. "Why is David furious?"

"We detected a blast in French Polynesia, and our scientists—"

"A nuclear blast?"

"Yes, a test, underground."

"Old news, I already know what's going on."

"The Prime Minister just found out. He's denouncing the test tomorrow."

"Remind him to denounce the four nuclear explosions that were detonated on the Mururoa Atoll the last few weeks. Then tell Lange he owes me one." She hung up. When would her moles learn? People didn't want to read about nuclear explosions, they wanted to read about the guy next door, chopping his wife up into porterhouse steaks and cooking her on the barbee.

She called her secretary again, who said, "The Hooker case is in the papers again."

"Hooker? Refresh me."

When her secretary finished with the details, Clancy thought, Interesting—and on the way north to Calgary, I'll hit Tehama, see what I can dredge up on Hooker, then take a break. The Ortega scoop will set me up financially for the rest of the year.

Clancy thought, Ng's been spotted in Toronto, but witnesses have been wrong before. My hunch is he's still headed west. He has a relative in Calgary, and he thinks that the police don't know that fact.

She smiled. *Business with pleasure . . . I haven't been to the Calgary Stampede in ages.*

THURSDAY, JUNE 13, 1985, 10:00 A.M.

Ng's lawyer, Garrick Lew, who represented him in the 1984 shoplifting case in San Leandro, told a reporter from the *San Francisco Examiner,* "Ng was a quiet, reserved type of guy. It's totally bewildering as to how he's described today."

FRIDAY, JUNE 14, 1985, 11:00 A.M.

Another grueling week of work had gone by on Blue Mountain Road. Ballard said to Eisenmann, "Sorry to bother you, but there's a woman at the barricade that wants to talk to someone."

That's me, Eisenmann thought, someone, not even a name anymore.

He escorted the woman, about fifty, plump, wearing a colorful peasant dress and a straw hat, to the interview area.

The woman settled into a chair. She kept unzipping and zipping her purse. She said, "I've been so worried since I read the papers."

Eisenmann asked, "Why are you worried?"

The woman opened her purse and pulled out a strand of pearls. "I'm worried about these."

Puzzled, Eisenmann examined the necklace, then gave it back to the woman. He wondered, Who does she think I am, a jewelry appraiser? He asked, "Do you think they're fake?"

"No, but I bought them here."

"Here?" Eisenmann said.

"Here," the woman said with finality. "I saw a notice at the Academy Club, that's a bar in West Point. The notice was on the bulletin board. It was for a yard sale, giving this address. I also bought a ring."

Eisenmann eyed the strand of pearls the woman was twisting nervously in her hand. He said, "A ring?"

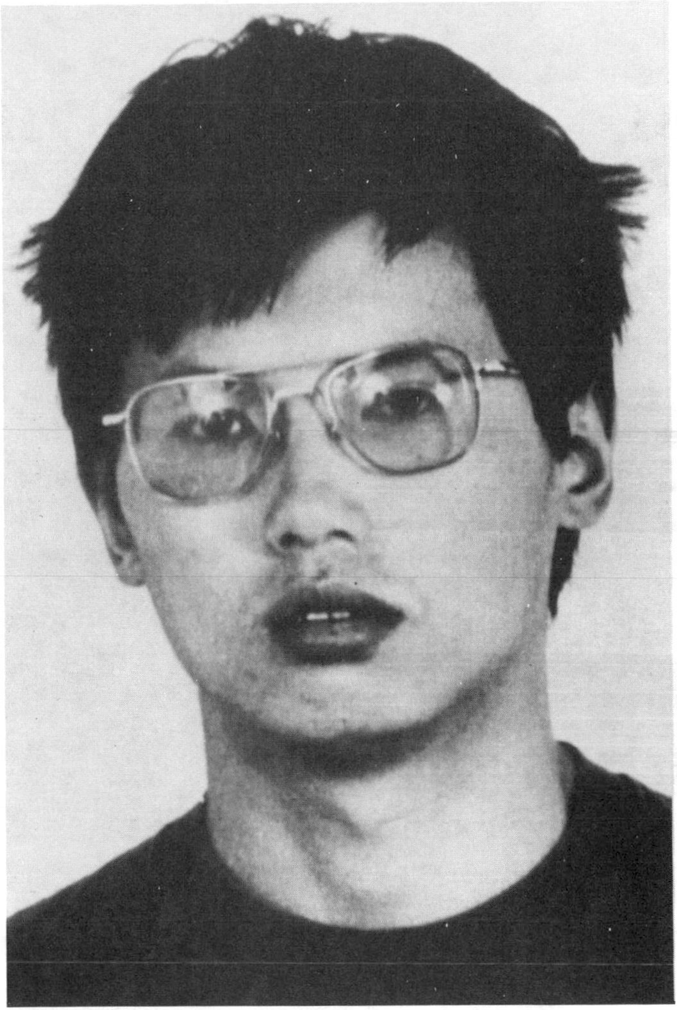

Charles Chitat Ng was booked by Daly City police for shoplifting in 1984, after finishing his sentence at Leavenworth. (Reuters/Bettman)

The Balazs cabin near Wilseyville, with its ominous bunker, became the center of a massive investigation in June, 1985 when missing persons were traced here. *(San Francisco Chronicle* / Mike Maloney)

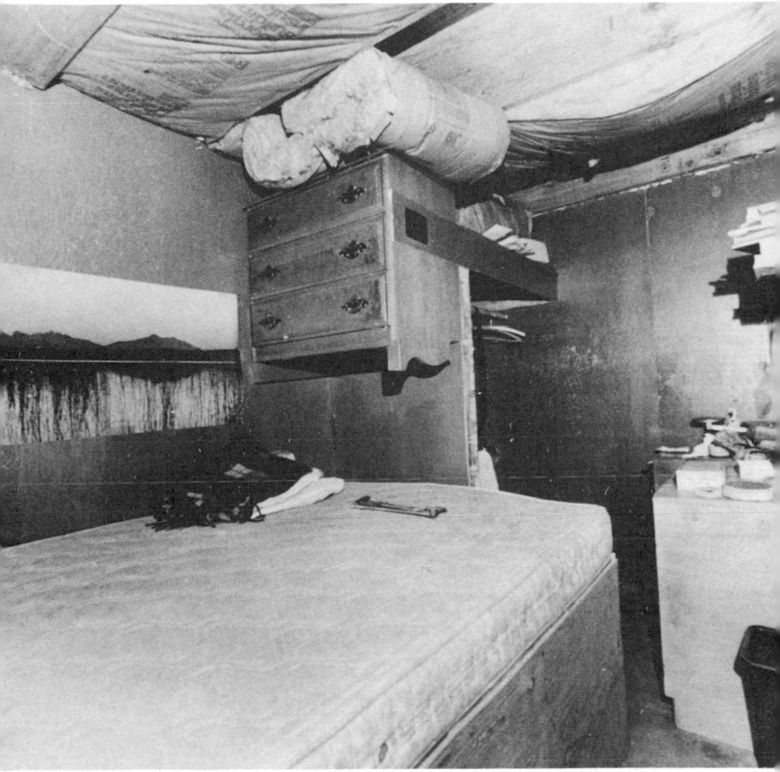

Early in the investigation, a hidden cell was discovered in the bunker, complete with a one-way mirror used to view the victims. (AP/Wide World)

During the first week, forensic experts identified bone fragments of four victims unearthed in a telephone-line trench. (AP/Wide World)

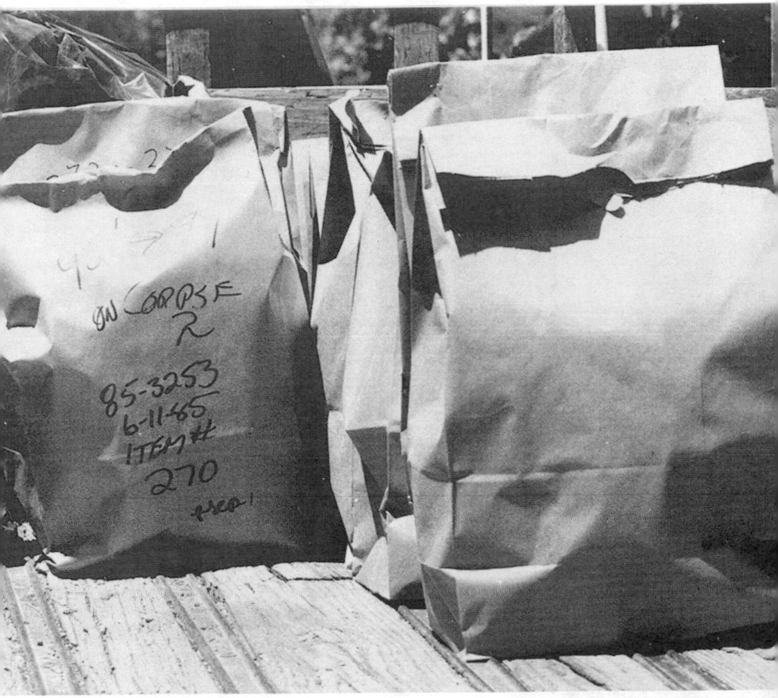

Remains of victims were catalogued at the site for shipment to San Francisco for further tests to determine age and sex. (*San Francisco Chronicle* / Mike Maloney)

Photographs of numerous women were found in the bunker, and were published by police in hopes of identifying victims. All of them were located and found safe. *(San Francisco Chronicle)*

Ng hid out in a lean-to hut in Fish Creek Park in Calgary before his capture in a bungled robbery in the city in 1985. (*San Francisco Chronicle* / Steve Ringman)

During preliminary hearings in San Andreas in October, 1992, Ng was confined in an extraordinary cage when not in the courtroom—a practice termed "barbarous" by a federal magistrate. (AP/Wide World)

"Yes."

"What about the pearls?"

"I bought them a couple of months ago."

"Here?"

"Yes, at another yard sale. I thought the man's name was Charlie Gunnar, but when I heard on the—"

"How many times have you been here?"

The woman frowned, concentrating, then, "Six, maybe eight times. About once a month."

Eisenmann rubbed his temples. Lake was holding yard sales to peddle the jewelry he took off his victims. He was selling the merchandise while he was standing on top of their graves. He felt his cheeks flush.

He remembered Parker showing him a finger bone. The coroner had said, "This was hacked off the hand. Ring finger—I guess he was after the wedding and engagement rings."

The plump woman said, "I don't know what to do. I keep thinking, these pearls might have belonged to one of those poor women who died here. I can't sleep at nights, and . . . I don't know why, but I feel guilty."

Transference, Eisenmann thought, and it caused heavy-duty guilt. He said, "Are you religious?"

"Catholic."

"Then make a donation to your parish church, light a candle to the Blessed Mother." Eisenmann stood and waved an arm, encompassing the entire area. He started to say, "Pray for the departed souls. . . ." But he couldn't play that role.

He mumbled, "Pray for me."

SATURDAY, JUNE 15, 1985, 11:30 A.M.

A group of officers in the interview area suddenly started shouting.

Ballard left his command post and went over to investigate. He heard a radio blaring. The announcer said, "One of Claralyn Balazs's attorneys, Stan Pozanski, said today: 'We have decided before she makes any further comment she must be granted full state and federal immunity. In recent days, there have been death threats against our client.' "

The announcer continued, "We have the last statement Ms. Balazs made." Claralyn's voice came over the speaker. "I have cooperated with the police to the best of my ability. I wish to express my concern to the people affected by this situation."

"Situation?" Ballard said. "I thought this was a killing field, not a situation."

The announcer's tinny voice went on, "Claralyn 'Cricket' Balazs's other attorney, Chris Carroll, said, 'The ball is now in the various agencies' court. We will settle for nothing less than blanket immunity'."

The radio was snapped off. One officer said, "I want blanket immunity from my debts."

Another added, "I want immunity from criminals."

Ballard thought, All I want is a blanket and three days' sleep. As he walked by the autopsy table, Parker pointed at a skull. There were tufts of hair popping out in a random pattern. "See the bullet hole."

He saw the small, circular hole, just behind where an ear once was.

Parker said, "One bullet, right behind the ear. I'll bet dinner that it's still inside the cranium." He peered at the skull. "Maybe not, the angle could have sent the slug across the inside of the skull to exit out of the bottom of the jaw—soft tissue all the way."

The coroner bent down to within a few inches of the skull. "I was wrong, this hole is too small for a heavy-punching caliber. It looks like the size of a .22. Then it would just tumble around, smashing and tearing. No way would it have oomph to go all the way across the brain matter."

Ballard sighed and returned to his command post. Ten minutes later Dr. Parker stood in front of him. His hands were stuffed into his pockets. He was hunched slightly forward, peering over his wire-framed glasses.

"Yes?" Ballard asked.

"I've made an ID."

"Fantastic. Who?"

"Jacobson."

"Who?"

"Randy Jacobson."

Sheriff Ballard opened a file. Could he have possibly missed a name? He knew them all by heart—that grisly litany of horror—Paul Cosner, Harvey Dubs, Sean . . .

He knew, absolutely, that there was no Randy Jacobson in his mind or on his list. Then it popped up from wherever it had been elusively hiding. He pawed through his files and found the inventory of identifications from Paul Cosner's Honda Prelude. There it was: under the front seat a First Interstate Bank card in the name of Randy Jacobson.

Parker said, "We got Randy Jacobson's fingerprints from S.F. Missing Persons. No question, the guy on our table with a bullet in his head is Randy Jacobson." He handed over the file.

Ballard read: *Randy Jacobson, white, 35, Vietnam War veteran. Missing for six months. Last known address: the Pink Palace, San Francisco.*

The Pink Palace, Ballard thought. I know that place well. It's a run-down "project" near the Haight-Ashbury district, in San Francisco.

He continued to read: *Two other residents of the Pink Palace, Maurice Rock, 38, and Cheryl Okoro, 26, disappeared at the same time. An investigator learned from other residents of the housing unit that Lake frequently stayed there too. Last February Lake hired the three people to help him finish a job he was working on in the mountains.*

Three more. Pink Palace.

Ballard rubbed his chin. His mind was burning with the knowledge that there was a connection between the Pink Palace and three more bodies.

It will come, he thought, just like the Miranda connection had.

SUNDAY, JUNE 16, 1985, 10:30 A.M., FATHER'S DAY. It was now two full weeks since the case broke. Criminal investigations the size of the Blue Mountain Road massacre inevitably bog down. It was becoming compartmentalized. One officer did nothing but itemize, another sift dirt, another photograph. The overall direction and information the case was taking was lost to some of the officers in the field. They hated the heat and the stench.

Eisenmann suddenly remembered the two photos taken at the juvenile hall. Whatever happened to them? Were any of them identified? Were any of them missing? He found Ballard by a flatbed truck. The truck was filled with evidence being shipped to San Francisco.

Ballard said, "You mean you haven't heard? The papers ran the photos. We've been able to identify seventeen of the twenty-one photos. And the wonderful news is, they've located all the women. All seventeen are alive, they're fine."

"Then why were the photographs taken in Lake's bunker?"

"We'll find out, we're plowing our way through puzzle after puzzle. We'll learn everything in the end."

The officers gathered at the interview area for lunch. One asked Sheriff Ballard, "How long do you think this will go on?"

Eisenmann thought, We have positive proof linking Paul Cosner, the three Dubses, Charlie Gunnar, Donald Lake, Robin Stapley, Randy Jacobson, Maurice Rock, Cheryl Okoro, Lonnie Bond, his common-in-law wife Brenda O'Connor, their kid, Lonnie Jr., to this place. And we have physical evidence, driver's licenses, credit cards, linking twelve more here, like Michael Carroll and his girlfriend Kathleen Allen.

But we haven't come up with anything major in days.

Ballard said, "I know what you're all feeling. The emotional part of the constant digging, sifting, thinking, sometimes I feel like kicking a tree."

Detective Copland turned to Eisenmann. "You guys from the big city who handle child abuse and homicide build up a coldness—"

Eisenmann said, "Don't you believe it."

"It still hits you, what people do to other people?"

"It still hits me," Eisenmann said. "This is a hell of a way to spend Father's Day."

Bunning said, "I have three kids."

"So do I," Copland said.

"When you have a child of your own," Bunning said, "you start to think—how could anyone do that?"

Detective Steve Mathews said, "You think about the terror in the victims' minds, it's incredible. I play video games at night, just to get my mind off it."

"You do?" Larry Copland said. "I talk to my wife. Sometimes, after the paperwork at night, I don't get home till midnight. She'll still be up, she'll listen while I get it out of me. We'll talk till two. I know it sounds corny, but if she wouldn't be doing that . . ." He trailed off.

This is helping, Eisenmann thought, they all feel the same thing I do—revulsion.

MONDAY, JUNE 17, 1985, 2:00 P.M., CENTRAL STANDARD TIME.

Charlie Chitat Ng had wasted another precious morning and was getting nowhere in the Asian quarter in Toronto. Too many people are taking too close a look at me, he thought.

He'd cropped his hair close. He'd plucked his eyebrows even more dramatically than he had earlier. He'd started wearing a hat.

People still stared too long when he walked by.

He realized that going to the Asian community in Toronto was a mistake. Caucasians couldn't tell the subtle differences in an Oriental. But Chinese knew Chinese, and Japanese knew Japanese, and Koreans knew Koreans. And they saw through alterations.

Time to move, he thought. But how?

No plane, too much of a trail.

Rent a car?

He realized that he had pushed using the phony ID in the name of Kimoto too far already.

Bus? Too many people.

Charlie Ng pictured in his mind the last time he'd ridden a bus—the people reading their books, the people asleep, the people doing crossword puzzles.

The bus, he thought, is cheap, it's direct, and it's usually very anonymous.

And that is exactly what he needed.

He went to the Toronto bus station. He paused, bought a ticket to Sudbury. There he would buy a ticket to Moosonee, but get off the bus in Timmins.

He was going to take a convoluted route to Calgary.

Chapter Thirteen

WEDNESDAY, JUNE 19, 1985, 10:00 A.M.

THE VARIOUS LEVELS OF LAW ENFORCEMENT working on the case—federal, state, county—denied Claralyn Balazs's petition for blanket immunity.

California State Attorney General John Van de Kamp said, "This is an overwhelming case—so enormous that systems, including a computer, have to be developed to deal with it. The problem is one of magnitude. You have to continue the investigation to find out how big it really is. This thing went from a burglary to atrocities."

The following day, Ballard proved the point about atrocities. He made copies of the infamous diary and sent them to all levels of law enforcement.

He thought, I've had this thing for two weeks and still can't stomach finishing it. It's your job, his conscience whispered.

He opened it and read how Lake described himself as a forgotten man, now in his second year as a fugitive, with a daily routine that was "dull, day-to-day." In an ominous aside, Lake pictured himself as "still" having death "in my pocket." His goal remained the achievement of his fantasy life, but he thought himself a has-been—older, fatter, "not much wiser." Where he would wind up, he didn't know, but he was confident he could avoid capture. Only the "weird things" bothered him—whatever they were, if they came out it was all over and he would kill himself.

Ballard closed the diary and thought, let the lawyers and the psychiatrists figure it out.

SUNDAY, JUNE 23, 1985, 2:00 P.M., CENTRAL STANDARD TIME.

Sergeant John Clarke of the Metropolitan Toronto Police, made a joint statement with the Royal Canadian Mounties, "We know Charlie Chitat Ng is hiding in one of the three Asian communities in our city." It was too late for the afternoon papers, but the story made headlines on Monday morning in Sacramento, San Francisco, and San Andreas. Ng now had been reported "seen" in several places in the Midwest. Which way would he jump?

MONDAY, JUNE 24, 1985, 8:00 A.M.

Using an infrared camera, the makeshift crime lab in San Andreas found a hot spot directly under the bunker.

"About six-by-six-by-six feet," the technician informed Ballard. "In the center, directly under the reinforced floor. We did a couple of core samples. That floor's made of rebar, wire mesh, and concrete."

"Tear it down."

"The whole bunker?"

"Yes, but get an architect here and have him sketch the layout. Have him build a miniature replica, and have photographs taken of every angle on that thing."

"What do you think's under there, Sheriff?"

"After spending weeks here, I wouldn't be surprised at anything we found."

By the following morning, the architect had finished his drawings. A backhoe scooped dirt from the rear of the bunker. An eight-man crew of officers, four from Calaveras and four from San Francisco, started to dismantle it, cinder block by cinder block.

* * *

Eisenmann's phone on the deck of the Balazs house rang. A voice whispered, "I don't want to get involved, but you guys should know about—"

"Who are you?" Eisenmann asked. *This guy sounds like he's making an obscene phone call.*

"None of your business," the husky voice said. "I just want you to know that Jeff Gerald and Cliff Peranteau have been missing for months."

"Why does that have to do—"

"They both worked for the Dennis Moving Company, that's where Ng worked."

"Why do you think Ng was involved?"

"I don't think, I know. I was standing there when Ng asked if they wanted to pick up extra cash. I've never seen them again."

Eisenmann pictured the scene: Four guys, shooting the breeze between assignments—one of them describing a mountain cabin where the living is easy and the pay is great—just for building a cinder-block house. Only they didn't know they'd be digging their own graves. He said, "Thank you, are you sure you can't tell me who you—"

"No way. Just you and the other cops get off your fat asses and start doing something."

WEDNESDAY, JUNE 26, 1985, 2:00 P.M., ONTARIO, CANADA.

Charlie Chitat Ng got off the bus in Timmins. He bought four new bus tickets: one to Quebec, one to Montreal, one to Vancouver, and one to Edmonton. The bus to Edmonton was leaving last. He boarded each bus, he kept his head down, wore dark glasses, and slouched. He made sure he was seen, then slipped out the window of the toilet in the rear.

When he boarded the bus for Edmonton, he kept his head high, still wore dark glasses, but walked with confidence to the last seat at the rear. He put his carryon grip in the seat beside him, curled up in the corner, and tried to sleep.

THURSDAY, JUNE 27, 1985, 11:00 A.M., SAN FRANCISCO.

Homicide investigators, working from the anonymous phone tip, interviewed all the employees of the Dennis Moving Service. Hector Salcedo, a long-time worker at the company, said, "I dropped Clifford Peranteau off at his house. Cliff was supposed to go to work that afternoon. That was the nineteenth of January this year. He never showed up for work again."

"Did you try to contact him?"

"I tried to call his house a couple of times. No answer. I went around to his house in mid-afternoon. Cliff had a Suzuki motorcycle. It was there on the nineteenth, but Cliff wasn't. A few days later when I went back again the motorcycle was gone."

That afternoon in Wilseyville, the oak-framed mirrors hanging in the spare bedroom were identified as belonging to Mr. Peranteau. The Cross pen and pencil set monogrammed with the initials C.R.P. that was found in Ng's apartment on Lennox was also presumed to be Clifford Peranteau's.

The film in the camera found in the telephone trench had been developed. One photo was a nondescript street scene obviously shot through a window. The San Francisco investigators received the photo the next day and went back to the moving company. They showed it to Salcedo. He didn't recognize the scene.

The investigators spoke with Jerry Gonzalez, another employee of Dennis Moving, and his brother Robert. They had sold Peranteau a turntable which was later found at the Wilseyville property.

Jerry Gonzalez said, "I heard Ng and Peranteau quarreling, back around Thanksgiving. Cliff called Ng a goddamned Chinaman. I remember Cliff saying, 'I should never have gotten you this job.' "

The photo of the nondescript window scene was shown to Gonzalez. He did not recognize it.

Mike Fitzgerald, another employee, said that he also heard Ng and Cliff arguing, two months later, in mid-January. Ng was angry because he thought Peranteau was sloughing off on the job.

Kenneth Bruce, who also worked at Dennis Moving, told the investigators that Cliff was going to watch the Super Bowl with him and Rick Doedens.

Rick Doedens told the investigators that Cliff Peranteau never showed on Super Bowl Sunday. "However," he added, "I got a letter from Cliff on January twenty-eighth. In it was a stamped, self-addressed envelope. Cliff wanted me to send him his winnings on a Super Bowl bet."

The investigators asked if Mr. Doedens still had the original envelope. He gave it to them. It was postmarked Wilseyville, California. The self-addressed envelope was made out to P.O. Box 349, Mokelumne Hill, California.

The investigators showed both Rick Doedens and Kenneth Bruce the scene from the film discovered in the telephone trench. Neither recognized it.

Calaveras investigators contacted Wanda Davis, the postmaster of Mokelumne Hill. Her records showed that a post office box, 349, was opened on January 20, 1985, in the name of Clifford Peranteau. The box was closed shortly thereafter.

The investigators next located a Cynthia Basharr, a friend of Cliff Peranteau's. She had not seen or heard from him since January 15. She said, "Cliff said he was going to Tahoe with Charlie."

She also did not recognize the nondescript scene in the photo.

The investigators spoke once again with workers at the moving company, this time with owner Dennis Goza. He didn't know where the photograph was taken. But he did confirm that during this time there was only one Charlie working at Dennis Moving and that was Charlie Ng.

Clifford Peranteau had been scheduled to work on January 19, but never showed up.

Dennis Goza added, "I did receive a letter from him though, later."

"You did? What did it say?"

"He wanted his last paycheck to be sent to a P.O. box. He even included a return envelope. He wrote that he had a new girlfriend, a new job, and a new place to live."

"Did you send the paycheck?"

"No way. How could I know the letter was from Cliff?"

"Did you keep the envelope?"

Goza rummaged in his file cabinet. "Here it is, P.O. Box 349, Mokelumne Hill, California."

"Do you know where Mokelumne Hill is?"

"Up in the Mother Lode somewhere."

"It's a few miles north of San Andreas."

SATURDAY, JUNE 29, 1985, 11:00 A.M., TEHAMA COUNTY, CALIFORNIA.

In the late morning of another hot day, Tomasina Boyd Clancy sat in her hotel room in Red Bluff, Tehama County, California, finishing her article on Cameron Hooker. It was a wrap-up piece, worth a little on the West Coast, but she knew this type of case didn't make the East Coast papers. It was certainly big news in this northern California town, known only to travelers as a stopping point on Interstate 5 near the Oregon border.

She picked up her typescript and read: *Cameron Hooker is accused of keeping—*

She stopped, crossed out *keeping* and jotted in *entombing.* Much better.

She continued to read: *entombing Colleen Stan for seven years while he used her as his sex slave. Colleen was informed today by Tehama County prosecutors that charges might be reduced through plea bargaining. Assemblyman Richard Katz, Democrat, San Fernando Valley, said, "He would be out in less years than he held the woman captive, and that's absurd."*

And absurd it is. The problem is money, or lack of it. Although Supervisor Pettinger is on record as denying the plea bargain is to save money, he did add, "We have made studies that possibly the costs of this trial could financially break the county."

You can't have it both ways, Pettinger, is it money—or not?

Clancy shrugged. Not the best thing she'd ever written. It just might cover the cost of the hotel room. You couldn't win 'em all, a big one here, a little one there.

She called the airport and booked a flight to Sacramento and then on to Calgary.

MONDAY, JULY 1, 1985, 2:00 P.M.

Three weeks after the fugitive had disappeared into Canada, the Charlie Ng case suddenly swept the mighty into its vortex. The FBI held an afternoon press conference in San Francisco and formally accused the Pentagon and the Navy of malfeasance. Ng was born in Hong Kong, he was a British subject, he should have been deported after serving his prison term for stealing the weapons in Hawaii. And he should never have been recruited by the Marine Corps in the first place.

An information officer for the FBI said, "Who knows, if he was sent back to Hong Kong, maybe none of this would have happened, or at least not in this country."

The Pentagon released a stony, "No comment."

TUESDAY, JULY 2, 1985, 10:00 A.M.

Ballard looked into the late morning sun over the mountain cabin, hotter than ever.

From the top of the hill covered with Mountain Misery, Copland waved at the sheriff. The case was taking another dramatic turn—exactly one month after it had broken.

Copland said to Ballard, "I was probing the ground with a rod and hit something." He pointed. At his feet, still recessed into their holes, were three pieces of Tupperware. He knelt, pried the lid off one. The pot was filled with silver dollars. The second was also brimming with silver dollars.

Ballard called a crew of officers to the spot. They quickly dug up the area around the Tupperware pots. A white, five-gallon, plastic bucket came up. More silver dollars. A metal pipe twelve inches in diameter was unearthed, with an AR-15 inside. In all, 1,863 silver dollars were counted, plus wallets and credit cards. Among the debris was a Social Security card in the name of Jeffrey Gerald.

Ballard spat out the words. "Gerald, he worked at the moving company with Ng."

The sheriff ordered several deputies to make ever larger concentric sweeps from ground zero—the bunker. The search was extended more than half a mile from the center. One of Copland's crew soon came across a small section of ground downhill that seemed to have been disturbed.

Here the detectives dug up a rectangular-shaped Tupperware-type container. It was crammed with a variety of items, but Copland immediately focused on an envelope with the return address of the Philo motel where Lake had worked in 1984. Copland stared at the envelope in disbelief. The name Cosner was written on the outside. He gingerly removed a pair of glasses. Then he saw that the AAA automobile club card, a Pac Tel card, a Banker's Life Insurance card, and some business cards for Marin Motors of San Rafael, all were in the name of Paul Cosner.

"So that's it," Ballard said somberly, "the end of the trail in the Cosner case. Call Irene Brunn." The sheriff looked down the hill and thought, We haven't identified a body as Cosner's yet, but it's here, buried or chopped up or burned.

The other items in the Tupperware container were equally ominous: a Ruger Mark II .22 caliber semiautomatic handgun, with the serial number ground down, a holster, a clip of twelve rounds of .22 caliber ammunition, and a silencer.

WEDNESDAY, JULY 3, 1985, NOON.

The following day, at lunch, the shoptalk turned to the "hot spot" under the bunker. The concrete bunker was gone, dismantled block by block. The reinforced floor was gone, jackhammered into rubble. Where the floor had once been, a backhoe had dug a deep hole.

Irene stood beside the open pit. There was nothing but clay, earth and rotting timber. The "hot spot" picked up by the infrared sensors was only the chemical decomposition of wood. Brunn turned to Eisenmann. "The only false lead we've had yet."

Eisenmann glanced at his watch and thought, At least two more hours to go. I have to sit down. He walked to the interview area. He sank into a chair and rubbed the back of his neck. The muscles were tense, rock-hard.

Sheriff Ballard joined him.

Eisenmann said, "You look pleased with yourself."

"I am. I think I just figured out what PP one, two, and three refer to in Lake's diary. PP stands for Pink Palace, and one, two, and three for the three people Lake recruited to help build the bunker: Jacobson, Rock, and Okoro."

"When will it end?"

"It will end. In a way it already has. I've been thinking a lot lately. Lake and Ng get nailed June second, one dies, the other flees. Neither ever comes back here again. When you arrived, the dungeon was empty, there's no one chained to the bed in the house. Coincidence? I don't think so. The women were kept for a while, a week, a month, before they were killed."

"What are you driving at, Sheriff?"

"I think Lake was in the Bay Area on a hunt. He lured the men up here with promises of easy money. Maybe even sex. And he probably had to drug the women. We've identified all but two of the twenty-one photos of women found in the bunker. All nineteen are alive, all accounted for. They could have become victims. Officer Wright deserves a medal."

The remaining two were later found, also alive and well.

"You look tired."

"I am," Ballard said.

"Take tomorrow off."

Ballard nodded. "I've decided to let everybody take tomorrow off, for the Fourth of July."

"Independence Day? I've lost complete track of time."

"Are you going to go to the parade?"

"I'm going to go to bed."

That same day, in San Francisco, Lloyd Cunningham, who worked for the San Francisco police as a questions-document examiner, was performing a series of tests on the Olympia typewriter found at the Wilseyville property.

He compared the typewriting on the letter that had been sent to Rick Doedens and the self-addressed envelope containing the request for Cliff Peranteau's Super Bowl winnings. He also compared the type with the letter received by Dennis Goza, owner of Dennis Moving, requesting Cliff's wages.

When he was finished, Cunningham wrote a succinct report: *In my opinion, all the letters I examined were typed on the Olympia typewriter.*

FRIDAY, JULY 5, 1985, SACRAMENTO.
The California legislature unanimously approved a grant of half a million dollars to Calaveras County to help defray the cost of the ongoing criminal investigation of what was now called the Lake-Ng case.

Senator John Garamendi, Democrat, Walnut Grove, said, "They just don't have the resources to fund even a part of that investigation." He added that these funds were not for the costs of a trial.

In 1971, mass murderer Juan Corona had killed

twenty-five itinerant farm workers to save paying them the $1.65 an hour that was their due. It had cost Sutter County five million dollars to bring him to trial.

At noon on the day of the vote in Sacramento, two large five-gallon buckets were dug up near the spot where Larry Copland found the Tupperware containers. Inside one was a first-aid kit, ammunition, and a knife. Inside the other was an electric skill saw, a three-foot tree-trimmer blade, and a mattock. All three tools were covered with a maroon stain.

The crime lab did tests. It was blood. It was human.

Another partially decomposed body was found in a shallow grave. Coroner Parker determined that it was a white woman, dead less than a year, and that she was not Brenda O'Connor, Kathleen Allen, or Deborah Dubs.

The FBI obtained a search warrant for six P.O. boxes, all believed to be mail drops of Lake's. Two boxes were at the Wilseyville post office, two in Pioneer, one box in Railroad Flat, and one in Mokelumne Hill.

Fifty pieces of mail were seized.

In San Francisco the police department obtained a search warrant for Claralyn's house in San Mateo. They removed six bags of evidence—among which were duplicate copies of the photographs taken of the two girls at the juvenile hall, in San Mateo where Cricket worked. Along with several innocuous audio cassettes, there were implements of a darker nature: whips, leather restraints, two vibrators, and a chain. They were taken to the property office at Seventh and Bryant in the City.

Claralyn Balazs was not home at the time. She was on a cruise ship sailing through the Mexican Riviera.

SATURDAY, JULY 6, 1985, 1:00 P.M.

After her morning flight from Sacramento, Tomasina Boyd Clancy rented a car at the Calgary International Airport and drove down 2A into town. She crossed the

Trans-Canada Highway and turned left on MacLeod Trail.

She could see the Calgary tower, with its red and white and black bands on the bulbous globe at the top. I love this town, she thought; a half-million of the friendliest people on earth.

She remembered landing a fat check, back in the seventies, when she'd scooped the plan to destroy the slum on Calgary's east side. She had gotten wonderful ink out of the juxtaposition of a rich town, with 450 oil companies headquartered in Calgary, and the east side hovels. Side-by-side photos of the oil companies' skyscrapers and the lean-tos of the poor graphically underlined the shocking disparity. Churchill Park, with its open space and low-rent housing for the elderly, replaced the run-down dumps.

Calgary did not have a large Asian population, Clancy knew. Most of its citizens were English, with doses of Dutch, Scandinavians, and French.

On this warm July day, the city was teeming with people, in vans, in motor homes, in tents. The Calgary Stampede had started, and more than a hundred thousand visitors congregated to watch the best cowboys in North America fall off bucking bulls.

She checked her map, found the right street, and parked in front of a modest house. The lawn was trimmed; marigolds crammed the planter box.

I'm not going to be coy, Clancy thought, coy got you zilch.

She rang the bell. No answer. She leaned on the doorbell. An Asian woman answered. Clancy asked, "Have you seen Charlie Chitat Ng?"

"No, no, go away." The woman slammed the door.

Clancy thought, I was right, Charlie the cheetah is in Calgary someplace!

Chapter Fourteen

SATURDAY, JULY 6, 1985, 1:10 P.M., CALGARY, ALBERTA.

THE FBI'S SPECIAL AGENT IN CHARGE SAT IN Special Agent Karen Alexander's car, parked half a block from Ng's sister's house. They watched Tomasina Clancy leave the house and drive off.

Karen said, "How did she beat us here?"

"If anyone has a nose for news," the SAC said, "it's that woman. She shows up at every major case I've ever handled. If she's here, I'll bet Ng's here too."

"Do we still interview Ng's sister?"

"No, Clancy's spooked her. Just stake out the front and rear of the house. Don't forget the father's import-export office."

Karen started the car, turned on the radio and headed toward downtown Calgary. She listened absentmindedly to the national news, then gulped.

The radio blared, "In San Francisco last night, Stan Pozanski, one of Claralyn Balazs's attorneys, said he was advising his client 'not to take the oath' at her upcoming grand jury investigation, 'and to invoke her Fifth Amendment rights. I'm also advising her to invoke marital privilege.'

"When asked if Ms. Balazs was divorced from Leonard Lake, Pozanski replied, 'So what? She usually follows our instructions.' "

The SAC smiled at Karen, settled back in the passenger seat and closed his eyes. The legal battle was beginning; parry and thrust, lunge and retreat. The complex issues involved, besides proof of guilt, were enormous.

How difficult would it be to extradite Ng back to the U.S.? He vaguely remembered a treaty signed years ago, in the early seventies, between Canada and the United States. Extradition rights had been part of that treaty. . . .

SATURDAY, JULY 6, 1985, 1:30 P.M., SAN JOSE, CALIFORNIA.

During their interview with Dennis Goza, San Francisco investigators learned that another employee had left his job without notice. Jeffrey Gerald had worked at the Dennis Moving Service with Charlie Ng. His roommate was a woman named Terry Kailer.

Kailer told the investigator, "On February twenty-fourth, Jeff received a number of phone calls. He told me they were from Charlie, a guy he worked with. Charlie wanted him to go to Stockton to help somebody move. The pay was a hundred dollars. He took a bus up there. I've not seen or heard from him since."

"Can you think of anything else?"

"A few days later, on February twenty-seventh, I came home around six o'clock in the evening. Most of Jeff's stuff had been taken from the apartment."

"So you assumed he came back and split."

Kailer shuddered. "It must have been somebody else. . . ."

The investigator waited for Kailer to compose herself, then told her that the work jacket found in the rear of Paul Cosner's car had been identified as having belonged to Jeff. Also identified as Jeff's were the guitar and guitar case found in the Wilseyville residence. And the book discovered at Ng's Lennox apartment by Officer DeFillipo was also traced to Jeff Gerald.

The investigator took out the mysterious photograph that had been developed from the camera found in the telephone trench. They matched it to the scene outside the window in Terry Kailer's apartment. No luck.

Kailer examined the photo carefully, then brightened. "I know that place. That's the view out of Jeff's old apartment."

SATURDAY, JULY 6, 1985, 2:00 P.M.

A car with Federal Bureau of Investigation plates drove up to the mountain cabin. An agent from the San Francisco office delivered a profile to Sheriff Ballard.

The sheriff saw that it wasn't from the Behavioral Science Unit of the FBI. That team got involved only to profile a serial killer and identify the potential psychological makeup of the suspected perpetrator. Lake and Ng were already known entities.

Ballard studied the two sheets of paper intently. He had not run across this kind of profile before in the investigation:

Leonard Lake, White Male Adult

1. Studied Survivalist Activities
2. Lake would raid marijuana plants from the growers in many counties: Humboldt, Mendocino, Calaveras.
3. Lake was a member of the Society for Creative Anachronism (SCA).
4. Lake wanted to totally dominate and control females. He was more interested in psychological domination. He played mind games, using degradation, both psychical and mental, so they knew he was in control.

Charles Chitat Ng, Asian Male Adult

1. Considers himself a survivalist
2. Studied the following:
    a) Martial Arts
    b) Nuclear Warfare
    c) Firearms

3. Suspect displays a deep hatred towards blacks, women, and children.
4. Has intense need to physically abuse as well as dominate females
5. Favorite sayings:
   a) "No Kill, No Thrill"
   b) "No Gun, No Fun"
   c) "Mommy cries, Daddy dies, Baby fries"
6. Suspect believed to be agent for many homicides in which victims were shot. He is considered to be "The Executioner."

SATURDAY, JULY 6, 1985, 2:30 P.M., CALGARY, ALBERTA.

Charlie Chitat Ng had been hiding out in a public park ten miles south of Calgary. It was now mid-afternoon and he was hungry.

SATURDAY, JULY 6, 1985, 3:00 P.M.

Larry Copland walked across the spring grass, now brown, and the Mountain Misery to Ballard's desk. "There's a Mountie waiting at the barricade."

"A Mountie?"

"Royal Canadian Mounted Police."

Ballard thought, Next comes Scotland Yard. He went to the foot of the road. The Mountie wasn't dressed in high boots, red coat, pants with the yellow stripe, and wide-brimmed hat—as he had visualized. He wore a short-sleeve sports shirt and gray slacks.

The Mountie showed his credentials and said, "I'm here about the Ng matter. I've been sent down to view these tapes they're all talking about."

Ballard led the Mountie up the very well-beaten path that ran from Lake's house to Bo Carter's cabin. He asked, "Would you like a cocktail?"

"It's still afternoon, Sheriff."

Ballard turned on the TV and VCR. He ran the first tape.

After a few minutes the Mountie said, "Why, I see it now, they're celebrating Easter."

The Mountie listened to Lake rant about the survival of the fittest and the inevitability of nuclear war. When the tape ended, he said, "That fellow's quite odd. He's not the one we're looking for?"

Ballard slipped the second tape into the slot. "No, he's long dead." He started the tape.

The Mountie watched silently. A woman was chained to a chair. Leonard Lake paced in front of her. Charlie Ng stood off to the side. Lake began talking about how the woman should "cooperate" or be buried with a round in her head in the same place they "buried Mike." Lake proclaimed he was not going to be caught because there were no witnesses. He called it a little "crude" but shrugged it off as the reality of the situation.

The tape ran on. Lake chastised the helpless young woman for beating on the door of the cell in the concrete bunker. She had bent the hinges and he'd had to pound them back straight. She was told not to do that again, or she'd get a severe whipping.

On the screen, Lake began a diatribe about his resolve never to be taken alive. He bragged to the defenseless woman before him that he had previously shown her the cyanide pills, implying that he was willing to use them at any time to do himself in if the law came down on him. He hoped that no one would ever catch him at these "weird things," but if they did he'd just die. And, of course, he said, she would die, too, but that would be "immaterial."

Sheriff Ballard pushed the pause button. "We now have substantial proof that the woman you're looking at is Kathleen Allen, of Milpitas. The Mike referred to at the beginning of the tape is Michael Carroll. Carroll served in the Marine Corps with Ng. They also served time in the stockade together."

Ballard added, "We have established a trail that follows Allen, from Milpitas to this site." He opened his notebook. "Kathleen worked at the Milpitas Safeway.

She was seen leaving work with a stranger on April fourteenth. A coworker asked her where she was going."

Ballard paused, checked his notes, then continued, "Kathleen said that she was going to the mountains, her boyfriend was in trouble. This guy was just giving her a lift. The coworker said, 'You call me, because if you don't call me, I'm calling the police.' Kathleen got into a car. She was never seen or heard from again."

Ballard pushed the VCR's play button.

Lake now addressed Charles Ng, asking him if he had the keys to the handcuffs on Kathy Allen. Ng's voice was heard off-camera saying yes. Now Lake began his best imitation of a smiling torturer, first asking Kathy to stand up, then apologizing for being "clumsy" at his little game. He commanded her to stay on her feet, then to undress for "us." He wanted, he went on, to see what "we bought."

The scene on the camera moved inexorably on. Relishing every step, Lake and Ng forced the terrified woman to strip, then tossed her various pieces of lingerie to wiggle into. The woman had trouble working her legs into one of the flimsy outfits.

The screen turned snowy. The Mountie said, "Ah, that is it, I see. Then—"

"That's not it," Ballard said. "That's only the first part."

The screen flickered back to life, showing the same room as before, the same chair, the same backdrop of wallpaper depicting the scene of a forest in fall.

Only this time there was a different woman chained to the chair.

Lake spoke, apparently answering a question from the woman about what happened to her boyfriend. He denied doing anything with or to him.

The woman had long hair, a pleasant face, a well-proportioned body for all to see. She nodded at Ng and asked what Ng had done with her boyfriend. When Ng said he hadn't done anything, she broke in immediately to confront him. "Did you guys kill him?"

Lake insisted they hadn't.

Ballard pushed the pause button. He said, "We have positively identified this woman as Brenda O'Connor. She was married to Lonnie Bond, as a common-law wife. They had a baby, Lonnie Bond Junior. They all lived next door with a man named Robin Stapley. She told friends that she feared Lake. Her husband was a painter and had to take out-of-town jobs." Ballard referred to his notes again. "Trini Ferrero was a friend of Brenda O'Connor's. She told police, in an interview, that Brenda said Lake told her he wanted to take pictures of her and him and the baby 'doin' things together."

"Doin'?" the Mountie said. "I am unfamiliar with the term 'doin'.' "

"We're not positive, but we think Lake meant he wanted to take movies of them making love."

"With the baby?"

"With the baby. Brenda's friends told us that every time her husband left for an overnight painting job, Lake would come over, bang on the windows and doors and shout sexual advances at her."

Ballard pushed the play button on the VCR.

Brenda O'Connor was now sobbing, her anguish unbearable as she pleaded to know why they were doing this to her. Again Lake answered for both men with a cruel smile, saying it was because they hated her. The plural was clear.

The videotape relentlessly played on.

Ballard went out onto the porch. He'd seen the tape often enough. He breathed in the fresh mountain air. It cleansed his lungs but not his mind.

When he reentered the room, the picture on the TV still showed Brenda in the chair. When she spoke, it was in desperation, promising to do anything they wanted if only she had her baby back. Lake broke in on her sobbing plea: she was going to have to do anything they wanted, in any case. Then came the ominous complaint from Lake that the house would be dirty with the baby around.

. . . She screamed back that her baby couldn't live without her.

"He's gonna learn," Lake said.

In the background a scratchy sound was heard overriding the voices on the tape.

The Mountie asked, in a hoarse voice, "Is that important?"

Ballard answered, "We filtered out the static. Ng just went into the shower, he's yelling at Lake that there's something wrong with the water."

The screen went snowy white.

The Mountie said, "Was anyone actually shown being killed on a video?"

"No, but some things trigger the imagination worse than actually seeing them. I gave a press conference yesterday. I said something like, 'A nightmare. One thing led to another and it snowballed. I don't think anyone could have guessed what was on the tapes. Lord knows, I didn't. It was vicious, vicious, vicious.' "

SATURDAY, JULY 6, 1985, 4:00 P.M., CALGARY, ALBERTA.

John Patrick "Sean" Doyle, forty-six, a part-time security guard at the Hudson Bay department store in Calgary, was halfway through his afternoon shift. He worked full-time as an English, art, and science high-school teacher. He picked up extra money as a guard during the busy ten days of the Calgary Stampede.

He stood next to another security guard. They had both been watching an Asian man, wearing a light blue knapsack, steal the store blind.

So far the man had taken two cans of fried herring, one can of baked beans, a Swiss army knife, two boxes of cookies, a braided cord, three miniature packs of Vitabath, and a packet of breadsticks.

The two guards watched him slip a can of lighter fluid and a wedge of cheese into the knapsack.

Sean said, "That bloody thing holds a lot."

The second guard said, "He's as oblivious to us as if we were on the moon. How long do you want to wait?"

The Asian man slipped a bottle of Pepsi-Cola into his knapsack.

"You want to do it, or me?"

"I'll do it," Sean said, "back me up." He approached the man, who backed away. Sean said, "Please, stop moving. I'd like to look into your knapsack."

"No."

"Why not?"

"It's mine."

Sean grabbed the bag.

"No!" the man repeated. "That's mine."

"You've been shoplifting. I watched you put things in the bag."

"Let me get my wallet," the Chinese man said, and reached into the knapsack.

The second guard shouted, "Sean, he's got a gun."

Sean saw the black shape being pulled from the knapsack. He grabbed the gun.

The two men grappled for it for a moment, then there was an explosion. The bullet lodged in an overhead fixture.

The two men fell to the floor, still fighting for the gun.

Sean thought wildly, This guy's really strong for being so small. He looked down. The barrel was being forced toward his chest.

Random thought, fueled by terror, fired through his brain. *Good God, I'm going to die. Over beans and herring. Where's my partner?*

Sean felt the strength come as adrenaline came roaring to the rescue. He shoved with all his energy, forcing the gun to the floor. There was another explosion, Sean felt a flash of heat in his hand.

His partner swarmed over them and got a choke hold around the shoplifter's neck.

Sean stood up. He was dizzy. He was holding a .22

caliber Ruger in one hand. His other hand was pumping bright red blood.

Two hours later, at the Calgary Metropolitan Police Station, Sean learned that he had helped apprehend Charlie Chitat Ng.

Chapter Fifteen

SATURDAY, JULY 6, 1985, 4:30 P.M.

SHERIFF BALLARD PUT DOWN THE PHONE and shouted, "They got him, the Canadians captured Ng!"

Officers rushed in from all sides. Ballard gave them the details, then ordered, "Let's call it a day." They raced for their cars and the Black Bart Hotel's bar.

At the bar, Ballard drained half his beer in his first gulp—from sheer joy as much as thirst. He wore a mustache of foam. He grinned. "It's all been worth it."

"Every agonizing minute of it."

Officers surrounded Ballard. "When do you think they'll ship him back, Sheriff?"

"No problem, a few days for the paperwork. Ng was caught committing a crime in Canada, they'll have to straighten that mess up first."

"Who you going to send to get him?"

Another deputy added, "I'll volunteer, and I'll do it for free. I'll even pay for my trip out of my own pocket."

"Me too."

Ballard held up a hand. "I'll make that decision when the time comes. I want to congratulate all of you on a fine job. But Ng's capture doesn't mean the work's finished. Have fun tonight, but tomorrow we're back in the trenches."

SATURDAY, JULY 6, 1985, 6:30 P.M.

Larry Copland, Steve Mathews, and Bob Bunning drove down a dirt road adjacent to Blue Mountain Road six-tenths of a mile from Lake's house. They noticed ground had been dug up. When they got out of the car, the smell hit them.

Dirt had been clawed away by coyotes. The cooking process that the body undergoes after death had proceeded normally. The decomposed stench was trapped underground until coyotes performed a partial exhumation, allowing the sweet, acrid odor to contaminate the mountain air.

Mathews got a camcorder out of the trunk of the car. He set it up on a tripod. Using the car's radio, Bunning called the command post and filled Ballard in on the discovery.

They began a careful excavation. They uncovered a sleeping bag. They halted work, posted a guard, and returned to the Wilseyville property.

The next day they returned with Dr. Boyd Stephens. He carried a tape recorder. Hundreds of giant bluebottle flies circled aimlessly.

The coroner began, "Coroner's Case Number 2521-85. Body enclosed in a blue-colored sleeping bag with a zipper across two sides. Bag is tied around the head region with gray-colored duct tape. Similar tape is about the ankle and lower region."

The sleeping bag was moved. To everyone's surprise, another sleeping bag appeared below the first. Dr. Stephens said, "There's no dirt between the bodies. This suggests they were buried at the same time."

The sleeping bag was removed from the first body. Stephens spoke into his tape recorder, "Body clothed in a shirt, an undershirt, pants, and socks. A green plastic garbage bag is enclosing the head and upper trunk. The hands are handcuffed at the back. The ankles are tied with rope."

The green plastic garbage bag was pulled away. Dr.

Stephens bent over the corpse and said, "Around the neck there is a leather cord which contains a red rubber ball which has been made in such a fashion as to be consistent with a mouth gag. There appears to be a single gunshot wound to the head."

The coroner turned to the second sleeping bag. "Coroner's Case Number 2522-85. Body enclosed in a red-colored sleeping bag. Bag is quite damp."

The red-colored sleeping bag was opened. Stephens said, "The feet and hands are taped together with gray duct tape. There are two plastic bags about the body. The first is a large-sized garbage liner that's been cut open, and the cut portion of the bag is adjacent to the left anterior surface of the body. The second green-colored plastic garbage bag is across the head and shoulders."

The garbage bags were removed.

Stephens said, "Around the neck is another leather thong holding a red-rubber-ball mouth gag."

The coroner knelt and examined the face. "There appears to be a close-contact gunshot wound to the dental ridge. A second gunshot wound is located just above the right eyebrow. A third gunshot wound through the right supraclavicular space and clavicle." With his right forefinger he traced the two slender bones, each articulating with the sternum and a scapula and forming the anterior part of the shoulder. "A fourth gunshot wound involves the right lateral fibula and tibia." He pointed at the corpse's calf.

He leaned to within inches of the leg. "The route of the projectile appears to be across the left posterior parietal region, approximately 2.5 centimeters lateral to the vertex and slightly behind it. By aligning across the repositioned calvarium, the most likely area of impact, the course of the bullet would be from up to down, from back to front would be approximately ten degrees, and from left to right by approximately forty degrees. The wound is consistent with those made by a .22 caliber firearm."

"What do you make of it?" one deputy asked another.

"I don't like to guess, but if I had to venture something,

I'd say that the bullets in the leg and shoulder were fired first, while the victim was on the run. The shot came from behind, the shooter was on higher ground and to the left of the victim."

"Then the head and mouth shots administered the coup de grace."

SUNDAY, JULY 7, 1985, 6:00 A.M.

The first brief chill of dawn was filled with happy talk, and the Blue Mountain Road Gang, as they now called themselves, was rekindled with energy. Officers who, twenty-four hours earlier, were bone tired, now heaved to their work.

They were expectant. Something was happening that would wrap this all up. The FBI announced that Ng's extradition proceedings would begin immediately.

Sheriff Ballard studied the time sheets lying on his desk. This thing is killing my department, he thought.

Every one of his patrolmen not assigned to the Ng case was working a twelve-hour shift, seven days a week. The Ng task force was working more than twelve hours a day.

I'm facing bankruptcy, he thought. The state had allocated a half million, but they were parceling it out in a funny way. Even though Assemblyman Norm Waters and Senator John Garamendi, with an assist from San Francisco Mayor Diane Feinstein, had helped push through the request for state funds, Calaveras County was to pay a percentage of the initial cost, called a platform. After reaching this platform the state would pick up ninety percent of the costs. The platform was based on .0125 percent of the full value of taxable property in the county. This totaled $70,746.

The sheriff was granting days off to his personnel on a review of each specific request.

He had received a lot of help. The number of telephone calls coming in was enormous. FBI agents had been sent to handle the overload. Two Department of

Justice agents had been sent. A media hot line had been set up. A prerecorded message of the latest information was available.

The Office of Emergency Services had provided a van with five mobile work stations. These lines were dedicated to law enforcement calls only.

Even with help, the county was still facing a disastrous economic shortfall.

Sheriff Ballard pushed aside the problems of money and opened Lake's diary. Most of the entries had been made in 1983.

The sheriff tapped a pencil against an entry that read: *Operation Fish, the murder of Charles Gunnar.*

In May of 1983, Lake had written in the diary, *Operation Fish completed.*

Investigators on the Ng task force learned that Lake had formed a guardianship for Charles Gunnar's children. He explained that their dad had moved to a remote mountain and would never return. He took letters from those children to their dad, and brought letters back purported to be written by their dad. He asked for money from them. Whether they sent money, no one knew yet.

They never saw their dad again.

At the Wilseyville property, more items were found in the ever-widening search perimeter. A key was unearthed. An ID for Mike Carroll was found. The key was tested and found to open Mike Carroll's house nearby.

A small Buddha turned up under a rock. Near it a ceramic fish and a candlestick holder were unearthed. Then a Pennsylvania license plate with the personalized plate: CINDY. All were traced back to Cliff Peranteau.

D.A. Investigator John Crawford had been trying to find out whose child was in a photo found in the telephone trench. He had two clues: her name, Stephanie Jennine Carr—and a date, 7/81.

He contacted the California Department of Vital Statistics. They checked their records for a possible match to the photograph.

Nothing.

Crawford then sent letters to the remaining forty-nine states. He received an answer from Pennsylvania. An officer with the Abington Police Department, Joseph Dalton, called. He placed Crawford in contact with Donna Mullen.

Stephanie Jennine Carr was Donna Mullen's daughter. She told Crawford that she had dated Cliff Peranteau from 1978 to 1981. She had given Cliff a picture of her daughter. It was the one found in the telephone trench.

Investigators simultaneously interviewed Judy Emerson, the landlady of Robin Scott Stapley.

She stated, "Last April eighteenth I saw Scott loading his pickup—"

"What kind of pickup?"

"A gray Chevrolet. I again saw Scott the next day around noon. He told me he was going to the mountains. That's the last time I ever saw him."

"Do you know the license plate of the Chevrolet?"

"Yes, it was personalized: AHOYMTY."

A highway patrol check was run. On April 23, 1985, Kern County Highway Patrolman Wood Hicks made a report of an accident involving a Chevrolet truck with the license plate AHOYMTY.

Patrolman Hicks identified the driver of the vehicle as Charles Ng.

The Calaveras Sheriff's Department then contacted Dennis Goza, owner of the Dennis Moving Service to confirm the Chevy truck. His employment records showed that Charlie Ng took off from April 22 to April 27. There was a note in his files stating that Ng had phoned, saying that his parents had been in an accident in Los Angeles and he needed time off.

Phone records were again checked. It was discovered that at 7:21 on the evening of April 21, 1985, a call went to Dennis Goza's home phone. It was from the Wilseyville cabin.

SUNDAY, JULY 7, 1985, 1:00 P.M., CALGARY, ALBERTA.

The party mood of the Stampede was in the air, and the entire town was braced for the annual holiday. It was the Mardi Gras of the Northwest, appropriately between the Fourth of July and Bastille Day. The city's population of 600,000 seemed to double overnight, to the delight of bar owners and of everyone who had a room to rent.

The stars were the finest rodeo performers in North America. Encamped in their trailers and motor homes, they milled around the stadium. Just as at other events of great civic pride—such as European soccer matches or victory parades for U.S. baseball teams—the fans were ready to bust loose.

The constabulary looked the other way at revelers, for the most part. Yet the Remand Centre in downtown Calgary had already collected its share of drunks. It was a jail, by any other name. In the States it would have been called the Hall of Justice, a combination of city prison and police headquarters.

On its seventh floor there was a prisoner, brought in just last evening, who had nothing to do with the Stampede. He was a mere shoplifter.

Despite the manacles on his legs and arms, Charles Chitat Ng had the decency of a private cell and the right to make a phone call. He asked for a phone, and placed the call that might still save him. Or at least buy him some time.

Attorney Charlie Stewart was the president of the Calgary Defense Lawyers Association. Ever since he had read the headlines in the Sunday paper, page one, he had expected this call. Only he guessed it would come from San Francisco, or from a relative, not from Ng himself. Yes, he told the man with the high-pitched, slightly British accent, he would come down to the jail. And yes, he would recommend a lawyer to represent him.

Stewart immediately phoned the Calgary police station to ask if his client had been questioned.

"You'd better get down here," the desk sergeant said. "As soon as the detectives from the States get off the plane, they're going to have at 'im."

SUNDAY, JULY 7, 1985, 9:00 P.M. CALGARY, ALBERTA.

Tomasina Clancy checked her watch. The detectives had been closeted with Ng for five hours. As soon as she stepped out the door, she knew—with her luck—the interrogation would break up. But she walked over to the Hudson Bay store anyway, just to get some air—and maybe some color.

It could have been Mervyn's, in Hayward, California. Near there, Ng had been accused of lifting two waterbed sheets. Clancy knew that Claralyn Balazs had bailed Ng out of jail and that charge was later dropped, but who was the lawyer that stood up for him then?

Sure enough, when she got back to the Remand Centre, six somber men were filing out of the interrogation room. She recognized Ron McFall, a detective from Calaveras County, the guy with the Dick Tracy chin. With him was deputy Nutall. And there were Brosch and Erdelatz from San Francisco. Who were the other two?

No chance for an exclusive story here, Clancy thought. Reporters of every shape and size jammed into the room. She recognized familiar faces from the *Sacramento Bee* and the *Los Angeles Times.* The *Chronicle,* as usual, would rely on a wire service rather than get their news direct. But that's what she liked about San Francisco: it was as provincial as, well, Calgary.

"There'll be a press conference tomorrow, after the morning arraignment," shouted a tall, thin man with a name tag on his lapel. *R. C. Tarrant,* Clancy wrote on her notepad, wondering if it stood for Royal Canadian.

"What did Ng say?" yelled a man in front. "Did he confess?"

"The hearing will be tomorrow," one of the Canadian detectives answered, waving off Tarrant. "But I can tell you this, and maybe we can get out of here. Ng didn't say a thing. He has been well advised to keep his mouth shut."

"And you are?" the man persisted.

"Detective Roy Anderson."

"Mr. Anderson!" a woman shouted. "Do you think Ng will try to kill himself, like Lake did?"

"We're not giving him many opportunities—"

"Will he be extradited?"

"Please," Tarrant interjected. "I promise you a press conference tomorrow. We will not jeopardize this case by any further comments at this time."

When will Ng be brought back to California? Clancy thought. That is the question.

At that very moment, the reporter from the *Times* blurted out the same words at Tarrant.

"All right," he said. "And let's end it there. I'll say this: if everything goes swimmingly, and there's no opposition to it, you're looking at perhaps two to four weeks."

"Bullshit!" came a cry from the back of the room. "What do you mean no opposition? What do you think these damn lawyers are for?"

"I beg your pardon?"

"Who has Ng hired? I heard it's Dan MacLeod."

"I have no information about that, sir. I believe Mr. Stewart has advised his client to ask for a week's delay, in which time he can select representation and give him time to prepare a case."

"So nothing's going to happen tomorrow?" another frustrated reporter shouted.

"I'm afraid I've said all I can, except to commend the two security officers at the Bay store who subdued Mr. Ng yesterday."

An audible groan went around the room.

Tarrant persisted, "It was a very busy day at the store.

It was a miracle no one was injured, and there could have been deaths if more shots were fired."

A young man edging against Clancy whispered to her, "A few more gratuitous lines like that and you might as well drop 'alleged' from the story."

Tarrant strode from the stage. The milling reporters left to file bylines.

Clancy sidled out a door and watched Tarrant enter a room down the hall. She followed and entered without knocking.

He looked up from his desk. "Who are you?"

"A reporter who got stiffed during the interview. I have a few questions."

"Tomorrow."

She gave him his card.

He said, "Just a few."

"What about Ng's sister? Is she being charged?"

"No."

"How did Ng get here?"

"Apparently he's been in town for a while. We can't rule out the possibility that somebody may have aided him or harbored him here."

Clancy studied the unwavering eyes before her. I'm being stonewalled, she thought. First Ng's sister isn't being charged, then a switch to "someone may have aided him."

MONDAY, JULY 8, 1985, 9:00 A.M.

Investigator John Crawford flew to San Diego. He went to the home of Tori Doolin. She had phoned and wanted to get something off her chest.

She explained that she was a friend of Robin Scott Stapley's and that she had had occasion to visit Lonnie Bond and Brenda at their place off of Blue Mountain Road. She had seen Leonard Lake's photo in the papers and knew him as Charles Gunnar.

She said, "I know the date—it was April twenty-fourth, 1985, eight-thirty in the morning. A man named Charles

Gunnar and an Oriental male, who I later found out was Charlie Ng, came to my door. They rang the doorbell. I said, 'Who is it?' The reply was, 'Charles,' I asked, 'Charles who?' because I didn't know any Charles. He said, 'Charles from up north.' I opened the door but left the chain on. I recognized him as the man that I had seen at the house next door to Lonnie's. I opened the door. I invited them in. Charles Gunnar came in and said his friend would rather wait in the car. Charles Ng left and went back to the car."

"What happened next?" Crawford prompted.

"Gunnar told me that he had found the three of them —Lonnie Bond, Brenda O'Connor, and Robin Scott Stapley—dead. He said he and his friend, Ng, cleaned up the mess and burnt the bodies Indian style. He said the baby was missing."

Crawford asked, "How do you know Lake was referring to Ng when Lake said he and his friend had cleaned up the bodies?"

"Lake referred to Ng as a good friend from the Marines, and that it was him, the good friend from the Marines, who was there and helped them clean up the mess."

"What happened next?"

"He said that there were clothes all over the place. There was no ID left on any of the people. He said no guns were found there. He told me he wanted to make it look like Scott moved, so that the police wouldn't come snooping around up there. Plus, he wanted the pink slip on Scott's truck. He wanted Scott's diploma. He wanted Scott's favorite bike. He wanted all of Scott's clothes. He wanted the receipt for a gun Scott had bought from him when he had been up there on vacation."

"Did you give those items to him?"

"I told him I couldn't get into Scott's safe. He gave me Scott's keys, which allowed me to get into the closet where Scott's safe was. I let him take Scott's clothes. I didn't know where the receipt for the gun was. I later found the receipt."

She handed it to Crawford, who read: "Sold to Scott Stapley, a Walther pistol, model PPK/S, nine millimeter, Serial Number 1562315." It was signed Charles Gunnar.

He asked, "What did the man you knew as Charles Gunnar do when you couldn't find this receipt?"

"He became very upset, about the receipt and the other things he wanted. He said, 'Well, if you find them, will you please call me or will you, you know, send them to me?' He asked for the pink slip to the truck."

"Did you give it to him?"

"No. And he got very upset. He told me the truck had been in an accident. And he had driven the truck to San Diego. I walked out to the truck with him. He showed me where it had been wrecked. Ng walked around the truck with us and never said a word. The truck looked like someone had hit an oak tree up by the left front, the driver's door."

"What was the license plate number?"

"It was personalized: AHOYMTY."

She gave Crawford a receipt for repairs to a camera owned by Scott, Serial Number 5022594.

A check was run. It was learned from the Calgary police that a camera had been discovered on Ng at the time of his capture. The serial number: 5022594.

MONDAY, JULY 9, 1985, 1:00 P.M., CALGARY, ALBERTA.

Provincial Court Judge Edward Adolphe removed his glasses and peered at the three-page document that had been presented by the prosecutor. It was one he had seen many times. "Mr. Delong, may I ask why you have asked for a psychiatric examination?"

"If it please the bench, there have been a number of troubling reports in the press about the state of mind of Mr. Ng. We intend to charge him with crimes of a most serious nature. It is our belief that it is in the interest of justice to establish Mr. Ng's mental fitness before he is charged."

"Is there any objection from counsel?"

Brian Devlin and Don MacLeod, in flowing black robes topped by white, starched collars, rose and bowed respectfully to the bench. "I can speak for both of us, your honor. Our client has no objection. We are familiar with Dr. Feinman's credentials."

Judge Adolphe referred again to the document. "You state that you can conduct this examination in less than half an hour?"

"Quite," the psychiatrist answered.

"Then we will have a thirty-minute recess. Please clear the courtroom."

Thirty minutes later the psychiatrist delivered his report in front of a full courtroom. "Mr. Ng is mentally competent to stand trial," he said briskly. A murmur went through the room, and Judge Adolphe raised his gavel menacingly.

Charles Chitat Ng sat impassively in the handsome wood-paneled docket. His pitch-black hair was tousled, as if he had just gotten out of bed. His face was squat, almost pudgy. The cuffs on his wrists were joined by a short chain in front of him, limiting the range of his arms to his lap. His legs were similarly restricted at the ankles. His pajamalike, gray clothing was in stark contrast to the robes of the prosecutor, Manfred Delong, of the judge, and of the two defense attorneys.

The droning of the prosecutor ran on. Canadian charges: attempted robbery, robbery, possession of a firearm, attempted murder.

TUESDAY, JULY 9, 1985, NOON.

A hushed group of officers huddled around the radio on the porch of the mountain cabin. A stiff breeze swayed the limbs of the surrounding trees.

It was a news special from a Sacramento station. "Charlie Chitat Ng's defense attorney, Brian Devlin, said that Ng is using his option to be tried before a jury in the Queen's Bench Court. Devlin said, 'The charge of attempted murder of the Hudson Bay department store's security guard is ludicrous, they're really holding Ng for shoplifting. I am requesting bail be set.' "

One of the deputies said, "What bullshit."

"Don't worry about it," another said, "it will never happen."

The radio announcer continued, "Len Westerberg, Canadian immigration spokesman, said, 'No action against the gentleman will be taken until court in Canada is completed.' "

"The gentleman?" Ballard said in a dull voice.

The officers milling about silently shook their heads.

The broadcaster continued, "This interview was just sent to us a few minutes ago by reporter Tomasina Clancy. She talked with a Canadian spokesman for the court, who stated, 'Canadian Justice Minister John Cosbie will face a huge legal problem if our southern neighbors charge Ng with a capital crime. In the 1976 treaty with the United States, Canada has the right to refuse extradition of someone accused of a capital crime that carries the death penalty. We Canadians feel strongly enough about barbaric state-sanctioned executions to have outlawed them in our own country.' "

"Sheriff, does that mean what I think it means."

"I think so."

"This can't possibly be happening."

"It is." The baseball scores came on. Ballard turned the radio off. The officers drifted back to work, in silent anger.

One stopped in front of Ballard and said, "You mean Ng is going to hide behind Canada's laws? There's a possibility that we may never get him back? That he may never stand trial?"

"That's a possibility," Ballard said in a tired voice.

"It kind of makes you long for the good old days when you just tossed a rope over the sturdy branch of an oak tree."

"Law enforcement's come a long way since then."

"Too bad the criminal hasn't."

Chapter Sixteen

WEDNESDAY, JULY 10, 1985, 11:00 A.M., SAN FRANCISCO.

ATTORNEY STAN POZANSKI STRODE DOWN the City Hall steps with Claralyn Balazs in tow. A knot of reporters waited for them on the sidewalk.

"How'd it go?" a woman from the *Sacramento Bee* asked.

Claralyn held her purse in front of her face as a photographer approached.

"There's not much we can tell you," Pozanski answered for her. "We advised our client to refuse to take the oath."

"You mean she took the Fifth again?"

"That and she cited marital privilege."

"You've got to be kidding, she divorced Lake long ago."

"A grand jury doesn't set time limits to their questions." Pozanski shrugged. "You'll recall that my client has already given hours of testimony to the San Francisco police."

The *Bee* reporter persisted. "Have you seen where Ballard says Ms. Balazs is a suspect?"

"Ballard?"

"Claud Ballard, Sheriff of Calaveras County."

"Ask him to talk to the San Francisco police."

"Ms. Balazs," reporter began, "why did you bail Ng out?"

"That is an inflammatory and insulting question," Pozanski answered.

FRIDAY, JULY 12, 1985, 2:30 P.M., CALAVERAS COUNTY.

Justice Court Judge Douglas Mewhinney was a familiar figure in San Andreas. Tall, thin, almost gaunt, with a well-trimmed mustache and beard, and black hair barely tinged with gray, he was Lincolnesque to some and a humorless monk to others. But no one could fault his judicial bearing. He had grown up here and, like many a gold-country judge before him, seemed destined since boyhood to take his rightful place in the courts.

But Judge Mewhinney's forebears, for all the stories of the gunslingers of the last century, could not have imagined the outlaws that would jam the courts in the 1980s.

The arraignments each morning involved the usual DUIs and domestic violence cases. But more and more there were drug busts and execution-style killings. Real estate promoters had sold retirement homes like junk bonds in the sixties and seventies here. Nowadays, there was a good chance that the proverbial "cabin in the woods" would be an amphetamine factory.

Now this.

Mewhinney had studied the warrant the District Attorney's Office had presented Wednesday. John Martin and his deputy, Ron Krelle, had worked on it feverishly since Monday, taking cues from McFall and Nutall in Calgary about how the case was proceeding there.

Things were happening lightning fast on all fronts. It was difficult to calculate what effect the warrants might have on extradition.

Judge Mewhinney noted that the warrant didn't allege special circumstances. Those were the key words that drove the death penalty: things like multiple murders, or the killing of a law enforcement officer.

Mewhinney entered the courtroom for his scheduled appearance and immediately signed the warrants, for transmittal to Calgary. Charles Ng's San Francisco attorneys were in court to receive copies. Garrick Lew had represented Ng long before, and, ever since his visit from the FBI in early June, he had been expecting this day. No one knew if Ng's father had been paying for representation, for Lew had a reputation for taking on plenty of *pro bono* work. Michael Burt was appointed to the case from the San Francisco Public Defender's Office. There was now a definite shape to the case, something they could grapple with.

The declaration began: *Charles Chitat Ng is charged on two counts of violation of Section 187 of the Penal Code of the State of California, a felony. They were the murders of Brenda O'Connor and Kathleen Allen.*

Before closing the hearing, Mewhinney reminded the court that he had issued a gag order the day before. "All investigators, detectives, patrolmen, and officers of the court are off limits."

"Your honor?" a man began as he stood in the second row.

"You are?"

"John Galvin, representing McClatchy Newspapers. We have filed a brief against the gag order."

SUNDAY, JULY 14, 1985, 10:00 A.M.

Coroner Boyd Stephens had returned from Calaveras County to where he did most of his work: the basement of the San Francisco Hall of Justice. He was now wearing his other hat: Chief Medical Examiner. He opened a metal wall drawer and pulled out the shelf. The body was transferred to a metal table. He looked at the toe tag. The corpse was numbered: Coroner's Case 2521-85.

Using an overhead microphone, he read the pertinent information into a tape recorder.

The medical examiner bent and peered at the body. Bits of red dirt were scattered about the decaying flesh. Using the tools of his craft, he obtained pieces of epidermis with friction ridges.

He washed the pieces of skin. Then he took the skin, which he had removed from the fingertips of the deceased, and put them on his own fingertips. He rolled on ink, then rolled his fingers onto fingerprint cards.

The results were faxed to Cheryl Steuer, who worked for the Criminal Identification and Information section at the California Department of Justice.

Steuer had the fingerprints of Lonnie Bond on file. This was because California Penal Code requires law enforcement agencies to send arrest and booking information, dates of arrest, charges of arrest, the arresting agent, as well as the fingerprints of the arrested to the state office.

She compared these originals with the faxed copies sent to her by Stephens. She found ten points of similarity between the fingerprints of Coroner's Case Number 2521-85 and the known fingerprints of Lonnie Wayne Bond, date of birth 12-2-57.

Lieutenant Thomas Murphy, who for ten years had taught fingerprint identification at the City College of San Francisco, stared at a transparency.

Murphy then looked at the accompanying card: Robin Scott Stapley, DOB 8-16-58, California driver's license N4547300. He had received this information from CI&I at the Department of Justice.

He put the transparency next to a fingerprint card faxed to him by Coroner Stephens.

They matched.

The two bodies found in red and blue sleeping bags six-tenths of a mile from the mountain cabin, on the Heale property, had been identified.

MONDAY, JULY 15, 1985, 5:00 P.M., SAN FRANCISCO. Ephraim Margolin seldom read the *Sacramento Bee,* but now it was the basic source for how the criminal proceedings were going in Calgary. As attorney for his friend Garrick Lew, he was following the Ng case carefully. He knew that Lew was in Canada. He knew that this would have international repercussions.

Murder, sex, torture—the stuff of page one news.

This was clearly a news story that was not going to evaporate. He handed the paper back to Tomasina Clancy with a smile. "To answer your question, yes, I have appeared in extradition cases."

"You've seen what the state deputy attorney said about extraditing Ng?"

"I haven't. Who's he?"

"Nelson Kempsky. I'll quote from the *Bee.* 'It could take a few months, and at the fastest, it's unlikely to take less than a month.' "

"When did he say that? Does he know something the rest of us don't know?"

"Last Monday, after a press conference, he used the occasion to bring up John Belushi—"

"What's the reference?"

"Belushi died more than three years ago, in a Los Angeles hotel room. I covered the story for a TV special. It was a Canadian gal that spent the night with him, and supposedly fed him heroin and cocaine."

"She fled to Canada?"

"Back to her home in Toronto. Cathy Evelyn Smith was her name. And Kempsky pointed out in that newspaper story that Smith fought off extradition for a year and a half."

"So what's this talk about a few months? Now, I've appeared before the tribunal in The Hague on extradition cases. I get up there and say, 'Look, we are not a lawless country'. I try to tell them we have a strict code of law, we have constitutional rights for the accused. You'd be surprised how tough it is to get through to them. When we electrocute people here, they imagine we're still in the Wild West. My job is to tell them, quite simply, 'We are not a barbaric nation'."

Clancy was taken aback by the famed defense attorney's mood. He was philosophical, in contrast to the tense belligerence of his counterparts in Boston, New

York, and Washington, D.C. A call came, he picked up the phone with a nod to her, swiveled around in his chair, and agreed to a date for a lecture in Rome.

Clancy knew telephone mannerisms from years of being put on hold. There was no recognition in his face that he had been on stage in front of her. He went back at once to the conversation, as if he had just arranged to have a haircut.

"Tell me, Mr. Margolin, is it as difficult for lawyers to predict what's going to happen in these cases as it is for the rest of us?"

"Maybe even more so. *You* have time to read the papers."

MONDAY, JULY 15, 1985, 3:00 P.M., CALGARY, ALBERTA.

Brian Devlin and Don MacLeod, Ng's Canadian court-appointed attorneys, gathered their papers as soon as Provincial Judge Edward Adolphe left the courtroom. Ng's arraignment on the charges of attempted murder of the Hudson Bay guard and attempted robbery had just concluded. Anticipating the clamor of reporters, Devlin turned to the spectators and announced a press conference in five minutes.

With bailiffs flanking him cautiously, Ng shuffled off the stand and left by the same door. It had been an easy day for the court reporter.

Motion by the defense to delay the first hearing until September: granted.

Motion by the defense for a "ban on publication": taken under advisement.

"There's nothing unusual about a ban on publication," MacLeod told the reporters in the crowded hallway. "At this stage, I'd request it for any of my clients."

"Would that include foreign press?" a woman from Associated Press asked.

MacLeod hesitated. "You've got a point. I don't suppose anything you printed in the States would affect potential jurors here."

"You're going to ask for a jury trial?"

"Before the Queen's bench, yes. That's our current position."

"How long is that going to take?"

"As long as an attempted-murder trial takes."

"And what about extradition?" the Associated Press reporter persisted.

"Your guess is as good as mine."

Chapter Seventeen

DECEMBER 16, 1985, 10:00 A.M., CALGARY, ALBERTA.

FIVE MONTHS HAD GONE BY QUICKLY IN THE time frame of the legal system. After a second delay to allow defense attorneys to prepare their case, Charles Ng was brought before Court of Queen's Bench Judge Allen Sulatycky. The defense had changed its tactics: instead of a jury, a single judge would decide whether Ng had attempted to murder a Hudson Bay guard.

It had become apparent in these five months that the first attempts of California jurisdictions to file extradition papers were premature. It would be at least a year before all the charges from Calaveras County would be assembled.

The defense had no need to delay, to postpone for another half a year by forcing a preliminary hearing. The defense had a very good chance of protecting Ng from a California death penalty simply by allowing a Canadian court to sentence Ng on a charge less than murder.

Two of the four charges brought before the Queen's bench could result in life sentences: attempted murder and robbery while armed. Calaveras County had originally rushed through two murder charges against Ng, and six more had been added since July 15.

"Canada has rightfully refused," defense attorney Don MacLeod told reporters, "to extradite anyone facing capital punishment for at least the past twenty-three years."

Before entering the courtroom, he added, "And the 1976 treaty with the United States leaves no doubt about our future intentions. This is our law. We intend to argue for it vigorously."

The Queen's bench proceedings moved swiftly. Extradition loomed in the background, but it played no part in the matter-of-fact presentation of the case.

Prosecutor Manfred DeLong introduced seven law enforcement officers of various jurisdictions as witnesses. Their demonstration of the events of five months before was mercifully brief. John Patrick "Sean" Doyle, the affable security guard and part-time teacher who had pinioned Ng in the Bay store had told his story in the press many times over. He was led through the account again by attorney Don MacLeod.

After the noon break, Doyle was subjected to a curious line of cross-examination. "During the struggle with the defendant," Brian Devlin asked, "Could you tell where your hands were?"

"My hands were wrestling against the gun he was trying to point at me," Doyle answered, bewildered.

"But can you tell us for certain whether your hands were on the gun handle, on the barrel, or perhaps on the trigger?"

Now the point was obvious. "They were not on the trigger—"

"Do you know exactly where your hands were, Mr. Doyle?" Devlin persisted.

"No."

The prosecution rested its case. MacLeod and Devlin asked for a recess to consult with their client. They returned in a few minutes to announce, "The defense elects not to call any evidence." The spectators recognized the code words. Ng would not be put on the stand.

Devlin focused his summation, a few minutes later, on the fact that Ng was armed, but not pointing a gun, during the scuffle. Was it attempted murder? If a gun goes off in an altercation, he argued, surely there is no premeditation.

How could it be termed "armed robbery"?

"If a person steals from a newsstand and happens to have a gun in his coat, for whatever reason," Devlin asked, "can it be called "armed robbery"?"

Then he tempered his defense with an apology. "I realize that the argument has never been dealt with in our courts, but it is a reasonable one."

The reporters in the courtroom had already accepted the inevitable: it wasn't going to stand as "robbery at gunpoint." The prosecution had been snookered into an exaggerated charge.

The following morning, Judge Sulatycky ruled that Charles Chitat Ng was guilty of shoplifting and assault, for which he would serve a prison term of four and one half years in the Prince Albert, Saskatchewan, provincial prison.

About a week later, the convicted Britisher, whom the American press had finally stopped defining as a "former U.S. Marine," celebrated his twenty-second birthday in jail. It was Christmas Eve.

FEBRUARY 26, 1986, AUSTIN, TEXAS.

Police Sergeant Russell Schmidt had tracked down Tori Doolin at her new address. The information he was using had been sent to him by Calaveras D.A. Investigator John Crawford.

The Texas policeman knocked on the door and Tori Doolin answered. He introduced himself and asked her if he could show her a photo lineup. He explained it was in reference to thc casc that had concluded two months before in Calgary.

She agreed.

He spread six photos of Asian males out on the coffee table.

She studied them, then pointed at the one numbered 15350-F. "That's the man I saw in my apartment with Leonard Lake on April twenty-fourth, last year."

"In San Diego?"

"Yes."

"Are you sure that's the man who was with Lake?"

"Well, I thought his name was Charles Gunnar at the time."

"No, I mean about the Asian?"

"Yes, that's Charlie."

"Do you remember anything you forgot to tell when you last spoke to the police?"

Doolin thought back to the interview she had in San Diego about the Bond family, the couple with the baby who Lake told her he had found dead. "Yes," she said, "Lake actually told me where he found the bodies. He said, 'Brenda was found in the house, Lonnie—' "

"What house?"

"Lonnie's house, next door to Lake's. He said, 'Lonnie was found on the front balcony, and Scott was found outside the back door. There were no guns or drugs around.' "

"And no mention of the baby. . . ."

MAY 26, 1986, SAN ANDREAS, CALIFORNIA. Sheriff Claud Ballard finally had a chance to respond to criticism from the press about lack of progress in extraditing Charles Ng. "It's been almost a year since these ghastly things happened," he told a press conference at the County Administrative Headquarters. "But we now have a breakthrough in extradition evidence."

The reporters pulled out their notebooks. The scene was noticeably different from a year ago in the same room. Ballard noticed the regular reporters among the press, but there was no one from San Francisco or Los Angeles, let alone the national media. "Extradition" was a big boring word.

"I'm happy to announce," he began, "that we are going to release the videotapes to Canadian officials responsible for holding Charles Ng."

"Videotapes? How many?" the reporter from the *Sacramento Bee* asked.

"One."

"What about capital punishment in California? Won't the Canadians gag on that?"

"We intend to show that the nightmare in Calaveras County overrides any objection against bringing murder charges with possibility of execution."

"On what grounds?" the reporter persisted.

"The public has a right to self-defense against sheer viciousness like this."

FRIDAY, FEBRUARY 27, 1987, OTTAWA.

A videotape of torture, said an Ottawa newspaper, was included in more than one thousand items or pages of evidence submitted by the United States State Department to the Canadian Department of Justice. The press, of course, hadn't seen the tape, and had to rely on rumors from unnamed police officers. But after seeing the eye bolts anchored on the floor of the master bedroom of the cabin on Blue Mountain Road, reporters had little trouble speculating on the scenes of sexual assault the tapes would eventually reveal.

The counsel for the Canadian department said to reporters, "We are prepared to recommend to the Ministry of Justice, after we have had a chance to analyze these records, that the Court of Queen's Bench issue a warrant to Edmonton to release prisoner Ng to us for extradition to the United States."

In Calgary, attorney Don MacLeod demurred. "We're dealing with very complex issues here. Very complex. When you're looking at the nature and number of the charges here, and how serious they are, you can expect both sides to look at every issue carefully."

"What do you see as the next step, and the outcome?" a reporter asked.

"The fall of 1987 will not be the end of it."

The fall of 1987 wasn't the end of it. Neither was the

fall of 1988, 1989, 1990, or 1991. The Canadian government and the United States continued to argue over Charles Ng. But he was safe, for now, serving his four and a half year sentence.

He spent his prison time studying criminal law.

Chapter Eighteen

MONDAY, SEPTEMBER 26, 1991, OTTAWA.

THE STORY HAD BEEN OUT OF THE HEADlines for years. Charles Ng was in jail in Saskatchewan Penitentiary, in Prince Albert. His four and a half year sentence was over, and now he was in limbo between Canada and the United States.

These were the long years for the families who had come to Calgary for the trial. Some had exhausted their life savings on the interminable trips. All of them kept in their nightmares the face of the accused—the boyish face with the upturned, defiant chin and lips, the steady, emotionless black eyes, the mop of hair falling in bunches over his forehead. And above all, the demeanor of intensity, of self-containment, in the face of the most lurid accusations in memory.

It had taken years, as lawyers had predicted, for the final extradition papers to arrive on the proper Canadian bench. But now the matter had finally come to a head. The Conservative Party in Canada had approved a resolution asking for the return of the death penalty. As in many of the states, public opinion polls in many provinces favored the return.

Minister of Justice Kim Campbell had ruled that the extradition papers were persuasive, but her decision was subject to a Supreme Court ruling. Defense attorney Donald MacLeod had made sure of that. He cited the Charter of Rights and Freedoms Act, passed in 1976. He argued that extradition would violate Ng's rights under that charter by subjecting him to cruel and unusual punishment—carefully choosing phrases that were clear to his U.S. counterparts.

Ng now had to appear before the high court, represented by a lawyer from Montreal, Julius Grey. Amnesty International had mounted a campaign for Ng ever since June of 1990, when Minister Campbell decided enough was enough. Campbell's predecessors as Ministers of Justice, John Crosbie and Douglas Lewis, had rebuffed efforts to release Ng if the United States would agree that the death penalty would not be an option after extradition. And the U.S. persisted in leaving the death penalty as an option of U.S. courts. Both of the former ministers of justice had argued that Canada would become "a haven for murderers trying to escape justice."

At ten o'clock in the morning, reporters made their way through the demonstrations to hear the court's ruling in person, and perhaps interview some of the justices. They were not disappointed. "The ruling is conclusive," said a spokeswoman for the court. "The court has concluded that Ng may be extradited to the United States without assurances that he will not be subject to being executed."

"What was the vote? Unanimous?"

"The vote was four for the majority with three dissents."

In Calgary, reporters were waiting at MacLeod's offices. He was nonplussed. "We still have a final appeal."

"Higher than the Supreme Court?"

"We are going to the United Nations," he said. "The Committee on Human Rights has agreed to hear our case. We intend to pursue all the avenues open to us."

SEPTEMBER 26, 1991, 10:30 A.M., SASKATCHEWAN

Calaveras County Sheriff Bill Nutall nervously waited in the warden's office at the Saskatchewan provincial prison. A phone call was promised from the Minister of Justice.

Sheriff Claud Ballard had passed away a year earlier—and his affidavits on Ng had legally gone with him. But Nutall knew the case was still solid.

The first news was already in: the Supreme Court had voted 4–3 to "refuse to condemn the death penalty," as the media was framing the decision. Now, Nutall had anticipated, the real decision would come. The ball was now in the court of Justice Minister Kim Campbell. She could act on the court decision, or she could demur, as had her predecessors.

The phone call came. "You may release the prisoner in question to United States authorities, at your pleasure."

At first there was pandemonium in the prison, as the California officials who had come with Sheriff Nutall began the inevitable congratulations, mixed with rumors about yet another legal hurdle. But Nutall had already made up his mind: he had reserved a flight at the airport. He signed the documents allowing him to take custody of the prisoner. He called for his car to be positioned by a side door. In minutes the prisoner was brought through the door. The car sped to the airport.

When Ng recognized some of the deputies surrounding him at the airport, he knew what was happening. He had seen them at the trial in Calgary.

Charles Chitat Ng saw the airplane on the runway. Still in his gray-brown jumpsuit, collar turned up, he bristled as he was hustled toward the plane.

There was a brief scuffle, but Ng was forcibly reminded that he was wearing hand and leg restraints. His head dropped. He shuffled to the waiting aircraft.

The speed of Campbell's decision and the subsequent immediate flight out of Canada caught Ng's Canadian attorneys by surprise. The Royal Canadian Mounted Police were back at their stations before MacLeod could denounce the haste of the exit. MacLeod hastily called a press conference and pointed to the dissenting opinions. "This amounts to an indefensible abdication of moral responsibility," Justice Peter Cory had written that morning.

MacLeod was now out of the case. There would be no appeal to the United Nations.

SEPTEMBER 26, 1991, NOON, GARDEN GROVE, CALIFORNIA.

The phone call seemed to be a trick. It had the sound of a real estate promotion, or an offer of aluminum siding for the house. Then the man identified himself.

He was a reporter for a radio station in Ottawa. "Have you heard the news?" he asked.

Dwight and Lola Stapley were both on the phone. They had been aware that the Ng case was nearing finality in Ottawa. No! They couldn't believe it! The Supreme Court had voted against Ng?

"Better yet," the reporter said, "Ng is already on his way to California."

Dwight had retired as an elementary school principal a few years before. "Yes," he said to the reporter, "I'll look forward to the trial."

Lola said she was skeptical of when it might happen. But they agreed it was a most happy day. "We've aged fifty years in the last six."

Sharon Sellito had harried the press and the police over the injustice of it all. She had not endeared herself to either with her frank criticisms of how the search for her brother, Paul Cosner, had been carried out. She was still unrepentant in her outrage. Her vivacious, outgoing manner gave her easy access to reporters, and she used them to try to obtain some recompense for her brother's disappearance.

His body had never been found. She said, "All I want for Ng is to tell us, by God, where they buried my brother. Then maybe we can give him a proper burial. Watching Ng go through the legal system is like running a triathlon. The first leg was the horror of the murders. The second was the horror of the Canadian justice system and how long it took to get him back here. The third and final leg will be getting the justice system started in California."

In Canada, Sharon's words were echoed by police associations and public organizations demanding the death penalty.

In Oakland, California, close to some of the crime scenes, a national group, Citizens for Law and Order, cheered the decision as another support for victims' rights. "For some of these people, it's not even over when the trial is over," said the president, Phyllis Callos. "For some, it has to be the final sentence. For others, it's not over until the death sentence is carried out."

She continued, "It's not how long it takes, but the assurance that there will be an eventual resolution. Each person needs the final act that will set them free."

TUESDAY, NOVEMBER 5, 1991, SACRAMENTO, CALIFORNIA.

Six weeks after Charlie Ng's return to California, Channel 13, KOVR, announced a special showing of *Inside Edition.* The station made an unusual warning: the show was about the sexually violent history of the prisoner at Folsom and should not be viewed by children.

Inside Edition had run the controversial segment the previous evening in many national markets. The new aspect of the story was the introduction of a player who hadn't been heard from before—a former cellmate of Ng's at Fort Leavenworth, Kansas. The cellmate related graphic details of the sexual torture of several women which he said were told to him by Ng.

The unidentified ex-prisoner claimed he was a friend of Ng's for several months during 1982. Ng had been sentenced there in 1982 for stealing military weapons in Hawaii. It was after he left Leavenworth that Ng hooked up again with Leonard Lake.

Prison confessions cannot be authenticated by any records, most law enforcement people agreed. But there was speculation. "There is even talk about this guy being a key witness in the trial that's coming up in Calaveras County," a Sacramento officer argued.

"I doubt that," another rebutted. "It's part of the hype."

Yet the *Inside Edition* segment stirred up the Ng mania once again, after years of quietude. The former cellmate of Ng's said Ng bragged about using pliers and other common tools to disfigure women as they screamed in agony. "I don't think sex to him was very important. . . . The torture, the pure terror, he wanted to see terror. He wanted to see them beg, to plead."

Perhaps the only factual impact of this television tabloid show was the information about Ng's personality. Until now, Ng had been an enigma. He was stone-faced in court in Canada. There were reports of his law studies in prison, but little else. Now the Leavenworth story, as far as it could be believed, painted a different and frightening picture.

"He seemed like he hated everyone and everything," the former cellmate said. "Gays, drug users and dealers, ethnic groups. He can kill and not even think about it. People would whisper and move away from him. People were scared of him," the former prisoner averred. He claimed Ng had called him after he got out, continuing to describe his escapades of violence. He said he was terrified of Ng, even with Ng behind bars.

WEDNESDAY, NOVEMBER 10, 1991, EDMONTON, CANADA.

As the court appearance of Ng in Calaveras County loomed, further defamatory reports came from another ex-inmate, this time in Canada. Attorneys close to the case discounted, however, the possibility that this kind of testimony would ever be allowed in an American court.

The *Edmonton Journal* published a complete version of the story, including drawings that Ng purportedly made in his jail cell. "It's pretty damning stuff," one of the sources of the information said, "but whether it can be used is a question."

Ng's fellow prisoner in Canada claimed that Ng had bragged that he would never be returned to the U.S. He was quoted as saying that he would kill a guard or a fellow prisoner first. That brought a potential sentence of twenty-five years to life in Canada. The same fellow prisoner said that, when he was to be released, Ng tried to hire him. Charlie gave him a list with seventy-seven names on it—law enforcement officials, lawyers.

Ng wanted them killed, the ex-prisoner claimed.

The proximity of the Canadian revelations with those from Leavenworth also raised some eyebrows. "It's like a bombing—everyone wants to get into the act," a psychologist said. The FBI responded vigorously to the suggestion that the complaints of a former inmate of Leavenworth went unheeded in 1983–84, and thus led to the Wilseyville massacre.

"Charlie had a reputation when he came in," the former Leavenworth inmate said to a newspaper reporter, following up on the *Inside Edition* show. "He was the best martial-arts guy I've ever seen, and he would do a lot of showboating, spin kicks and all that.

"This was in 1983. I contacted the FBI when I got out in January," the informant said. He told them Ng had been discussing murders and torturing women.

Ng talked about a compound, "out in the woods somewhere," where there would be a torture chamber, the "whole nine yards." Photos sent by Leonard Lake reportedly confirmed that the plan was already under way.

The FBI spokeswoman told the news media that "talk is no crime." An agent in the Kansas City office said, "There's really nothing you can do."

He was right.

Chapter Nineteen

MONDAY, MARCH 4, 1992, 8:00 A.M., CALAVERAS COUNTY.

AT STOCKTON, EPHRAIM MARGOLIN TURNED onto Highway 4 and headed toward Angel's Camp. San Andreas was another ten or eleven miles north, on Highway 49.

He was to appear in court in an hour—on behalf of a man accused of the most vicious murders in the history of the state. He was prepared to say that justice could be best served by allowing the accused to choose his own attorneys, reinstating Garrick Lew and Michael Burt, who had represented Ng seven years ago, in San Francisco, in San Andreas, in Calgary. But Judge Douglas Mewhinney—the same judge who had issued the search warrant in 1985 that opened the case—had ruled in November 1991 that new attorneys were needed. His arguments at the time seemed unimpeachable. Lew had never defended a capital case. Burt was now traveling back and forth from San Francisco to Los Angeles representing Ramirez, the so-called Night Stalker. Ng was persuaded that Lew and Burt could represent him best, but Mewhinney obviously thought otherwise.

Was the judge worried about further delay, further obfuscation by the accused? Margolin was prepared to argue that there was already something hideously wrong about new attorneys having to go through twenty thousand pages of documents and research some six hundred witnesses.

What if Mewhinney countered that the two new attorneys had already done that work in preparing for the preliminary hearing—due to start next month? In California such a hearing is equivalent to a grand jury indictment. The purpose is to satisfy the court that the evidence warrants the charges and a trial.

The skeleton of the case had formed in Margolin's mind. He had to search for a parallel, a comparison in some other field to the *enormity* of this case. He couldn't approach the bench and say "this is different." He had to say how different.

Margolin pulled into the Government Center in San Andreas, noticing the TV camera crew in front of the courtroom. He went through the elaborate security system and entered the courtroom, joining two attorneys whom he had never met, at the defense table. In front of him, in his orange jumpsuit, was Charlie Chitat Ng.

Judge Mewhinney entered.

Margolin approached the bench tentatively. An idea had been forming reluctantly in his mind. This court had to look beyond the normal rules of the justice system, just as, in other fields, the normal rules sometimes have to be abandoned. *Is it overkill? Is my analogy ridiculous? Am I being seduced by the audacity of my creative argument? Am I trying to make legal history and not legal sense for the accused?*

Margolin knew that every attorney had to search himself before he tried something novel in front of a judge.

"Your honor," he began, "we are all aware of the danger of bringing certain attorneys into a case." He noticed that Mewhinney was chary of smiling. The seriousness of his demeanor was a danger sign: humor was not the answer.

"I represent two attorneys, Garrick Lew and Michael Burt, whom the accused, Charles Ng, wishes to reinstate. I fully realize that you have already ruled on Mr. Ng's request to be represented by these two attorneys. I realize that you have appointed the present attorneys, Mr. Webster and Mr. Marovich, and that they have been laboring on their preparations for the preliminary hearing.

"However, Mr. Lew had been Charles Ng's attorney for several years prior to that time. When an all-points bulletin went out for him in 1985, Mr. Lew was de facto Mr. Ng's attorney."

"And Mr. Burt's appearance in this case also dates from 1985?"

"Yes."

"You intend to argue to reinstate Mr. Burt as well?"

"Exactly, and I would like to begin by reviewing your argumentation at that time."

"Unless you have something new, may we go on?"

James Webster rose. "Your honor, in view of the personal nature of this matter, the possibility of personalities being discussed, I move that these proceedings be *in camera.*"

There was a groan from the small band of reporters present. Mewhinney paused to take that into account, then turned to Margolin. "Is this acceptable to you, sir?"

"I will be brief, your honor. Three minutes should be enough."

The courtroom was cleared. Only the defendant, the usual guards, the defense attorneys, the Deputy Attorney General of the state, and the prosecuting attorney were the audience for Margolin, Mewhinney, and the court reporter. Margolin began, "A man is about to go on trial for his life. We gassed one less than a year ago at San Quentin. A man in this danger should have his day in court. I'd like to emphasize, your honor, that the request I am about to make runs counter to what I or any other sane defense attorney aims for in a case of this kind."

Mewhinney raised both eyebrows. The handful of onlookers were silent. Margolin let the thought sink in for ten seconds.

"We all know," Margolin said at last, "what the defense aims for. Delay. The longer the delay, the greater the chance that the defense might break down the case. And that the defendant might live."

Mewhinney stared at Margolin as if to ask him to come to the point.

"Your honor, *I'm* going to ask you to speed this trial up. I'm moving that we *avoid* further delay. I could argue point by point why my clients—attorneys Lew and Burt—have no problem with workload or lack of experience. I could try to make my case by reviewing the almost eight years of experience that my clients have had with this case. But I'm not going to do that. For centuries we were content as a human race with the ordinary laws of physics. The laws of large objects. Sir Isaac Newton laid out the principles of gravity, which explained the movement of every heavenly body."

Mewhinney peered over his glasses at the bushy-haired, husky attorney.

Margolin steamed ahead. "Two thousand years before Newton, Euclid showed us proofs of geometry. All these things have served us well. Then along came Einstein. My point is obvious. Just as in physics we had to abandon the ordinary rules to deal with the microscopic world of Einstein and the black holes of astronomers, so here we have to deal with a case that breaks all the boundaries by making decisions that also break normal boundaries."

Mewhinney nodded.

"We now think of astronomy as megaphysics, your honor. This is a *megacase.* Plain common sense recommends that we break the rules you have cited and abide by the request Mr. Ng has made. Your honor, I move that Garrick Lew and Michael Burt, *in the interest of speed and justice,* be reinstated as counsel for the defense."

Margolin pulled back his cuff and looked at his watch. It *had* been three minutes.

The following morning the court ruled that Charles Ng's original attorneys be reappointed to the defense.

Mewhinney knew that Webster and Marovich were virtually required to appeal. The appeal was made to the California Supreme Court.

With uncharacteristic speed, the high court voted 4–3 against the lower court ruling, thus keeping Burt and Lew from assuming Ng's defense.

The Attorney General's Office in Sacramento reacted immediately to the decision.

"We're obviously pleased," said spokesman Dave Puglia. "The Attorney General and the District Attorney will be seeking a new date for a preliminary hearing in Calaveras County. . . ."

Margolin was aghast at the court's action. "The people of California may be bloodthirsty," he said, "and may want capital punishment. And certainly the Ng case is not a pretty case. But I do not think the people of California ever authorized or wanted a wholesale abandonment of fairness in preparation for trial."

THURSDAY, OCTOBER 8, 1992, NOON.

I need background material, Clancy thought. She would hit Folsom prison and see for herself Ng's prison accommodations. She would see if he was being treated inhumanely. *And if I can't see Ng, at least I'll see how the typical prisoners live.*

Clancy veered east through Sacramento onto Highway 50, the South Lake Tahoe route over the Sierras. She watched for the Folsom turnoff and sped up Old 50, past the legacy of rapacity of the gold dredging machines of a hundred years or more ago. For miles one entire side of the highway was nothing but mounds of gravel spat out by barges working the American River.

The town of Folsom was a pleasant gentrification of the Old West, with saloons as harmless and prettified as miniature golf courses. East of the town, up a gradual rise, stood the citadels of the old and the new prison. Like the walled cities of Europe, these fortresses were there to control the invaders—some on the outside, some inside.

Clancy drove straight to the gate of Old Folsom Prison. She looked at the drab landscape.

The guard asked, "What's your business?"

"I'm a reporter. I'm looking for background material on Charles Ng. I made an appointment with Theresa Rochas, the warden. Call the public information officer."

Public Information Officer Chuck Winters met Clancy at the Victorian gate of the old prison. It was the one she had seen in movies, on postcards. The squat tower presided over an ornate grating whose spikes stepped up like the pipes of a cathedral organ to a central point.

Clancy showed her driver's license at the gate room and had her hand stamped. She signed a document stating that she understood that if she was taken hostage, her life would not be bartered for. She was issued a pass. As she followed Winters inside the yard, two images flashed before her ominously. On the left was an imposing hill with crosses at the top: she could make out several men seeming to wander aimlessly on trails around it. Straight ahead, some two hundred feet below, was a cavernous rock quarry.

She couldn't detect any movement in the vast pit before her, but her mind's eye could. She imagined huge blocks of stone being hauled on wooden planks up toward the stone buildings to her right.

The two walked cautiously down the macadam pathway to a stark fortress close to the river. Its lower blocks were crudely chiseled, as if to discourage leaning against them —or climbing them.

The information officer was prepared to talk about security—it was the question everybody asked. "The hills allow for vantage points, for gun towers. I hope you don't mind looking at some heavy artillery later."

Wait a minute, Clancy said to herself. There's a group of guys in the yard just above us, playing basketball and handball. "The artillery doesn't scare me as much as—"

"As the guys in the blue jeans? There'll be guards moving around through all the buildings."

Winters opened a gate for her and described the daily routine of the convicts as they moved along.

Am I really going in there? she said to herself. No eye contact, for God's sake. I wonder who they think I am, carrying a notepad and walking nonchalantly into their all-male sanctuary. Thank God I dressed down—business suit and ankle-length raincoat.

Men lounged at picnic tables. Men played handball, basketball, lifted weights. There were blacks and Hispanics. The only Caucasians she saw were bearded, all of them seemingly sporting tattoos.

"Where are the white men?" she asked instinctively.

"We're about a third, a third, and a third, four thousand all told."

"Really? Maybe that's what happens to your eye-count when you're a minority."

Clancy was surprised at the number of female guards she saw walking the yard. But they had unisex uniforms of trousers and formless shirts. *Wow—the days when pants were thought sexy. Now they're the muumuus of the nineties.*

Thcy cntered a huge building that could have been the hangar for a dirigible. "We've got a thousand guards to handle four thousand prisoners. There are a hundred blind spots in this old fortress. Corners. Change rooms. Showers."

She wondered, How will my obituary read if one of these guys milling around me—a rapist, a murderer—suddenly psyched himself up to take all his aggressions and resentments out on a woman? A woman who had signed a release form on her life. A woman who seemed to be inspecting them like a, well, journalist.

Winters pointed straight up, to the top of the building. "This is the largest prison structure west of the Mississippi. Those cellblocks are stacked seven rows high."

To Clancy it looked most like a sort of Victoria Station, with spidery webs of steel rising up to support a corrugated iron ceiling. Instead of the floor bustling with trains and passengers, there were these independent cellblocks packed in under the giant canopy. The bleakness of the Industrial Age hovered over it all.

She said, "A scene from a Dickens novel could have inspired this. It's not intentional, of course. But just having to live in something that looks like an abandoned factory is grim enough."

"Remember," Winters said, "these are bad people. A lot have killed people. That's why they're here." He led her down the concrete walkway between the cellblocks, discussing changes that had occurred in the prison system in California.

In her peripheral vision Clancy noticed a man sitting on a toilet, staring at her inquisitively, from the end of a cell.

Each cell is about four feet wide, she figured, and about seven or eight feet deep. The bunks are two feet wide, and they take up about half the width of the cell. Those bunks, fully six feet long, run virtually to the back wall. There is no room in the cell for a chair, let alone a table. Only the bare hole of a toilet stands at the end of each cell, like a raised drain.

And then there is this, she said to herself, dictating her article to herself, there is this: the second bunk, on top. Not one, but two men, call this thirty square feet home. Stacked two to a cell, stacked seven or so rows on top of each other.

Winters interrupted her ruminations. "In the old days, there wasn't any yard. No hoops. No handball court. Let me show you the first cellblock."

"Vintage?"

"Designed and built in 1856. Hard to believe they built prisons this solid when the gold mines were still using timber trestles that are now mostly gone." Winters turned down a passageway and the two emerged in a smaller building. "The roof was put on later. These used to be open to the weather."

Clancy peered down a row of cast-iron doors that looked like the covers of ovens. She took a tentative step down the aisle. "These old grates are just for atmosphere," she said, and then noticed a movement behind one of them. The forged iron clasps on the doors were enormous.

"These are still used," Winters told her. "For honor prisoners. One man to a cell—a little privacy."

"But this is a dungeon!"

"What kind of a view do you get from the main cell-block?"

Clancy had almost forgotten why she was here. She had been swept up in the history of the place. "How about Ng?"

"He's in the administrative segregation unit, maximum security, of course. But it's not far from this. He's lucky on one count: no one shares a cell with him."

"I want to talk to him."

"Fat chance."

"Why not?"

"There's a gag order regarding him the size of the Grand Canyon."

"I'm not included in the gag order."

"Why not?"

"I'm not with the police or the court, I'm a journalist."

"If you can get his lawyers' permission, then, and only then, can you get in."

"Who have they let Ng talk to?"

"No one."

They moved through another passageway into the mess hall. Prisoners from the last lunch crowd were being patted down as they left the cavernous hall.

"See those floors?" Winters said. The huge room was institutionally scrubbed, and concrete floors virtually polished. It smelled like a combination of Lysol and burnt milk. "Five years ago you'd have to kick your way through garbage in here. And in the cellblock area you'd hold something over your head to keep from getting hit by all kinds of shit."

"What changed?" she asked incredulously.

"We tried to weed out the offenders. Reward the guys

who kept the joint clean, punish those that didn't with a trip to Pelican Bay."

"Pelican Bay?"

"California's new Alcatraz. The end of the line. Prisoners there spend twenty-two and a half hours in their cells."

Sensory deprivation, Clancy thought as she looked around the mess hall. "I still can't get over women guards being in here."

"It took some getting used to. But most people would agree it's had a positive influence. It's no longer a sexless void."

That's good, Clancy thought. No, that's bad. That's not life. None of this place is life.

They walked back through the checkpoints, showing ID at each gate. She thanked him for the tour, at the same time gleaning facts about Ng's confinement. But she had seen enough. She picked up Highway 49 at Placerville and headed south into a driving rain. She was going to court in the morning.

Charlie Chitat Ng was going to court again, except this time it was in the U.S., this time it was in San Andreas, this time it was in the county where the crimes were committed: Calaveras.

She had purposely avoided the first four days of testimony in the preliminary hearing. She would read the transcripts later.

She thought, I'll dig up the local reporter, Matt Hedgers, and have him fill me in. I may not need the transcripts.

She remembered back to 1985. Matt usually had a beer after work in the Black Bart Hotel. First stop, she thought. Get the background, then the spice: the videotapes. Tomorrow they're showing the infamous videotapes.

Chapter Twenty

THURSDAY, OCTOBER 8, 1992, 6:45 P.M.

CLANCY CHECKED INTO THE BLACK BART Hotel and immediately entered the bar. It was well past Happy Hour. She found the local reporter, Matt Hedgers, where she had hoped: sitting alone at the end of the bar. She ordered a martini for herself and another beer for him. "Been going to the trial?" she asked.

"Preliminary hearing, and yes I'll have another."

"What'd I miss?"

"Four days of testimony. Deputy Larry Copland's and Irene Brunn's."

"And?"

"The defense has been challenging 'chain of evidence' all week. One of the first articles discovered in Paul Cosner's Honda was the P G and E slip—if the defense could have had the judge strike that, the original reason for going to the Wilseyville property was out, and so was all the evidence found there."

"What did Judge Mewhinney rule?"

"Denied. Against the weight of evidence, not the admissibility. Then the defense attacked the foundation of the affidavits taken in the Canadian extradition hearings. If one wedge was forced into that testimony, then all the affidavits would be in question."

"Why bother? If the defense tossed a cloud over Copland's testimony of what Officer Wright or Detective

Hopper said or did in front of a judge, it did not eliminate the testimony. Just Copland's ability to deliver it."

Hedgers said, "Time. This was all about time. People die. Sheriff Claud Ballard is dead, his affidavit stricken. The top Calaveras law enforcement representative, in June of 'eighty-five, is six feet under, and buried with him is his testimony. Daniel Wright could die. He could be shot in the line of duty. He could eat his own gun. It happens to cops every day in America."

Clancy sipped her drink. "Did they talk about the Dubses?"

"For two days."

The Dubses' disappearance was almost like a Sherlock Holmes mystery. Clancy reflected. A man leaves work, goes home to his wife and child, and two minutes later none are heard or seen again. She asked, "What evidence was found in the apartment? Was there blood? Were there any weapons? Knives, shell casings? How'd they die?"

Hedgers shrugged. "The neighbor across the street, Dorice Murphy, IDed Ng as the Asian man leaving the Dubses' apartment. She also said the house remained dark that night, no lights, and that was very unusual. The tenant downstairs, Barbara Speaker, IDed him as the Asian man also. But no physical clues were found in the flat. Not a drop of blood. No one saw bodies being taken out."

Clancy had a good imagination. She could visualize events in words—that was her job. Conjecture, she thought, conjecture.

What did happen? The Dubses' bodies were never found. With observant neighbors like Dorice Murphy and Barbara Speaker, it would not have been easy to spirit away a year-old infant, let alone two adults.

One possibility: Harvey Dubs leaves work at the Graphic Company and heads home. He has a potential buyer coming over at a quarter to six. He parks his car in front of his house on Yukon Street. He's eager to see his son. Sean's brought a new joy to his life in the last year.

Harvey enters his house. His wife, Deborah, waves at him. She has the telephone cradled under her chin as she bustles about the kitchen preparing dinner.

"Are you talking to Karen Tuck?" Harvey calls.

"Yes."

He grins. Very few people, besides her parents, have known Deborah as long as Karen Tuck.

Harvey goes into the bathroom. He starts washing his hands.

Deborah stirs the stew she's cooking. She listens as Karen excitedly tells her what happened to her that day.

The doorbell rings. Deborah says, "Karen, got to hang up. The people who called about the video equipment are here."

What happened to the Dubses next? Clancy wondered.

Was Leonard Lake at their door?

Was Charlie Ng at their door?

Could someone just walk into a house and kill everyone?

Deborah answers the door—the potential buyer, or buyers, enter—the door swings shut—then a bullet is fired, without warning, into her head? Then another bullet crashes into Harvey's head as he leaves the bathroom? Then a final bullet extinguishes the baby Sean's life?

For what?

A camcorder?

Impossible.

But what else made sense?

Deborah Dubs was alive at 5:45—Karen Tuck's testimony. The house remained dark that night—Dorice Murphy's testimony.

The Dubses weren't selling a car, like Paul Cosner. A car allowed mobility, misdirection, seclusion.

But video equipment?

Three lives snuffed for a few bits of electronics?

Possible. But where were the bodies? And how were the bodies brought out of the house? And not seen?

Clancy had covered stories that involved dissection of the victims. It was completely possible that a whacked-up body could be crammed into a very small container. But if the body had been carved up, where was the physical evidence left at the scene?

Was it possible that Harvey, Deborah, and Sean had been led away from the scene? Alive? Then killed later, at a different location?

More than possible.

Even with such attentive neighbors. The timing would have to be lucky, not intentional.

Potential sequence: the Dubs family is led down the stairs, at gunpoint. Dorice Murphy takes that particular moment to turn her attention to the dinner she is cooking. Barbara Speaker takes that particular moment to take a shower, and cannot hear the tramp of many footsteps on the stairs of the flat overhead. . . .

Possible.

But improbable.

But the only other explanation was that the Dubses were killed in their apartment. Then their bodies moved. But there was no physical evidence. Police could trace microscopic transfers of evidence.

Who could know?

Who really knew?

Clancy knew that the Dubses were dead. Leonard Lake was dead. Was the only person on earth who knew . . . Charlie Ng? Or was the Asian man referred to in Dorice Murphy's and Barbara Speaker's testimony someone else?

Random thoughts battered her.

Better a hundred guilty men go free than an innocent man be found guilty.

Innocent until proven guilty.

The law of the land.

FRIDAY, OCTOBER 9, 1992, 9:30 A.M.

Tomasina Clancy was late getting to the Government Center. She circled the parking lot looking for a space.

Full.

There were TV satellite trucks everywhere. She had to drive back and park on the street. She hurried to the courthouse, tossed her earrings onto a plate, and walked through the metal detector.

The alarm went off.

A deputy sheriff said, "Take off your shoes."

"My shoes?"

"The metal brads that hold the heels on are setting—"

"They don't set off the metal detector at the airport."

"You're not taking a plane. These things have different sensitive levels."

"So this one's set at—"

"The highest level."

Clancy took off her shoes. She walked through the metal detector. The alarm went off again. She said, "Now what?"

The deputy shrugged. "You'll have to be patted down."

She eyed the middle-aged man. "By you?"

"No, by her." He pointed to a female deputy sheriff standing nearby.

Clancy followed her to an empty room. The deputy sheriff frisked her and said, "You're clean."

Clancy noticed the patch above her right shirt pocket: Deputy Volunteer. She asked, "You're not a regular deputy?"

"No, a bunch of us locals volunteered for this duty to help out the Sheriff's Department. Which is broke."

Clancy walked through the metal detector, picked up her purse, put on her shoes, and entered the courtroom. It was packed. A deputy asked her if she was a member of the press. She hated being catalogued, so she shook her head. He pointed to the right side of the courtroom and sat in the last row.

The opposite side was filled with men and women clutching notebooks and furiously scribbling. The front three rows on Clancy's side were reserved for people she recognized as relatives of the victims.

Clancy glanced at the man sitting to the right of her.

He had a coat on his lap. She could make out the stock of some sort of weapon. She smiled at him; he glared back.

She scanned the courtroom. Another plainclothes cop was sitting alone in the jury box. His weapon, a black Uzi, was held at port arms. Two uniformed deputy sheriffs stood at the rear door, another at the door that gave access to the judge's chambers.

Three more uniformed men sat in a triangle around the accused. Each had a sidearm, each stared unwaveringly at Charles Ng. The defendant was shackled to his chair. His head was bent over a thick file on the table in front of him.

Clancy ticked off the players in her mind: Next to Ng were his two lawyers, Thomas Marovich and James Webster. To their right was another table. At it sat Sharlene Honnaka, deputy attorney general of California, and John Martin, district attorney of Calaveras County. The judge was the Honorable Douglas Mewhinney. The court reporter was Linda James.

Clancy quickly tuned in to what was being said.

Judge Mewhinney said, "The court is going to admonish the persons who do remain that they are not to discuss any testimony about any object viewed."

Webster argued that showing the videotape would effect Ng's right to a fair trial.

Videotape! Clancy thought. I got here just in time.

The judge said, "I'm actually going to exclude people, a copy of the transcript is going to be provided."

A transcript? Clancy thought. I'd rather see the tape, but a transcript is better than nothing.

The judge finished with, "Anything said to anyone else could very definitely jeopardize the right to a fair trial in this case."

No way, Clancy thought. Maybe twenty years ago, but the Rodney King case changed all the rules. Most people on the planet watched that searingly vivid fifty-eight seconds, and comments in bars, churchyards, press rooms, and classrooms ran damn near one hundred percent that four police officers were guilty as hell. Yet a jury was unswayed, by public opinion and by the same fifty-eight seconds of videotape.

Whether the public, and the potential jury pool, saw the "M Ladies Kathy/Brenda" tape now, or in a courtroom later on, they would draw their own conclusions.

Clancy tuned into the events in the courtroom. Marovich said, "Your honor, Mr. Ng has indicated to me he has not had a hot meal since the preliminary hearing started. He had indicated he had cold pancakes and milk for breakfast on Tuesday. Of course, he got a bag lunch in court. When he got back to Folsom, it was a cold meat stew and cold rice. Yesterday morning, he had a sweet roll and milk. Again, a bag lunch here, a cold chicken pattie, mashed potatoes when he returned last night. This morning he indicated he had scrambled eggs, which was cold, and some sort of scalloped potatoes, which was the same. As I understand it, all his food is precooked, and it comes into administration segregation where it is supposedly heated up. He is on a different schedule than ninety-nine percent of the other inmates in 'ad seg' because of the early rise to get to court, and since the start of the preliminary hearing, the meals have been cold."

During Marovich's entire delivery, Clancy watched Sharon Sellito, Paul Cosner's sister. An attractive woman, her profile became progressively grimmer as the litany progressed of cold food Ng had been made to suffer through.

The judge, a man from the Department of Corrections, and the defense attorneys thrashed out a solution to Ng's meals.

The judge said, "That may solve the problem."

"Part of the problem," Marovich said. "We want Mr. Ng being able, when transported, to have a view of the horizon as to avoid motion sickness."

"Jesus Christ!" Sharon Sellito said in a loud, clear voice.

Clancy smiled at the shocked looks on the faces of the officers of the court. Ng did not turn his head. The judge looked slightly befuddled, vacillating from wanting to make an admonition to a victim's relative and realizing how it would look in the press.

The defense argued that Mr. Ng's dependency on scopolamine, to avoid car sickness, was making him drowsy.

Marovich said, "Mr. Ng indicates his feelings of anxiety, confusion, shakiness, psychological effects every time he arrives and is put in the cage. This affects his concentration, his ability to fully prepare and communicate with his attorneys."

Clancy had seen the morning papers. A picture showed Charlie Ng, wearing an orange jumpsuit, arms shackled to his waist, in a cage. The cage, six-by-four-by-three feet, was used to secure the prisoner during the morning recess, the lunch break, and the afternoon recess.

The judge refused to deny use of the cage for security reasons.

Marovich said, "Judge, I think I can express our view that the photo of Mr. Ng in the cage, we believe, is very relevant information."

"I understand that."

Marovich said, "That that type of what we believe is an excessive unconstitutional confinement is being applied to him."

Webster stood. "I saw videotapes of the bunker on TV last night. All the information that the news media had received up to the filing of the gag order was from the prosecution. On the other hand, as the court is I'm sure aware, it is not normal procedure for a defendant to put on any evidence at the preliminary hearing. So the total effect of this is that the—the news media is getting more of the prosecution's case and none of the defense side, even when we file a declaration as to why we need a continuance."

Mewhinney nodded. "I'll reconsider that declaration."

Webster held up a newspaper. "I think that the bottom line is that we don't want this case tried in the press."

Judge Mewhinney raised his eyebrows. "I definitely do not. I'm trying to prevent both sides from being tried in the press. I can only prevent that which has not occurred yet. I cannot go to the past and remedy those things."

Finally, Judge Mewhinney came to the word everyone had been waiting for.

Videotape.

A hush came over the room.

"Ladies and gentlemen," the judge said, "other than Mr. and Mrs. Stapley, if the remaining people will leave the courtroom, then we are going to show a videotape. The tape is labeled 'M Ladies Kathy/Brenda.' "

Webster responded, "Fine, your honor. As a matter of fact, for this portion of the preliminary hearing, under Nine seventy-seven, Mr. Ng would—well, actually—if possible, Mr. Ng would waive his presence, as well."

The judge was flabbergasted. "Nine seventy-seven specifically exempts the preliminary hearing as a procedure from which he could be excluded."

Webster and Marovich sat down.

The judge turned to the Stapleys. "The first portion of the tape does not deal with Mr. Stapley or Ms. O'Connor. And on that basis, I'm going to have you excluded from the first portion of the tape. When the second portion is played, you will be present and are entitled to be present. And a member of the bailiff's staff will be out to have you step in at that time."

The Stapleys both said, "We understand."

Clancy walked out to the courtyard and caught Sharon Sellito's eye. They looked at each other knowingly. At that very moment, inside the courtroom, the videotape was running.

Clancy said, "I'd like a quote on what you think about Ng's cage."

Ng had told U.S. Magistrate Peter A. Nowinski that he felt like an animal when he was put in the cage. The morning papers carried the magistrate's reply in a sidebar to the photograph of the cage. "The cage is beneath any concept of human dignity worthy of a civilized society except under the most demanding circumstances demonstrated by clear and convincing evidence of necessity."

Newsmen now began to cluster around Sellito.

Damn, Clancy thought, I lost an exclusive.

Microphones were thrust in Sharon's face. Random questions were fired—"What about Ng's food?"—"What about Ng getting sick?"—"What about the cage?"

Sharon's face was fixed in a battle between rage and humor. She said, "Actually, the cage may be a little too large and roomy for him."

Chapter Twenty-one

FRIDAY, OCTOBER 9, 1992, 10:00 A.M.

THE COURTROOM WAS ORDERED CLEARED BY Judge Mewhinney.

Clancy learned that Kathy Allen's sister had decided not to view the videotape.

Outside the courthouse a mob of media surrounded Diane Montemurro, Allen's sister. She said, "I don't want to see the pain that she went through. I just realized that I really don't want to. Hearing about it was bad enough."

Clancy had never covered a story involving anyone that was close to her. Her family tragedies and pain had been kept private.

She stared back at the Government Center and the courthouse.

What would I have done?

Would I have watched?

Would I have wanted to know?

To see?

Inside the courthouse the judge said, "The record will reflect that now present are Mr. Ng; his counsel; representatives of the people; the defense investigator, Mr. Stewart; the prosecution's investigator, Mr. Crawford; officer Copland, and officers of the court."

Webster said, "Your Honor—the court has denied our motion on authentication?"

"Yes."

Webster said, "I have another alternative to the problem of getting a correct version or transcript of the tape."

"Go ahead," the judge said.

"If the court reporter be allowed to go outside, that the tape be started. That if there is a portion where somebody raises their hand or yells 'stop', we stop the tape, the court reporter comes back in for the discussion."

"I appreciate the idea," the judge said. "Ms. Honnaka, in light of your point, and it is a well-taken point, ma'am, I am going to have you here to report the proceedings. You are not, however to take down the verbal portions of the tape, as we do have a transcript."

Webster said, "That's our question. Now we have a request. Due to Mr. Ng's housing conditions that are currently being litigated in this court and federal court and everywhere else, and the strange situation that he's under CDC personnel, we would request that for the playing of this tape, that CDC personnel that are in the courtroom be replaced just for the playing of the tape with sheriff's deputies."

"I'm not going to grant the request."

Webster once again tried to challenge the accuracy of what was on the court-submitted transcript of the videotape. He requested that Investigator Crawford, who was going to operate the tape, be instructed to stop and rewind as the defense challenged key words. He finished with, "I would like to say for the record that there are two television sets present in court that are both—it looks like both of them are going to be showing the tape. One of them is a very large-screened television, fifty inches or so.

"The other appears to be about twenty-five-inch, and that is sitting on top. The one on top is facing the audience where there—" Webster turned and stopped. The spectator seats were empty. He continued with, "—basically the people watching the top one would be Mr. Crawford and two CDC officials, Sergeant Mike Walker of the Sheriff's department. The rest of us, it would appear, would be watching the bottom one."

"Mr. Martin," the judge said, "You may proceed to play the tape."

The tape was stuck into the VHS. The screen filled with snow, then cleared. A commercial broadcast appeared.

Webster said, "I can't hear."

"Okay," the judge said. ". . . we'll stop the tape, and increase the volume. Back it so we can start again."

"I need to hear some audio."

"We can start," the judge said, "hopefully with the commercial television."

The commercial ended. The screen went blank, then depicted at first a white female sitting in a chair in what appeared to be the infamous living room in the house on Blue Mountain Road.

The woman's hands seemed to be cuffed behind her and Leonard Lake was heard and seen talking to her: "—money back, so to speak." Lake began a long monologue directed at the woman, beginning with the accusation that a man named Mike "owes us" something. Only Mike, unfortunately, can't pay. Using the woman's name, Kathy, Lake offers her a choice, but it's her last choice, he says: she can cooperate with them, do willingly everything they tell her to do, or in thirty days she will be drugged and blindfolded and turned loose back "in the city." That date, the fifteenth of May, is so certain, she can write it on her calendar. Lake claims to be unafraid of what she might do then, because she doesn't know where she is being held and doesn't even know his name. So what, he seems to say, that she knows Charlie's name. Her boyfriend Mike will have "disappeared gracefully" by that time. So Kathy is ordered to do what she's told or get a shot through her head. And here Lake forgets that he has just used the euphemism that Mike may "disappear." He promises Kathy that she will be buried in the same spot where they have already buried Mike.

The judge interrupted. "I'm sorry. Could you please stop the tape? Did everybody agree that the word three lines up was 'into your head' as opposed to 'through your head'?"

"That's what I heard, your honor," Honnaka said.

"Was 'into'?"

"That's what I heard."

"Thank you."

"Judge," Marovich said, "it sounded to our investigator Wilson Stewart as the word 'through'."

The judge said, "If you'll please back it up and we'll see if we can confirm if it is 'into' or 'through'."

The videotape was backed up and rerun.

The judge ordered, "Please stop the tape."

" 'Through'," Webster said, "your honor."

Honnaka said, "We still hear 'into'."

Webster said, "We have a 'through' vote over here."

Mewhinney sighed. "I'm going to back it up one more time, just very briefly. We'll see if we can get through it."

The videotape was backed up and run again.

Webster said, "Stop it. I still hear 'through,' your honor."

The judge was visibly annoyed. "We're going to note for the record that at that point it is either 'through' or 'into' and there's a disagreement.

"Then if you'd please proceed." The judge waved at Crawford and he started the tape again.

Lake continued speaking, complaining he was "scared, nervous." He bragged that they never planned on "fucking up" or getting caught, or at least that they were not intending to get caught. It was simple, he explained: there would be no witnesses.

And now came the worst part: they were counting on Kathy to use the information they had about Mike to get money from his bank account, and then cover their tracks by writing to the storage company that had Mike's furniture to circulate a story that Mike had simply gone "over the horizon." No one would wonder about it, Lake said; a story like that was "semi-acceptable." Meanwhile, Kathy was expected to take care of all the household chores, so to speak, at the cabin. That included sex—"you'll fuck for us." It wasn't much of a choice for her, Lake explained, unless she had "a death wish."

The woman said, "No, I . . ." and her words trailed off.

Webster broke in, "Can we stop that? Your honor, this transcript, after we get through with it, is going to be released to the public. At the top of page one of the transcript, on the left-hand side, it says, quote, 'Two women', close quote. And then it had 'L Lake' and 'N Ng', 'K Kathy', and 'B Brenda'. I would request that 'N' not be used at this point, but perhaps a question mark. And there is no proof whatsoever that this is Mr. Ng that's inaudible or some fourth person. And I don't think that throughout the tape that there would be a sign that there is not some fourth person there. Whether or not the Court can determine that this portion of the tape—that it is, in fact, Mr. Ng, there is another question."

Mewhinney answered, "I'll certainly reserve on that issue, then, after listening to the tape."

The videotape was backed up and restarted.

Lake's voice was heard again, presenting the option of "a death wish."

As the woman said, "No, I . . ." Webster broke in again. "Stop. I heard that as 'It is not much of a choice, unless you've got a death wish'. . . ."

When the videotape was restarted, Lake told Kathy that he liked her and didn't like lying to her. He would lay it all out in clear terms. It was a monologue in which Kathy's failure to respond only intensified Lake's insecurity. He alternated between toughness and self-doubt—and was speaking in the plural. They were "selfish bastards," he admitted, for using her for their own pleasure—and she would "probably think of worse names" for them, he said, over the next four weeks. But, Lake whined, they were nervous and "high-strung," and needed her to "do something about that."

So it was time for a decision, he said in a lawyerly conclusion: she could play ball with them and be a willing sexual prisoner, or force them to strap her to the bed.

Then they'd have to shoot her. "Sorry, lady," he apologized—"time's up." What was it going to be?

In a faint voice Kathy agreed that she would have to be "available."

That wasn't enough for Lake. He wanted her to spell out the sexual details on tape and from her own lips.

Kathy protested that she didn't know how to spell it out. She simply agreed to go along with whatever they wanted.

Lake apparently felt he had broken her will. Gloating over his little triumph, he rubbed it in. Her boyfriend, Mike, he said bluntly, "was an ass."

Kathy could only mumble incoherently.

Lake nodded as if to say he understood. Then he launched into an evaluation of her relationship with Mike, revealing his own jealousies. Mike was going to drop her soon, anyway. Just today or yesterday, Lake claimed, Mike told him he had had sex with a woman in a motel. Lake looked at Kathy for a reaction, then blurted that Mike could have been lying.

Kathy mumbled.

Lake turned to his partner off-screen and asked, matter-of-factly, if he had the keys for Kathy's handcuffs.

A high-timbred voice off stage said, "Uh huh."

On the screen Lake began putting leg irons on Kathy's feet, then removed the handcuffs.

"Stand up, Kathy," Lake ordered, swaggering into his role. He apologized for being "clumsy" at what was about to happen. He wanted Kathy to undress completely for him and his partner, and show them what they had bought.

"Undress for you?"

Lake spelled it out: he wanted her blouse off, then the bra, and then her jeans.

Marovich stood and said, "Judge? I believe that's 'Take your chains off', rather than 'Take your jeans off'."

"Back it up please."

The videotape was replayed.

The judge said, "It is 'chains'. Would you please stop

the tape. The last line on page three will now be 'take your chains', c-h-a-i-n-s, 'off', as opposed to 'Take your jeans off', j-e-a-n-s."

The videotape began again.

The voice off-stage commanded Kathy to remove her pants. And then Charlie Ng appeared on the screen.

Lake agreed that Kathy should remove her pants, but added that "we'll run it through the shower."

"Should I go, too?" Ng asked.

The judge said, "I'm sorry. If you'd please back it up. I'm concerned about whether it is 'run it' or 'run her through the shower'."

The videotape rolled, and the judge asked, "Everybody hears, 'We'll run it through the shower?' "

"Yes," Webster answered, "that's what I hear."

Martin agreed.

Marovich asked, "Could we run it through again, your honor?"

Marovich, Webster and the judge listened several more times to the unclear section of tape. Finally the judge made a determination: "Page four, 'Lake: "Sure, but we'll run her through the shower." "Should I go too?" "Oh, you want to take a shower with her? If you want." ' "

Honnaka insisted, "Well, your honor, the People still hear 'run it through the shower' instead of 'her'."

"Then we'll put a disagreement there of 'it' and 'her'."

Those in the courtroom worked their way through the tape, with frequent pauses and replays. After minutes of this, but only a few seconds further into the chronology unfolding on the TV screens, Lake acknowledged to Charlie that Kathy was being "wisely cooperative." Then he told Kathy that he and Charlie were going to do anything it took to bend her to their will. He complimented her on seeing it their way, but immediately announced some "ground rules." She was told to follow instructions without the slightest hesitation. If she created any problems, she would wind up dead.

Charlie Ng told Kathy to finish undressing. "Please,"

he added. Then he noted, apparently to Lake, that the "piece" was on the table nearby.

Webster objected, "I'm not agreeing that it is Mr. Ng saying that, but I believe the 'N' should be there. In other words, we're not agreeing that Mr. Ng is there at all."

"I understand," the judge said; "the Court, however, is going to find that it is Mr. Ng's voice after the portions we previously discussed."

He signalled the videotape to continue. Ng's dialogue was repeated.

"This is going to be a slow process, ladies and gentlemen; we're determined."

Webster said, "All right. While I'm thinking about it, I think that we should make the public aware of the fact that this is not an eight-hour tape, or however long it is going to take us. That someone or somehow we should time the tape and say the tape actually lasts, or this transcript lasts such and such, so many minutes. Because they're going to think that we've been in here watching this tape for hours."

"They may," the judge said. "The Court, for purposes of accuracy, will try to note its approximate time on the official document."

The videotape clicked on again. Kathy fumbled with the buttons on her clothes. She apologized for being shy.

Lake told her not to be. He was understanding. But she was going to take a shower. When Ng added that this wouldn't be the first time or the last, Lake admonished him not to make it hard for her. With an unctuous "please," he commanded her to continue undressing.

Kathy muttered, "Yeah."

"Panties, too," Lake said. He didn't want to have to make an example of how he would get her to cooperate. Then he began to give instructions about slippers, but his thought was cut off in mid-sentence as the tape ran out.

Webster said, "It says 'outside of the—' Is this where the tape stops?"

Honnaka answered, "And then goes to another scene later on."

"So," the judge said, "this is a separate, different scene?"

"That's correct."

"I would submit," Webster said, "that it should say that last line there, 'When you get out, there will be slippers outside of the, inaudible,' then the tape stops and a new scene. In a different room, perhaps. Another scene some time later, something to that effect."

The judge said, "It will read, 'Lake: "When you get out, they'll be slippers outside of the . . ." ' And then it will be dot dot dot, tape ends. New scene. Go ahead, Bailiff."

The videotape then cut to a bedroom. It showed a black-haired man on a bed with a woman sitting on his back.

The judge said, "Tape ends."

Webster said, "Tape ends, commercial television scene. It looks like an advertisement for a motel."

"Right, then we'll have a new scene. Tape ends. Commercial scene. And then new scene."

The videotape cut to another bedroom scene. The background identified the location as the bedroom at the Wilseyville house.

Lake strapped Kathy Allen to the bed. He began taking still photos of her, all the while indulging himself in a long monologue about his sexual proclivities, his disappointments, his abhorrence of what he was doing even as he subjected her to the dehumanizing video images he was meticulously creating. He punctuated his threats with requests to turn her head this way or that way, remarking occasionally, "not bad." The sadness in his voice mirrored the words in his diary: he always seemed to be ignored by the opposite sex. He said "not bad" again as he focused a shot on the defenseless woman.

He complained that he had tried to respect Kathy's feelings, but of course that wouldn't make any difference anyway, he conceded. And then he accused her of not doing things he expected of her.

Kathy was aghast. "What haven't I done?" she asked in disbelief.

Lake replied that he was referring to telling her not to beat on her cell door.

"Oh, geez!" she shot back.

Lake walked to the bureau in the bedroom and picked up a set of keys while she pleaded that she hadn't tried to force open the door. He replied coolly that he was afraid she had. Another long monologue ensued, with Kathy recorded on camera straining to understand Lake's growing paranoia. He explained that he had picked the latches for the cell door carefully, and now they appeared to be bent out of shape. The metal shouldn't have been deformed so easily, he said, so obviously she had put an "immense amount of pressure" on the door. That just wouldn't do. What if someone nearby had heard the banging? Perhaps that was impossible, given the distance from the nearest neighbor, but anyway it bothered him.

Again Lake's fatalism came back. They wouldn't take him alive, he repeated. He had cyanide pills, which he had showed her: death would be far better than to be captured "doing these weird things." But both of them would have to die in that case, and he would try to prevent that. What, Lake wondered aloud, did he have to do to prove to Kathy that he was serious about her not trying to escape?

Kathy had no illusions about her tormentor's sadistic streak. She answered immediately: did he want to hit her?

No, Lake said, he didn't have to ask permission for that. He didn't want to hurt her—but in the same breath he took it back: Beating her up would be a turn-on for him, a "great thrill," but he was having problems with that idea. He assured her that he wanted, even in these abject circumstances, to preserve some of her sanity. And then he confessed: he was having a "little war" within himself, a battle between what the "decent" thing to do might be and what his fantasies commanded him to do.

But for now the only decent thing to do was take a rest. It was Lake's best imitation of a joke.

Kathy cringed as Lake returned to the problem of the bent hinges. He was going to hammer them back in shape, and he didn't want them bent again. There would be no noise from the cell—he didn't want to "hear anything." In the strongest possible terms, he said, there would be hell to pay.

Lake then remembered something: on the first night of Kathy's imprisonment, his sexual demands had apparently been rebuffed. Remember, he said, I told you I wanted you to "drink me."

Webster broke in. "Your Honor, can we stop it?"

"Stop."

"I don't hear the word 'me' after 'drink'."

"Back it up just a little bit."

The tape was rewound a few seconds and then played.

Webster said, "It is there."

The videotape began again.

Lake now became petulant. He had apparently been rebuffed twice—first about his request to "drink me" and second about the bent hinges. Now he was going to get serious. If any noises were made from the cell—no matter who might hear them—Kathy would be "whipped very severely." He asked if she understood.

"I understand."

"Good!" Lake exclaimed, and then quickly reverted to his ruminations about his "sadistic tendencies." He advised Kathy that some women "are into pain," but he didn't think she was. So he would spare her—otherwise he'd feel guilty about yielding to his "lesser impulses." As he continued on in his self-analysis, he suddenly yelled, "Rats!" It was time for her to get out of the straps that held her to the bed.

Lake appeared solicitous for a man who had just abused a woman with his camera and his domineering persona. He asked if the straps were too tight, too binding.

Kathy told him they were cutting off her circulation.

Leonard Lake had something prepared for this moment. He told her to release herself from the straps—which she immediately did, this being a fantasy bondage scene—as he tossed her some "Frederick's of Hollywood"-style lingerie. These were the words that investigators used to describe the women's "intimate" apparel they found in the Wilseyville cabin in abundance. Now it was Kathy's turn to play the unwilling model for Lake's "lingerie" fantasies.

She started to comply.

Lake admitted the panties were very tight as he watched her efforts to struggle into them.

"Huh?" Kathy said. It was only around the legs, she said: her hips were wide. But then she faced a dilemma. She couldn't figure out which side of the panties were "up." Usually the elastic is on the upper side, she said.

Lake snapped some candid photos as the video rolled. But he seemed more interested in his adolescent life story than in the efforts of his captive to wriggle into her skimpy costume. The whole scene reminded him, he said, of his "IRS girlfriend." He quickly admitted that she was only three years old and he was nineteen when they first met. He was asked by the baby's mother to take her out to play; she ran into his room "naked as a puppy" and he tried to dress her. It was a disaster.

Kathy was barely listening to Lake's story as she struggled to put on the tight outfit. She asked if it was inside-out.

Lake was still in his reverie. He ignored Kathy as he told how the three-year-old's mother lectured him about putting the panties on backwards. He didn't know they had a front and a back. He assumed her shirt buttoned in the front, like a man's shirt. He put a pair of trousers on her that weren't supposed to be for play. In general, he said, he "blew it."

In the same breath Lake told Kathy, matter-of-factly, to "hop on the bed," then quickly added that he didn't see the little girl for another twenty years. At that point, presumably, she became his "IRS girlfriend." Lake assured Kathy that twenty years did a lot for a three-year-old, but nothing more was said of the relationship.

Lake said he would take a couple of pictures, then finish his "game" and have a cigarette. Ominously, he advised her against doing anything foolish, like smiling. He found her non-smiling, sultry look attractive, and assured her that the other guys probably did, too. A smiling woman, it would seem, would be a challenge to him.

What a gentleman! he seemed to imply. He pointed out that he hadn't taken any full nude photos.

Kathy said, "Uh huh."

It was the old cliché: a woman should always leave something to the imagination. Kathy agreed with him on this indisputable point.

"Right," Lake said, and took another picture. He handed her another panty and asked her to try it on. This is what he liked, he almost drooled; full nudes were not interesting, even the ones he had "acquired." He suggested that the panty might fit her, even if too small.

"It probably will."

"And . . ."

". . . problem."

"That's all right."

". . . years of practice."

Lake asked her to try to get the panties on, then suddenly turned the subject to religion. Was she still on that track?

Kathy put on new lingerie. She told Lake that, yes, she was talking about religion when Lake walked in on her that morning in the bathroom. She had been mumbling, she said.

He answered that the sounds from the bathroom brought him in. He thought she was about to prepare for a breakout—a "kamikaze wrist slash." He was going to advise her not to make trouble. What was she doing?

Kathy paused. "I was saying my morning prayer."

There was scarcely a pause in the attention of the prosecution, the defense, and the judge, but the room was unusually still. The videotape rolled on as if no one had heard the last sentence. The job of everyone in the courtroom was to compare text to sound on the screen—not to pass judgment. And yet . . . Again Lake's voice was heard. He ordered Kathy to "jump" in bed, to sit, to look at him. As she complied, he fiddled with the video camera on a tripod, complaining about how hard it was to adjust. Then he was satisfied with her pose, and told her to hold it. Now he wanted the bra off that she had just had so much trouble forcing herself into.

Lake asked her if she ever wore bras that fastened in front. Kathy must have thought it was a juvenile question, but she agreed that she had. This one, though, was posing a problem.

"It's trippy," she said.

Webster piped up. "Tricky?"

Judge Mewhinney asked to have the tape backed up. "I thought I still heard the word 'trippy'."

"It could be," Webster agreed. "It doesn't make sense, but that's what it sounds like."

"We'll leave it as 'trippy'. Go ahead."

The videotape was played.

Lake asked, "Can I help?"

Kathy continued to fumble. A string was stuck, she thought.

"Okay," Lake said. He told her to put her legs in front of her, to lean back on the bed. As she pulled the panties on, he applauded, "That's it."

He snapped a few more shots and promised her he'd have the photos for her to look at before she left. He told her to put her clothes on and get outside. Something was going to happen outside.

Kathy put on her jeans.

As Lake and Kathy prepared to go outside, he reminded her that she had "given up" smoking for the four days she had been in the cell. He suggested that she might want to have a smoke.

Kathy agreed that she was shaking from lack of nicotine. Lake continued to play with her. He advised her that after a month of this sort of abstinence she might lose the shakes. And that would be good for her.

Kathy said she didn't want to quit—not just yet.

Lake again returned to the plural "we." He said that "we" didn't care, but he would give her a cigarette "under protest." The irony hung in the air.

The judge called a halt. "That will be the end of the tape, and a new scene. It is now twelve o'clock. We will be back at one-thirty."

Webster said, "The next portion of the tape is the one which supposedly involves Mr. Stapley."

The judge said, "We'll have Mr. and Ms. Stapley come through, we'll play the portion right through without comment, let them go, and then we can go back through it and work out the transcript details. Court is in recess."

T.B. Clancy watched the lawyers leave the courthouse. *What,* she thought, *could they have possibly spent all morning on?*

The press congregated around Dwight and Lola Stapley. A dozen different voices fired questions simultaneously. A reporter asked point-blank, "Why have you decided to view the video?"

Dwight Stapley, the retired school teacher, said, "We're like people who are waiting for someone who is late, and we overimagine what we don't know. We've got to know. We know we can't change it, but maybe it will help if we can learn as much as we can. We know it's going to hurt."

Lola added, "To me, not knowing is the worst thing in the world. Maybe what I find out will be as bad. I have no idea what to expect."

Clancy saw Matt Hedgers hustle out of the courthouse entrance.

He smiled and held up a sheaf of papers. "I got a copy of the transcript."

"Can I follow you into town? I'll copy it, then you can turn it in to your paper."

"Sure."

Clancy glanced at the papers. The court had spent all morning on the tape and they had only gone through the first ten pages of the transcript.

Clancy would have to skip going to court that afternoon, anyway. The lawyers were going to play soundtrack detective again.

She decided to find a quiet place and read the Brenda O'Connor portion of the transcript.

Chapter Twenty-two

FRIDAY, OCTOBER 9, 1992, 2:00 P.M.

TOMASINA BOYD CLANCY SAT ON A RAISED stucco planter box in the Government Center's courtyard. The sun had come out. The rays from that distant star warmed her face.

She opened the transcript. It was titled M LADIES KATHY/ BRENDA.

She read the Kathy portion.

When she was finished she went inside to the bathroom and washed her hands. She splashed water on her face, then rinsed out her mouth.

She returned to her seat in the courtyard. She flipped to the section marked: *Brenda.* She read: *The second female subject observed on the tape is called Brenda. She appears in same room as Kathy. Brenda appears clothed at first and handcuffed with her hands behind her back. In the tape also observed is an Asian male, black straight hair, wearing no shirt. . . . The screen is at first filled with snow, then clears.*

Clancy turned the page and read the transcript:

Lake said, enigmatically, that he had nothing to do with "him."

Brenda asked what Lake's companion did with "him."

Ng denied doing anything.

Brenda persisted in asking if "you guys" had killed him.

Lake denied it. There was still no indication of who "him" might be.

"Are you going to let us go soon?" Brenda asked.

Us? thought Clancy. She'd said, 'let us go soon?' Who's us? Who's Brenda referring to? Lonnie Bond? Lonnie Bond Junior? Robin Scott Stapley?

She continued reading the transcript.

Lake said, "Probably not."

"Never?" Brenda asked. She asked if they were going to kill her; she had decided, it seemed, to face her enemy.

Lake answered that it was up to her.

She would have none of it. She confronted Ng directly, referring to him as "Charles." She demanded to know why he was doing this.

Lake answered for both men, without hesitation. He said they hated her.

Brenda wouldn't buy it. She and her family had never done anything to them, she said.

Lake told her to shut up.

As Brenda continued talking about her baby, Lake battered her with accusations that she was a problem in the neighborhood, that nobody liked her. When she volunteered that she would move away, Lake seemed to relish telling her that she had already been "closed down." "We," he said, "took Scott away." He identified the "we" as the "Star Route Gang." The post office designation for that part of Blue Mountain Road was "Star Route."

As Brenda continued to shake her head at the absurdity of this crime, Lake announced to her that her baby would be taken away.

"Taken away?" she asked, not ready to accept the enormity of what was going on.

Lake said there was a family in Fresno that needed a baby. And he snarled that they had one now. Ng chimed in that this was better than the baby being dead.

Brenda was stupefied. She couldn't believe that her baby was the one they were talking about. "My baby?" she asked.

Lake answered by giving her the same choice he had

given Kathy. She would be a slave for them, in every way, and if she refused to do anything they asked, they would simply tie her down, rape her, take her outside and shoot her.

Brenda whispered that she would cooperate. As Ng was heard to mumble something in the background, Lake laughed about how fast she had answered. But she was still defiant about her baby, demanding to know if they were really going to take the baby away.

Lake seemed to relish her torment. Yes, he said, because she wasn't a fit mother.

Again Brenda quizzed her captors, this time about her boyfriend Lonnie, and others she suspected had been "captured" by Lake. He answered with calculated euphemisms; they had been "taken away" to a place in the hills where they'd be chopping wood happily for the rest of their lives. Brenda grabbed onto this straw of hope; they hadn't been killed "or anything?", she asked.

Lake answered with tantalizing vagueness. He hadn't killed them, he said, but whether they would die was "their problem." But he implied that they were under his control, because they faced the "same choice" as she did.

And now Brenda revealed how she, Lonnie, and perhaps a third person, Stapley, had met their fate. She asked Lake if that was why they had been "invited over here for dinner."

As Lake nodded, Ng added that it was just part of "the game."

Game? Clancy rocked back and forth on her impromptu bench. Her brow felt damp. Her heart was racing. Part of the game? They invite their next-door neighbors over for dinner, Lonnie Bond and Robin Scott Stapley, Brenda, and the baby. Then what? Brenda gets tossed in the cell. Bond and Stapley get bullets in their heads and buried in sleeping bags six-tenths of a mile away.

And the baby?

Was Lonnie Bond Junior one of the small and as yet unidentified corpses found in the initial excavation?

She flipped open the document and continued to read.

As Clancy took in the next few pages, the words fell into the background as the scene in the bedroom became more vivid before her eyes. Dialogue no longer mattered; she could picture an angry young mother, bound like an animal, spitting defiance at two men who had taken her baby away.

What was wrong with them, Brenda yelled, that they were doing this to her? Lake shot back that they simply didn't like her. But now they were going to enjoy raping her. He promised to demonstrate why he was known as "fuck face," and he asked Ng to get "the manacles."

Brenda asked them to loosen the handcuffs, and began to cry about Lonnie. Lake boasted that he wasn't "gentle" with Lonnie, but that Lonnie was "at least alive" when he left the cabin. He conceded that he would remove the handcuffs as soon as Ng had her ankles in the manacles. Ng seemed anxious to get on with this task; if she was so hot, he would take her clothes off. As the taunting continued, Brenda again begged to see her baby. She refused to believe they would keep her baby to force her into sexual acts with them.

Ng fumbled to put the manacles on her, leaving the handcuffs in place. Lake explained that Brenda's baby was innocent but she was not. Again Brenda confronted them: they were crazy, she told them to their faces.

The reaction was instantaneous: Lake accused her again of being "an asshole" and Ng slashed at her T-shirt with a knife, ripping it away to reveal her bra. The taunting continued, with jokes about Ng being so crude as to have ruined a perfectly good shirt that Lake liked. When Brenda pleaded with Ng to leave her bra on, he responded by brandishing the knife again and cutting the bra off with one slash.

Ng seemed to enter the dialogue gleefully. When he was told to take the handcuffs off, since Brenda was fully confined by the leg restraints, he scolded her that crying would do no good. She could complain like "the rest of them."

Lake laughed that he was "hot as they come," and insisted that Ng get on with removing the cuffs. But Ng continued to flaunt his power over the captive. He leaned close to Brenda and threatened that he would get his "weapon" if she were stupid enough to try to resist. To emphasize his point, he placed some sort of a gun on the table next to him.

Brenda again demanded that the cuffs be removed. She was perspiring under the ceiling light that was needed for videotaping. She said she was feeling sick.

Lake answered, "Suffer!" And then he asked her to look at something, which he said he would show her only one time. He held up a black, coiled whip.

Brenda didn't flinch. So it's come to this, she as much as told him. They were going to "beat" her.

Lake admitted he might. Waving the whip, he started to say how "vicious" it was, but then he backed off. If only she would "cooperate. . . ."

Clancy heaved a sigh of relief: the transcript now turned to a scene that could well have been a spoof of a pornographic movie. Lake and Ng began to haggle over the prospect of taking a shower with Brenda. Ng said it was lucky for him. Lake demurred to his partner about who was going to go first. But what about the leg irons? Lake thought Brenda was sufficiently cowed to take a shower without her legs in irons.

My God, Clancy thought: this gal is still holding her own. As Lake demanded that she take her jeans off, Brenda again complained of the heat. She was going to pass out, she said—and that wouldn't do either of them any good, was the implication. So Lake directed her to a couch and moved the camera on her.

As the tawdry dialogue continued, it was becoming obvious to Lake and Ng that Brenda was stalling. Lake was irritated; he volunteered that his animosity toward her was at the breaking point and he was about to prove how serious he was by starting things out with a "nice firm whipping." As Ng laughed in the background, Lake again demanded that Brenda slip her jeans down.

But Brenda answered that she was too dizzy to do it. Ng suddenly became solicitous: he told Lake that her lips were pale and asked Brenda if she wanted some water.

Over Lake's objections, Brenda said that, yes, she would have something to drink. She pointed at a pack of cigarettes on the table, again changing the subject. She had been sick all day, she said, implying that she needed a smoke.

Amazingly, Lake took the bait. He chided her about how he thought she had given up smoking.

Brenda began vomiting. Lake was now at his wit's end; he told her to clean up her own mess. She protested that she was too dizzy and sweaty to do anything.

The heat apparently was getting to Lake, too. He asked Ng to turn off one of the lights in the room. After some fumbling, Ng found the right switch. Brenda seemed to be breathing easier.

Lake and Ng now began to compare Brenda's torso with Kathy's—arguing that Brenda might be older and had just had a baby, but still was "a little better." In the midst of their rambling dialogue, Brenda said that all she could feel was a "shush" in the top of her head. Ng offered her an aspirin, but Lake said no. Brenda, now sobbing, said she felt as if she were pregnant. Ng recoiled at the thought: there was no time for "that shit." And he didn't want to hear further complaints about what happened to her baby, or "it'll be history."

Brenda again begged for her baby, promising to "do anything," but Lake reverted to his boast that she would have to do what they wanted regardless of her promises. Besides, he argued, a baby just wasn't the thing to have in a dirty house. . . .

Brenda had stalled as long as she could. Over her pleas that her baby couldn't live without her, Lake and Ng forced her to strip and prepared for their fantasy shower. They informed her that she had to be "clean" before they had sex with her. That was the "house rule." Lake, Ng, and Brenda disappeared from the screen; the sounds of a shower running made the conversation inaudible. Except for one thing: as Brenda protested, Lake was heard to say, "Gobble down."

The rest of the transcript was banal: talk of towels and washing each other and worrying about something. Ng complained about the showerhead. Lake insisted that Brenda brush her teeth and use mouthwash. Finally the tape ended. There was a broad hint in the conversation that could be heard over the sounds of the shower that Brenda had asked Lake something about Ng. "Maybe he does," Lake answered.

Clancy swallowed, then swallowed again. Her imagination was flying. Her mouth was dry. Her heart was pounding. Her stomach was rolling. The bastards, she thought, the rotten business-as-usual bastards.

T.B. Clancy let the packet of loose papers fall to her lap, and looked across the courtyard. She had just visited another world, and the sunlight was all too bright a reminder of how far away that world was. She had to pause to force down the nausea that had swelled in her throat. Slowly, she got her bile under control, but not her emotions.

She stared again at the transcripts. Was Brenda's last question about Ng? When Lake told her that "maybe he does," was he talking about Ng having AIDS? No one could tell. But what did it matter? It was clear enough: Lake was captured on camera. Ng was there with him. They spoke in the plural about what they had been doing.

Chapter Twenty-three

THE PRELIMINARY HEARING BOGGED DOWN after the tapes were played. The sessions on Tuesday and Wednesday were held entirely *in camera.* Bizarrely, the discussions were over Ng's transportation, his shackles, the cage.

Deputy Sheriff Larry Copland was cross-examined Thursday and Friday. The ground covered was a rehash of early testimony. The defense continued to try to disqualify things as hearsay, double hearsay, and triple hearsay. The judge continued to cite Proposition 115, the initiative recently passed by California voters to speed up the judicial process. Before Prop 115, a preliminary hearing was as crowded as a trial, as every witness had to be present. Now, affidavits, including all sorts of hearsay, were allowed.

The press, with nothing new to cover, evaporated.

By October 20 the only reporters covering the event were Matt Hedgers from the *Calaveras Enterprise,* John Cox, from the *Sacramento Bee,* and T. B. Clancy.

OCTOBER 20, 1992, 9:30 A.M.

The bailiff called the courtroom to order as the hearings dragged toward the end of the second week. The judge took his seat behind the bench.

Marovich stood and said, "If I could speak. Before we

proceed, Mr. Ng is indicating to me, and he indicated to me when I first saw him earlier this morning about, I guess about nine-fifteen in the cage, when he was in the cage, that he's feeling ill at the present time, feeling nauseous, and from my personal observations, he does appear not to be mentally alert, as I've frequently found him. But he does appear having some mental problems, and he's told me of physical problems."

The judge asked, "Mr. Ng?"

"Yes."

"You're feeling nauseous at this time?"

"I'm just . . . I'm feeling kind of sick. . . . I think I've got the flu, I don't know, but I feel weak and tired, I can't concentrate. I didn't, I wasn't able to sleep last night for some reason, because of nightmares of being in a cage, so I—"

Marovich said, "Judge, when I first saw Mr. Ng a short time ago, he gave me a memo that's addressed to Mr. Webster and myself, but I would like to read at least portions of it as far as him explaining to Mr. Webster and myself how he feels right now."

"That's fine . . . Mr. Ng, that's fine. I'll let you do it in your own words, Mr. Ng. Mr. Ng, so you feel you have the flu; is that correct?"

"I've got a runny nose and I might have a temperature —I have a toothache too."

"Okay," the judge said. "And have you sought medical attention for the toothache?"

"Yes, I did, your honor, the doctor in the prison told me that he won't give me any medication, because he doesn't want me to feel drowsy. He doesn't want me to feel drowsy, so I didn't get any medical attention. I put in a request to see him this Monday. He didn't see me."

"And so let me understand. I don't understand, Mr. Ng, he did or did not see you?"

"He did not."

"He did not see you. How do you know he told you he didn't want to give you any medication if you didn't see him?"

"Through the MTA, the person that delivers medications."

"Okay. And then you indicated you have a runny nose?"

"Yeah."

"And what other symptoms do you conclude that you have the flu from?"

"Headache, nausea, stomach problems."

"Mr. Ng, the court is going to proceed today. If you feel that you need . . . if you feel nauseous, feel like you're going to throw up, if you'll just notify either of your attorneys at that point, then we'll recess at that point, gentlemen. On the—"

"Judge," Marovich interrupted, "for the record, we'd like to object to proceeding at this time. Obviously, given Mr. Ng's statement . . . and frankly, Judge, given my own personal observations, first having contact with him at quarter after nine this morning, I basically feel he is not really in any condition right now to meaningfully participate and assist us. I have dealt with him now for about a year, and I've seen him many times, and this morning is one of the times when I feel that he would have a great difficulty meaningfully participating in these proceedings this morning . . . or at least right now. I'm not saying all morning, but I'm saying right now."

Webster added, "Your honor, I have some . . . we've submitted two declarations, as the court is aware. They're short. I've just given them to the District Attorney. As far as the security motion that we have been doing in closed session, we have an additional . . . at least one additional exhibit, which we would be presenting to the court. I've just given a copy of the two to the District Attorney."

The judge said, "Well, let me deal with one thing at a time." Mewhinney ordered the court to proceed. Within a few minutes Charlie Ng fell asleep at the defense table.

Once again the hearing was mired in cross-examinations and recross-examinations.

Highway Patrolman Hicks testified to having been

called to the scene of an accident involving a pickup truck with the license plate AHOYMTY.

Mr. Crawford was cross-examined on the investigation he conducted involving Tori Doolin, the friend of Robin Scott Stapley who had moved to Austin, Texas.

A bombshell didn't drop until the end of October.

OCTOBER 28, 1992, 1:30 P.M.

The judge said, "The record will reflect Mr. Ng is present with his attorneys, Mr. Marovich and Mr. Webster. People represented by Mr. Martin and Ms. Honnaka, officers of the court."

Marovich said, "Your honor, before Mr. Webster starts, I'd like to mention several things to the court. Mr. Ng has some documents in the nature of a civil case that he wants to file, and we would request . . . he would request an order from this court that he be allowed access to the Superior Court Clerk's Office in some respect, whether that would involve the clerk coming down to the security area or even a bailiff, perhaps, delivering the papers to the Superior Court Clerk so that the civil action . . . so that he could file the civil action on his own behalf."

"Certainly," the judge said, "I'll allow him to hand it to the bailiff, and I'll direct that the bailiff hand it to the clerk in whatever form it is currently in."

Marovich continued, "The second part . . . the second point I wish to make is that the suit . . . the civil suit named myself and Mr. Webster as defendants. It's a . . . it's a civil suit for malpractice, wherein substantial damages are sought."

What! Clancy thought. Ng's suing his lawyers!

Marovich continued, "Mr. Webster and I have discussed this. . . . obviously, we haven't had time to research and really think about our position, vis-à-vis Mr. Ng, but in light of Mr. Ng having this suit prepared and ready to file, the fact that Mr. Webster and I are, in fact, named as the defendants in the suit with monetary damages being sought, we would request a continuance until tomorrow morning at nine-thirty so we can research this issue, look into it, as far as any potential violation of bar rules based on conflict of interest or anything along those lines."

Webster added, "Your honor, I just learned about this right just before, at lunch, and I don't, obviously, don't have the bar rules with me. But it seems to me that the bar rules are specific in that if you are sued by a client, that there is a conflict. I suppose that if, at some point a Superior Court judge were to say that the suit is spurious or obviously brought in the hopes of removing counsel, something to that effect, that that conflict would go away, but I don't know what to do in the meantime."

Judge Mewhinney answered, "We're going to proceed with the proceedings today, and then we'll take up the matter tomorrow morning at nine-thirty to allow you gentlemen to review any authorities and present them to the court, if you wish.

"Mr. Webster, do you wish to confer with Mr. Marovich, then, for a few minutes?"

Marovich said, "Judge, Mr. Webster and I share the view that there's potentially a real serious issue here of potential conflict, and we're both very, very reluctant to proceed this afternoon."

Webster said, "I don't think— In this case, of course, we haven't been served yet, but I haven't read the complaint word-for-word, but I believe Mr. Marovich has. I read the highlights, I think, right before lunch. Although it hasn't been filed and it hasn't been served, we know that it's here waiting to be filed and served, which, as Mr. Marovich indicated, could be done very expeditiously, and I certainly don't want to have the record look like we're proceeding because we haven't been served yet or anything like that, because I think it's clear that the intent to serve is there. We've already reviewed it and knew it was going to be filed."

"It's not my intention, Mr. Webster," the judge said, "to place you in a position of believing you're violating the bar rules. Ladies and gentlemen, we're going to be in recess at this time until two-thirty. That will give us forty-five minutes to make an initial review. Court is in recess until two-thirty P.M. The bailiff is directed to serve, or to provide the documentation which he has just received from Mr. Ng to the Court Clerk of the Superior Court. Court's in recess until two-thirty."

A slightly bewildered Clancy left the courtroom. She thought, If Ng can pull this off, then he has effectively end-run the judge's previous rulings on the Marsden motion. Marsden said that a defendant has the right to choose his attorneys. The defense couldn't continue to represent someone suing them. In effect he was firing his lawyers.

The court reconvened that day at two-thirty in the afternoon.

Judge Mewhinney said, "Court's again in session in the case of the People of the State of California versus Charles Chitat Ng, cases numbered C-851094 and F-204, consolidated. The record will reflect that Mr. Ng is presently present with his attorneys, Mr. Marovich and Mr. Webster, People represented by Mr. Martin and Ms. Honnaka. Mr. Ng, in regards to the civil suit, is it acceptable to you that I look at the civil complaint filed against your attorneys?"

"No," Ng said. "Your honor, I think this court have [sic] no jurisdiction, because I'm filing the matter in Superior Court."

"I understand that. It's a document of public record, Mr. Ng. The reason I want to look at it, Mr. Ng, is to determine whether it should be treated as a Marsden motion in addition to whatever else it's being treated as. That is, it's a civil suit against your counsel, but I just want to make sure, then, you do not wish this court to consider it for purposes of a Marsden motion; is that correct?"

Clancy scribbled in her notebook that Marsden equals right to choose one's attorneys. It sounded reasonable enough to her. She thought, There is a limit to how many attorneys can be given the gate.

Ng said, "I believe the items I mention in the lawsuit, some of them already have been mentioned or complained of in my previous Marsden."

Mewhinney asked Webster if he'd received a fax in reply to his ethical questions.

Webster answered, "Yes, your honor. We reviewed the fax and feel that it's not on point at all. The facts also contained three cites to other cases, which we've also reviewed, and find those not on point either. We have also, since taking the recess, been served, actually served with the lawsuit, which asks for a total of one million dollars in damages. We would ask the court a couple of things. Number one, we would ask the court to review the lawsuit. It's now a matter of public record. I have been served, and Mr. Marovich has been served."

The judge said, "On what basis would the court be reviewing it, to determine whether there is a conflict, or, what are you asking me to review it for?"

"The court has made a finding, and it's in regards to the finding as already made on the record. And that is to the effect of the court feels that this, the filing of this lawsuit against Mr. Marovich and myself, is another attempt to remove us as counsel, and in other words, it's a Marsden motion through another avenue, which the court has indicated is not the proper way to proceed on Marsden. The court made that finding without reviewing the lawsuit."

"That is correct."

"And I would ask the court to review that. I would also—"

"I'll certainly do that."

"I would also ask the court to allow us a day to do two things. Number one, Mr. Marovich and myself both need to find an attorney to represent us. This suit obviously has to be answered, and possibly a demurrer within thirty days of today. We also would like time, and it may be the same attorney, a malpractice attorney may also be able to advise us on the ethical problem, problems which we've related in the last couple of hours. If . . . I mean, I . . . it's late in the afternoon, I was thinking of just asking for the morning to do that, but I don't know if we'll be able to get in touch with anyone in the morning or this afternoon. I know how it is, trying to get ahold of lawyers. Half the time they're not in their office, you have to wait until lunchtime for them to get back or in the afternoon or whatever, so that we can discuss both the lawsuit, what it contains, and our ethical duties both to the client and the court to proceed in the matter while this is pending."

Clancy smiled. *Now we're hearing how hard it is to get a lawyer on the phone when you want him.*

"The court will review the lawsuit. The court has reviewed Case Number 18632, the Superior Court of California, In and for the County of Calaveras, the complaint—"

"And would the court take judicial notice of this lawsuit, your honor?"

Clancy winced. "Judicial notice"! All that meant was that they got Ng's lawsuit against them in the record. And now they had time off to get themselves a lawyer.

"The court will take judicial notice of it. In light of the allegations in the complaint, the court does not, at this time, relieve Mr. Webster and Mr. Marovich. The court finds there is not a conflict created by the filing of the lawsuit.

"After review of the lawsuit, it is consistent with Mr. Ng's statements here in open court that the issues previously raised by Marsden . . . It is, in fact, an attempt to revive those Marsden issues in a non-Marsden form. It is not the basis for removal of counsel. It is, in fact, an end run of Marsden, and the court is not going to relieve counsel on the basis of the filing of the lawsuit. Mister—"

End run, Clancy thought, exactly my words.

Ng interrupted the judge with, "May I be heard, your honor?"

"Mr. Ng, you want to be heard as to what issue?"

"The issue you just discussed."

"Okay."

"On the Marsden hearings, there was never any kind of evidentiary hearing as to—"

Clancy sat up straight. *"Evidentiary"? So the stories about Ng studying law in that Saskatchewan jail cell for six years weren't phony. This guy was fighting like hell for his life.*

The judge interrupted, "Do you want to do this in chambers as part of a Marsden motion, or do you want to do this in open court, Mr. Ng?"

"Open court."

"Okay. Because you have a right as to a Marsden hearing to have that *in camera.* This is not a Marsden hearing. This is a civil lawsuit that you have filed. The court has stated its findings. Now, Mr. Ng, are you going to be arguing a Marsden motion to me now here or presenting that, or are you going to be doing something else?"

Ng answered, "I want to make the record clear that on the Marsden motion, this judge never have [sic] granted me an evidentiary hearing so I can present evidence. You're making summary rulings finding that this two counsel are competent without inquiring to the, without giving me a chance to present the facts or the evidence; whereas, in this forum, I'm demanding this to be, even though it's the same allegation, I'm able to present evidence and to prove that the judge's findings are incorrect."

"Anything else, Mr. Ng?"

"And on that basis, I don't think . . . that's not an end run, so to speak, because this court has consistently told me in the Marsden motion that there's also appeal afterward, the suffer-now-and-grief-later policy, as it were. As of right now, all the Marsden issues that I have raised are still outstanding, that the complaint has not been redressed. And this judge is basically saying the Marsden is an appellate remedy, rather than immediate remedy. This suit here, is my only chances [sic] of immediate remedy on the cage, on shackles, on the failing of the lawyers to do the tasks they're supposed to do, to competently represent me. And I think I can differentiate that very clearly to you. That one of my point [sic] in the lawsuit is that counsel failed to file disqualification statement to this judge on time, and because of that, this judge has ruled that as untimely. And again, I just think that there's a conflict of interest here that will prohibit these two counsel from effectively representing me, if forced to do so."

Huh? Clancy thought. Give this guy credit for wielding the language—give or take a few plurals.

"Anything else, Mr. Ng?"

"Not at this time."

"In light of that statement, the court's ruling will stand. Mr. Webster, and Mr. Marovich, as to consulting with counsel, I'm going to proceed with the case at this time and allow you to consult with counsel, those are two things that can occur simultaneously. And we're going to continue on with that."

THURSDAY, OCTOBER 29, 1992, 9:30 A.M.

At the courthouse it was the same scene. Clancy was in her usual seat. Ng was led in. The handcuffs shackling him to his own waist were removed and relocked on his chair as he sat down.

The judge entered and the preliminary hearing started up again.

Webster said, "Your honor, before we start, I just found this morning, I haven't had a chance to look at the federal . . . federal books yet, but this is out of a book called *Professional Responsibility Between a Lawyer,* by John Wessley Hall Junior, it's by Lawyers Cooperative, Bancroft Whitney. On page 736, it's a footnote three that says, "In *United States* versus *Hurt,* H-u-r-t, 1976 App. D. C. 15, 543, Fed. 2d, 162, 167, new counsel on appeal alleged ineffective assistance at trial against former counsel. By the time the criminal case was remanded, trial counsel had sued new counsel for libel. New counsel sought to be relieved because of a conflict, but he was directed to proceed under threat of contempt. The Court of Appeals held that the accused was denied his constitutional right to counsel because of the pendency of the suit against his lawyer, notwithstanding the fact counsel had little to fear from the suit. The court concluded that counsel was, in fact, apprehensive of the suit, and he might not have advocated the accused's case fully, thereby prejudicing the rights of the accused. That seems to be the closest thing, closest case anyone has found on this point. And as I say, we haven't had a chance to review it. Does the law library in this county have Fed. 2d?"

"It does," answered the judge.

"I'd like to be able to take a look at that."

"I'll certainly allow you to do that, but not at this time. It's going to proceed. The case is not, in fact, on point. We are going to proceed. The court has ruled. Mr. Webster, your next question."

"The court, again, I want to make the record clear that, I think it's fairly clear from yesterday, but the court is ordering us to proceed."

"I am ordering you to proceed."

"And I'm . . . and I am proceeding, at this time, based on the fact that the court is ordering me to proceed, and I suspect that if I don't proceed, contempt proceedings will be instituted against me."

"That will be a logical progression."

This is the first time that I've ever heard a judge order a lawyer to defend his client, Clancy thought. This would be laughable if it didn't involve murder.

Ng said, "I've got a disqualification motion. Can you give me a minute to finish it up?"

"Certainly," the judge said.

A few minutes later Clancy learned that Ng was now seeking to disqualify Judge Mewhinney. *Don't like what's going on? Can't fire the lawyers? Fire the judge!*

The judge read the disqualification paper and said, "The Statement of Disqualification for Cause under Code of Civil Procedure Section 170.1, et seq. . . . copies will be made, and it will be received by the court and filed by the court. The basis of the disqualification is . . . in Paragraph Two, defendant filed a statement of disqualification against Douglas Mewhinney because appointed counsel Webster and Marovich have failed or refused to do so because of a conflict of interest. Reading Footnote One: 'There appears to be a symbiotic relationship between counsel and judge in this case! Paragraph Three: 'The reasons for disqualification of Judge Mewhinney are as attached three-page [sic] to Complaint about a California Judge. This judge should recuse himself because a complaint is about to be,' it appears that the word is 'launched,' Mr. Ng, 'against him with the commission on judicial formally.' The complaint, and its three handwritten pages, are also included and attached. Under Code of Civil Procedure Section 170.4(b), the complaint, or excuse me, motion on its face, does not state a basis for disqualification. It's ordered stricken. Copies will be made for Mr. Ng and for both counsel."

"So my motion," Charlie Ng said, "to request appointment of conflict-free counsel to rid this disqualification statement is denied."

Clancy left the courtroom.

She stood alone in the courtyard. She tried to imagine how a young Chinese man, accused of some hideous goings-on, but also caught in a culture gap, must feel about the California judicial system. She had no sympathy for him—not one bit.

But she wondered, This is justice?

Chapter Twenty-four

THURSDAY, NOVEMBER 12, 1992, 9:30 A.M.

CLANCY WAS BACK IN COURT AGAIN. SHE HAD tried to squeeze some work into the past two weeks of courtroom boredom, but her phones were quiet.

This was it, she thought, today would be the final arguments.

The judge asked, "Mr. Martin, Ms. Honnaka?"

Martin rose and assembled papers in his hand. "Thank you, your honor. It's the People's intention to discuss each of the homicides under two separate topical headings. The first will be corpus delecti, and the second will be probable cause to believe that this defendant committed the homicides.

"Starting with corpus delecti, the basic rule is succinctly stated in *People* v. *Ruiz,* R-u-i-z, a 1988 case at 44 Cal. 3d 589. And the quotation I am going to read is on page 611, which states: 'The corpus delecti rule is satisfied by the introduction of evidence which creates a reasonable inference that death could have been caused by a criminal agency, even in the presence of an equally plausible noncriminal explanation of the event.'

"And this rule applies even when, as some of the counts in this case have indicated, there is not a victim's body that has been located. The rule logically applies to such cases, otherwise a murderer who destroys or successfully conceals a victim's remains would escape any type of criminal liability."

Clancy had been through this before, but she was impressed with Martin's crisp way of laying it out.

"There have even been cases that go a step further. Not only have there been situations where there is no victim's body located, but there have been cases where there is no confession or no admission of the defendant. One example of such a case is the case of *People* v. *Scott*, which is stated in Justice Broussard's dissent in the Ruiz case. And the Scott case is a 1959 case at 176 Cal. App. 2d, 458, and in Scott, the prosecution not only proved the disappearance under mysterious circumstances of the victim, but also showed that the defendant had taken numerous steps, both before and after his wife's disappearance, establishing a scheme to steal her fortune, including the forging of numerous documents and conduct immediately after the disappearance, indicating that he was aware of the circumstances causing the disappearance.

"Turning to the evidence at the preliminary hearing, I'd like to speak first about Count Four involving Lonnie Bond Senior and Count Five, Robin Scott Stapley. As the evidence has shown, both of those victims have been positively identified by their fingerprints.

"Concerning Mr. Bond, the evidence has shown that he was shot once in the head. The recommended cause of death was, in fact, a gunshot wound to the head. Regarding Mr. Stapley, he was shot four times; shot twice in the head. And again, the recommended cause of death was multiple gunshot wounds.

"The manner in which those bodies were discovered indicate death other than by accidental, self-inflicted, or natural causes. As to both victims, their hands and feet were bound; in both, the presence of a ball gag was located, and they were concealed in a manner indicating some criminal agency; wrapped in sleeping bags, wrapped in plastic, buried together in a shallow grave. This clearly establishes unlawful killing by other parties.

"Count Two and Count Ten, the Count Two being the murder of Brenda O'Connor and Count Ten being the murder of Lonnie Bond Junior. Here we have both victims disappearing suddenly and we do have a criminal agency at work.

"This is seen from the videotape which was introduced into evidence. Brenda O'Connor is told if she doesn't cooperate, that she's going to be killed. It's obvious from the tape that she's not there voluntarily, criminal acts are being perpetrated against her on the tape. And the discovery and the condition of the bodies of Mr. Bond and Mr. Stapley are important concerning Brenda O'Connor and Lonnie Bond Junior, since mention is made of Mr. Stapley and Mr. Bond on the tape. And it indicates that the persons speaking on the tape know the circumstances of the death of both of these other victims.

"It's also admitted on the tape that the baby, Lonnie Bond Junior, is under the control of Leonard Lake and Charles Ng. Referring to the tape, she's told concerning Lonnie Bond Junior that, 'Your baby is sound asleep, like a rock.' Concerning Mr. Bond and Mr. Stapley, she's told by Leonard Lake that, 'We have closed you down, the Star Route Gang, if you want to call it that, we got together and we took you away. We took Scott away, Lonnie's going to earn a decent living for the rest of his life.'

"And concerning Lonnie Bond and Scott Stapley, again Brenda O'Connor is told by Leonard Lake, 'To be honest, for all I know, maybe they are dead right now.'

"And finally concerning Lonnie Bond, Brenda O'Connor asked, 'You didn't hurt Lonnie, did you?' Leonard Lake tells her, 'Well, to be honest, we weren't gentle with them, but to tell you he was alive when he, uh, walked out of here,' there's been admission that Leonard Lake and Charles Ng know about the bodies of Lonnie Bond and Scott Stapley.

"And concerning Brenda O'Connor and Lonnie Bond Junior, we have the evidence of the unidentifiable assorted human remains that were discovered on the premises at Wilseyville. It is reasonable for this court to infer that the death of Brenda O'Connor and Lonnie Bond Junior was pursuant to the same common plan and scheme and criminal agency which caused the death of Lonnie Bond Senior and Scott Stapley.

"Turning to Count One, Kathy Allen, again, we have her disappearing suddenly. It's not a voluntary disappearance, the evidence has shown that her sister had expected to hear from her. Her stepfather said she would not have forgotten to contact her mother on certain holidays.

"Again, we go back to the videotape. She's given the same choice that Brenda O'Connor is given, that she's to cooperate or be killed, that if she doesn't, she will be shot, and she would be buried, that they would put a round through or into her head. The videotape demonstrates that she too is being held against her will. The last scene involving her on the videotape, it's reasonable to infer that she's a victim, she's being forced to do things against her will on the tape.

"Again, it's reasonable for the court to infer, from the evidence, which points to the conclusion that this promise to kill, made by Leonard Lake and Charles Ng, was, in fact, carried out. The film was done at the property in Wilseyville. Outside, we have the human remains. And those human remains are not there because of deaths by natural causes."

Clancy loved the grim understatement. Now, she guessed, came the grisly details.

Martin said, "The testimony was that as to the unidentifiable human remains, they were burned. There were points of percussion, indicating that after the burning, the bones were crushed. They were then spread out across the property. This is an obvious attempt to conceal the fact of death.

"In addition, identification of Kathy Allen is located at the property. The same thing is true of Mike Carroll, the victim in Count Three. He's the boyfriend of Kathy Allen. He disappears suddenly, has not been seen since April the fourteenth of 1985."

Martin shifted his notes, paused, and looked up again. "And just going back for a moment to Kathy Allen, she went to Calaveras County because she was concerned, but her state of mind was that she believed Mike Carroll was missing. She was not intending to voluntarily disappear, but left to come to Calaveras County out of concern for Mike Carroll.

"But back to Mike Carroll, his house key was found in a trench in the property. His ID was found buried on the property. And these are items of identification that are commonly possessed on the person. His car is then sold. He takes no part in selling of the car. It is again reasonable for the court to infer that his death was caused by a criminal agency.

"Having established this corpus delecti, the statement of Leonard Lake made on the tape in the presence of Charles Ng becomes relevant and admissible. Kathy Allen is told that she would be taken out and buried in the same area that we buried Mike.

"Paul Cosner, the victim in Case F-204, he disappeared under mysterious circumstances. Concerning his last known whereabouts, he was meeting to show a car on November the second, 1984. After showing the car, he intended to have a date with his girlfriend. Instead of showing up for the date with his girlfriend, his sister is filling out a missing persons report on November the third, 1984. The car is also missing.

"When we catch up again with the vehicle, it's learned that there is a bullet hole in the headliner on the passenger's side. There's a bullet hole in the passenger door panel, there are bloodstains found about the front seat of the car.

"And again, we go back to Wilseyville, and we find items of Mr. Cosner's identification that have been buried. And again, these are items that are commonly possessed and closely associated with the person; the driver's license, the other items of identification. As to these items, it goes even further, his glasses are found with these items, certainly something that a person would continue to possess were they still alive.

"All of this evidence strongly suggests that Mr. Cosner is, in fact, the victim of foul play. And there's every reason to infer that he was killed and that his death was by a human criminal agency.

"The Dubs family. The victims in Counts Fifteen, Sixteen, and Seventeen. All three, an entire family, mysteriously disappeared. Mrs. Dubs is on the phone the last time anyone hears from her, that includes her friends, George and Karen Tuck, and her neighbors. The front door of the Dubs residence is open several days later. The key to that door is in the lock. And this is located there after a stranger walks from the house and there is property missing.

"There is a phone call to the office of Stan Pedrov, Mr. Dubs's employer, trying to make it appear as though the disappearance of the Dubs family is voluntary."

Very clever, Clancy thought, now he's going to deception and hence attempted cover-up, and hence guilt. Martin raised his voice. "There is every reason to believe that this phone call is just not the truth, because Mr. Pedrov said it was very unlike Harvey Dubs to leave work, not show up without any word. There was no information that the statements contained in the phone call concerning the Dubs family going to Washington matched with any personal information that was known about them.

"We have a man, Mr. Dubs, who has a wife and a small child. He didn't even ask for his last paycheck for the dates between July fifth to July twenty-fifth, 1984. All the facts and circumstances surrounding the disappearance of the entire Dubs family indicate that it's not a voluntary disappearance. And nothing, that is, it is nothing but consistent of death of all three by a criminal agency.

"And as I will discuss further, when I talk about conspiracy to kill, and this defendant's receipt of personal property, again, we have a link to Wilseyville, a connection to Wilseyville, where all the human remains are found. The Dubs family's personal property is found there. The cassette recorder with the serial number, the video duplicator, which was a very unique piece of personal property, as well as a video receipt made out to Harvey Dubs.

"Count Seven, Clifford Peranteau. Again, we have a person simply disappearing off the face of the earth. He's dropped off at midnight by his friend. He doesn't show up for work the following day, never shows up for work again. His friend, Mr. Salcedo, calls twice during the day that Mr. Peranteau is supposed to work, no answer to the phone. He goes to the residence. He cannot find Mr. Peranteau.

"Again, there is property missing from the victim's residence. The property is found in Wilseyville. Again, we have burnt remains, points of percussion, human remains scattered over the property. And again, we have a letter claiming that Cliff has voluntarily disappeared. The letter is sent to his employer, and it links this disappearance to Wilseyville because the typewriter in which the letter was typed was found at the Wilseyville property. Also at the property is the piece of paper found in the hidden cell in the bunker that says, 'Cliff, P.O. Box 349.'

"Mr. Peranteau's motorcycle is missing. And again, as in the case of Mr. Carroll, Mr. Peranteau is not involved in the selling of the motorcycle, nor is he involved in any negotiations to sell the motorcycle, but, in fact, it's sold by Leonard Lake at Wilseyville.

"There's no mention by Mr. Peranteau to his girlfriend, Cynthia Basharr, that he intends to voluntarily disappear or that he's planning any type of suicide. And again, it's reasonable to infer that his death was caused by a criminal agency.

"And lastly, as to corpus delecti, we have Count Nine, Jeffrey Gerald. He disappears February fourth, 1985. And his state of mind at that point is important. He intends to go to a moving job and return that evening. That is, he intends to be gone for the afternoon and then return. But he never shows up for work again. His roommate never sees him again, and his mother would have expected to hear from him, and she hasn't.

"Same ties to Wilseyville. His camera is found in the trench. It's identified as his by the film. A guitar which looks like one that he owned is found in the residence. A turntable similar to one he owned is found in the Wilseyville residence. Personal property turns up missing from his apartment. His Social Security card is found in the trench.

"Again, this court can infer that there's death by a criminal agency. And again, we have the multiple human remains at the Wilseyville property.

"The second part of the People's analysis is the probable cause to believe that this defendant is guilty of these murders. It is the People's theory the murders were committed pursuant to an overall conspiracy and common plan and scheme as to how these murders would be conducted and how the conspiracy would be conducted. It's a conspiracy between Charles Ng and Leonard Lake to murder people and to obtain each victim's personal property. And it is the obtaining of this personal property that is one of the common threads that links the defendant to each and every one of the alleged homicides."

Ah ha, Clancy thought, motive. Not random, crazy killings, like most serial killers, but cold, calculated.

Money, sex, survivalist fantasies.

Martin said, "The common plan involves a number of things: One is the receipt of the property, and also the sorting of the property. The evidence has shown that some of the property of the victims has been maintained by Charles Ng and Leonard Lake for their immediate use or conversion.

"Other property has been buried in protective containers that protect the items from the elements for possible retrieval and use at a later time. The other category of the stolen property is just simply discarded, because it can be inferred that Charles Ng and Leonard Lake had no use for this property.

"There is also the destruction and concealing of human remains that is a common element of these crimes. The common plan also involves attempts to misdirect friends and employers of the victims as to the cause of their disappearance. And also common to this plan is its home base, Wilseyville, California.

"One such as Charles Ng, involved in a common conspiracy plan and scheme which involves murder, necessarily has the sufficient premeditation and deliberation and express intent to kill that's necessary for a first-degree murder. In fact, this defendant's specific intent to kill is demonstrated on the videotape. Brenda O'Connor is told by Leonard Lake that if she doesn't cooperate, she would be shot. Charles Ng says, 'I'll get my weapon handy in case you try and play stupid.'

"The clearest example to show this agreement and this conspiracy between the defendant and Leonard Lake to commit murders and to obtain personal property, as well as the common plan and scheme is, in fact, the 'M Ladies' videotape. Kathy Allen is first depicted on that videotape with Leonard Lake and with Charles Ng, and with no one else, other than those two. The defendant is personally present when Leonard Lake tells Kathy Allen, 'We'll put a round in your head. We will bury you where we buried Mike.'

"Information concerning Mike Carroll's bank accounts is discussed with Kathy Allen. This is his property. There's discussion of the guy storing Mike Carroll's furniture, again, his property. Acts are perpetrated against Kathy Allen on the videotape that are participated in by both Leonard Lake and Charles Ng. Leonard Lake tells her, in this defendant's presence, 'We'll have you write letters.' And in fact, a letter is then received by John Gouveia, the foster brother of Mike Carroll, allegedly from Kathy Allen, saying that some people will be by to pick up Mike's property. It's a conspiracy not just to kill, but, also, to steal the property."

Killing to steal, jumped into Clancy's mind. These jerks killed for small potatoes—when it was easy for them. Almost risk free. They didn't have the guts to rob a bank.

They claimed to live by a warrior's code.

They were cowards.

"And," Martin continued, "after the disappearance of Kathy Allen and Mike Carroll, this defendant's conduct is highly relevant. He follows through on the attempts to get the property. He delivers car keys to Mike Carroll's car to the Blanks, and he aids in disposing of that property.

"Now, the scene with Kathy Allen does depict the residence in Wilseyville, but also the time and place is important to link the defendant, because we have phone calls going from that Wilseyville property on April the fourteenth and April the fifteenth, 1985, at a time when Kathy Allen is there. Calls going from the property to Charles Ng's employer, and Charles Ng did not work during that period of time.

"So how do we know that this conspiracy goes beyond the two crimes concerning Kathy Allen and Mike Carroll? How do we know that there is a common thread? Because the exact—almost the exact same pattern is seen on the videotape with Brenda O'Connor. She is given a choice very similar to the choice Kathy Allen is given. And again, the plural is used by Leonard Lake, 'We've closed you down, we've took you away. We've took Scott away.' "

Clancy noticed that even Martin's droll pattern of delivery couldn't dull the excitement of his argument. He was now using the grammar on the tapes in his linking of Lake and Ng.

The prosecutor said, "And again it's the same two, Leonard Lake and Charles Ng, engaged in a pattern of conduct with Kathy Allen, that is similar to other victims. In fact, there is reference made in the Brenda O'Connor portion of the tape back to the Kathy Allen portion. Leonard Lake says to Charles Ng, 'Now tell me, isn't she a little better than Kathy?' Charles Ng responds, 'Sort of, maybe a little, basically the same.'

"Concerning the conspiracy and common plan, Brenda O'Connor asks of Leonard Lake and Charles Ng, 'Is that why you invited us over here for dinner?' Leonard Lake says, 'Uh-huh.' Charles Ng answers, 'It's part of the game.'

"The court will recall what action this defendant is taking with Brenda O'Connor when she says, 'Don't cut my bra off.' His response to that is, 'You can cry and stuff like the rest of them.'

"Concerning her baby, this defendant also had something to say. He says, 'Just don't ask, or it will be history.' This is an express statement by this defendant tying him to the baby, Lonnie Bond Junior. It indicates that he and Leonard Lake have it. It indicates to the People that this child has been murdered just like its mother and father.

"Personal property is not discussed on the Brenda O'Connor portion of the videotape, but again, we have this defendant taking follow-up action concerning personal property of Brenda O'Connor, of Scott Stapley, and of Lonnie Bond. Scott Stapley's truck has been taken. This defendant is seen driving the truck by Wood Hicks on April the twenty-third, 1985.

"Leonard Lake and Charles Ng go down to the apartment that had been occupied by Scott Stapley and meet with Tori Doolin. There's an attempt made by Leonard Lake and Charles Ng waiting outside to clean out the personal property of Scott Stapley. And again, we have this attempt at misdirection.

"Leonard Lake, a coconspirator, in furtherance of his conspiracy with Charles Ng, says that the people at the house, the Carter house next door, are all dead, but he's attempting to mislead Tori Doolin concerning the cause of death. He says, he tells her further that all their identification was gone and their weapons just weren't found there.

"And what do we have? We have Lonnie Bond's First Interstate Bank card located at the defendant's residence. It indicates that he took the personal property of yet another victim that he has killed. Mr. Stapley's Ricoh camera is found with the defendant in Canada, when he fled from the United States, he took some victim's property with him."

The judge said, "I'm sorry, whose Ricoh camera?"

"Mr. Stapley's. Now, to go back, your honor, chronologically to the first homicides that are alleged in this case, and that, of course, is the Dubs family, how do we know at this early stage chronologically of the People's case that this defendant is involved? Well, again, Deborah Dubs finishes the phone call, which is the last time anyone has heard from her, and what is seen? This defendant is seen leaving the Dubs house at approximately that time.

"Dorice Murphy, I believe, sees a second person who is acting in conjunction with Charles Ng. And ultimately, the personal property from the house ends up in Wilseyville, California, and ends up in this defendant's apartment.

"How do we know that this is part and parcel of the same overall conspiracy? We know because the latter part of the conspiracy is absolutely established, as is this defendant's connection to it. The crime against the Dubses has the same earmarks as the latter portion of the conspiracy, which has absolutely been established, because the defendant has benefited personally in the Dubs case, just like with Mr. Stapley's camera, just like with Lonnie Bond's credit card. We have equipment consistent with equipment that the Dubs family owned, the same model, same make is seized at the defendant's Lennox Street residence. The defendant has videotapes that are matched to those owned by Mr. Dubs, not only in description, titlewise, but in handwriting.

"And back up to the Wilseyville property, we have the Captain Video receipt in the trench behind the bunker made out to Mr. Dubs, and it's in with other items that had been addressed or have the name of Charles Ng on them.

"Just like in the case of Kathy Allen, where there was an attempt to misdirect her employer concerning her disappearance. We have an attempt to make Harvey Dubs's employer believe that his disappearance and that of his family is a voluntary disappearance. And this attempt is made and the family is, in reality, dead. Like every other alleged victim, these victims are no different."

The idea of misdirection again, Clancy thought. It's a masterful piece of analysis of a killer's thought process.

Martin continued, "It's the People's position that their remains are located in Calaveras County. Because their property, like all the others, is located in Wilseyville. And Wilseyville is part of the common plan and scheme, because, it is, in fact, the home base of the conspiracy.

"There is another case, and the last citation I'm going to make in my argument. That's the case of *People* v. *Miller,* a 1990 case, 50 Cal. 3d 954, and at 985 the following language is set forth:

" 'The likelihood of a particular group of geographically proximate crimes being unrelated diminishes as those crimes are found to share more and more common characteristics.' "

That's the law? Clancy asked herself. Sounds a little weak when you've got both guys on a videotape.

"Next is Paul Cosner. There is a clear suggestion from the evidence that his death took place in the passenger seat of the Honda Prelude. The trajectory of both shots is from the backseat of that car. Blood is found in the car. He's taking his car out to show it to a prospective buyer, but yet Mr. Cosner is shot from the backseat, clearly suggesting the presence of someone in addition to the prospective buyer.

"And again, there is the common tie to Wilseyville. Although Mr. Cosner's items of identification are found approximately three miles away, there is a Philo Motel envelope with the name 'Cosner' written on it. Other envelopes with Philo Motel on them are found in the concrete bunker in the Wilseyville property.

"What else is found in Wilseyville? Well, a sun visor with a bullet hole, and when that sun visor is placed in Mr. Cosner's vehicle, the bullet hole in the sun visor and the bullet hole in the headliner of the vehicle match up.

"There are also .22 caliber slugs that are removed from Mr. Cosner's vehicle. And what is found with Mr. Cosner's identification? A .22 caliber pistol.

"We know that it's the same conspiracy that involves the Dubs family, Kathy Allen, Brenda O'Connor, Lonnie Bond, Scott Stapley. We know it's the same conspiracy, because we have the same two people, this defendant and Leonard Lake, who are continuing to use Mr. Cosner's vehicle to shoplift the vise seven months later. And this vehicle also matches the description of the vehicle that Kathy Allen left the Safeway store in April of 1985.

"Concerning Clifford Peranteau and the defendant's connection with his murder: the evidence again fits into this overall conspiracy. We have the tie to the Wilseyville property. We have items of Mr. Peranteau's property buried there in the trench. Some examples are the Buddha, the ceramic fish, the Pennsylvania license plates with 'Cindy' written on it. The notation, 'Cliff, P.O. Box 349,' is found in a hidden cell in the back portion of the bunker.

"We have two letters that go out, one to Mr. Goza, Mr. Peranteau's employer, and another to his friend Rick Doedens, both which have been typed on the Olympia typewriter found at the Wilseyville residence.

"Is there a tie to Charles Ng? Yes, there is. Charles Ng is the only tie between this victim and the Wilseyville property. And there is a tie, because Clifford Peranteau worked with Charles Ng at Dennis Moving, and the evidence has shown that Mr. Ng did not like Mr. Peranteau."

Huh? Clancy thought. What does "like" have to do with it?

Martin continued, "We have all the same earmarks as the other crimes. We have the misdirection, just like with Harvey Dubs's employer and Kathy Allen's employer. Just like the misdirection attempted with Tori Doolin. The misdirection concerning Mr. Peranteau is the letter received by Dennis Goza, indicating that he had found a new girlfriend, a new job, and a place to live, when, in fact, he was dead.

"This conspiracy fits with the same two persons, Leonard Lake and Charles Ng, because it fits the pattern. Mr. Peranteau's apartment is burglarized, property is taken, just like the others. Property is found buried in the trench. This defendant personally benefited from the stolen property, because Mr. Peranteau's pen and pencil set were found in his apartment with the initials 'CRP.' His motorcycle was sold by Leonard Lake. The oak framed mirrors missing from his apartment were found in Wilseyville. It follows along with all the others that this killing was done pursuant to the conspiracy between Charles Ng and Leonard Lake.

"And lastly, Jeffrey Gerald. Again, we have the ties to Wilseyville. His camera is found in the trench. A guitar similar to one that he had owned, and similar because the person who gave the affidavit concerning that was giving Mr. Gerald guitar lessons had he used that guitar. The turntable, looking very similar to one owned by Mr. Gerald, was found in the Wilseyville property. And his Social Security card was located in the trench.

"Again, not only do we have the tie to Wilseyville, but we have the tie to this defendant. It is the most apparent connection between Wilseyville and Jeff Gerald. The fact that he worked with Charles Ng, Charles Ng didn't like him, because he had retained his security when he came back to the job.

"And concerning Jeffrey Gerald, it's very interesting to take a look at the three uses that were made of the stolen property. There was the immediate use or conversion of the property, and there was the burying of other property in sealed containers for possible later retrieval. There is the discarding of the property. Jeffrey Gerald fits into this pattern.

"This count clearly fits the pattern, it fits the conspiracy, and the People believe that the defendant should be held to answer on all counts. Thank you, your honor."

Clancy thought, Not bad, not bad at all. Considering the complexity of the case, he summed it up rather tersely.

How would Webster and Marovich rebut?

She looked around the courtroom. The Stapleys were slumped back in their seats. Sharon Sellito was leaning forward, her elbows resting on the seat in front of her.

The relatives, Clancy thought, waiting for years, taking

each moment step by step. Now the hearing; the results foreordained.

A chill went through her. Were they? Were the results of all counts foreordained? What if the judge tossed some out?

How would Sharon Sellito feel if her brother's case was deemed insufficient evidence?

Or the Stapleys?

It would be a crushing blow. To have waited years, then let down.

Clancy thought, It would kill them emotionally.

Chapter Twenty-five

THURSDAY, NOVEMBER 12, 1992, 1:30 P.M.

AFTER THE USUAL PRELIMINARIES, MEWHINney nodded to the defendant's counsel. The prosecution had the morning. Now the defense had the afternoon. "Go ahead, Mr. Marovich."

"The prosecution evidence relative to the Cosner count indicated that Mr. Cosner disappeared on November the second, 1984. Reference was made to the sister, Sharon Sellito, who filed a missing persons report, his girlfriend, Marilyn Namba, who lived in the same Filbert Street apartment house, as did Mr. Cosner.

"Mr. Cosner indicated to Ms. Namba that he had a prospective purchaser for his car, he would be back shortly for dinner with her. He went out to show the car to someone and did not return. The evidence indicates that in June of 1985, some seven to eight months later, this car was found in South San Francisco, associated at that time with Mr. Lake.

"A subsequent search of the Wilseyville property indicated the presence of a sun visor with a hole in it. This was in middle to late June of 1985. Also a floor mat for a Honda was found in the carport area. The evidence doesn't indicate whether that floor mat was ever matched to the Honda itself. It does indicate that the sun visor was matched to the Honda Prelude vehicle that had been seized in South San Francisco on June second."

Where is all this going? Clancy asked herself. Is it going to be "Lake did it all"?

The answer came quickly. Marovich summarized the San Francisco Police Department's report on Cosner's car, then said, "I'm not disputing the District Attorney's argument relative to corpus delecti, as far as this sudden unexplained disappearance. But I am strongly disputing the District Attorney's version and interpretation of any connection or evidence pointing to a connection between Mr. Ng and the disappearance of Mr. Cosner.

"Relative to Kathy Allen, there is evidence that Kathy Allen was picked up in a similar-looking car at the Safeway in Milpitas. So in terms of the whereabouts, location of this particular vehicle, of the vehicle that Mr. Cosner went out to sell . . . there is no evidence for November, December, January, February, March, no evidence on this record of where that vehicle might have been during those five or plus months."

Interesting, Clancy thought. Didn't anybody in Wilseyville see that car? Didn't anybody see it parked there when they delivered things, or bought stuff at Lake's "garage sales"?

"After the search commenced at the Wilseyville property," Marovich continued, "properties in the general area of the county were searched, including the Heale property. Found on the Heale property were some Tupperware containers, one of which contained Mr. Cosner's ID, glasses, several other documents with his name on the . . . on the paperwork.

"The District Attorney . . . has made reference several times in his argument to human remains, to fragments of bone present on the property. However, it is without doubt that Mr. Cosner's body . . . has never been discovered.

"The hearsay testimony of Boyd Stephens . . . indicated that in addition to the bodies that were identified on the property . . . there were the remains of seven other persons; two children.

"One male remains unidentified, but was of a large

person. I think the record establishes that Mr. Cosner, I believe, weighed around 140 pounds and was around five-nine . . . was not a large person."

He has a point, Clancy thought. Where was Paul Cosner's body?

Marovich challenged the ballistic expert, a Mr. Grzybowski. "Mr. Crawford, the officer who testified to the hearsay conclusions and statements of Mr. Grzybowski, could not go beyond . . . in what is in the four corners of the affidavit. We have an opinion, a conclusion from Mr. Grzybowski, but that opinion or conclusion is sadly lacking, based on the absence of any information in the affidavit relative to how he reached his opinion. He talks about reproducible class and individual characteristics, comparing cartridge casings with the test firings from the cartridge casings found in the apartment. Nowhere is there any indication what those class or individual characteristics were, how many of each there were. . . ."

Clancy was puzzled. Why didn't this come out before? Better to have rock-solid evidence than something that could be rebutted.

Maybe, she thought, the ballistics man's findings were used as probabilities, to be combined with the other evidence, not circumstantial. But this was just the kind of thing juries don't like—and if this went to trial, all of this was on the record.

Clancy had met a few of the victims' relatives. She glanced over at Sharon Sellito. *I hope she's not let down. She's waited so long.*

Marovich continued, "Mr. Crawford . . . acknowledged that the Ruger Mark Two .22 caliber pistol, thousands of such weapons are commercially produced, the parts are interchangeable. He had no information, as part of his investigation, if the weapon in question retrieved at the Heale property had ever been into a repair shop, where parts were replaced, any indication of any purchaser, any owner, any transfers of that particular weapon.

"The ability of the defense to question the reliability

and veracity of the opinion given by Mr. Grzybowski was beyond the four corners. . . . It is an opinion of somebody who says he's done a lot of this and has a background in it, but the reliability, based on lack of information, lack of specific observations, comparisons, in our view, makes that opinion relative to the casings very suspect."

There's a phrase I like, Clancy noted professionally, "four corners." The defense has nothing to go on but what's inside the four corners of the affidavit. You draw a box from those four corners, and that's all the data the court can gather from the statement.

Again came Mr. Marovich's straining, almost high-pitched voice. "Mr. Martin indicates the existence of an agreement, an overall conspiracy. The conspiracy to kill and steal property involving common plans, to take personal property. . . . He starts with the 'M Ladies' tape."

The judge said, "I'd like to stop at this point. We're going to be in recess until three minutes after the hour. Court's in recess."

Clancy walked out into the courtyard. Matt Hedgers approached her and said, "Only a few more hours."

They speculated on a possible change of venue for the trial. Clancy asked, "Do you think the judge will bind over on all counts?"

"There's a chance of some of the charges being thrown out."

People were filing back into the courthouse. Matt Hedgers and Clancy followed them.

Mewhinney intoned the required language again. But, merely because the judge's decision was near at hand, the packed courtroom listened attentively to the words.

The judge said, "Court's again in session in the case of the People of the State of California versus Charles Chitat Ng, cases number C-851094 and F-204, consolidated.

"The record will reflect Mr. Ng is present with his attorneys, Mr. Marovich and Mr. Webster. People represented by Mr. Martin and Ms. Honnaka, officers of the court.

"Madam Reporter, if you'd please read back Mr. Marovich's last couple of sentences where he began a new subject area."

The court reporter, Linda James, obliged.

"Thank you, ma'am. Mr. Marovich."

Marovich said, "I indicated just before the break, the District Attorney refers to an agreement, an overall conspiracy, and starts with his example of that as the 'M Ladies' tape. Obviously, that's a graphic piece of evidence that has an impact. And it's understandable that the District Attorney would want to emphasize that as being evidence of this so-called conspiracy, common plan that he is espousing that existed between Mr. Lake and Mr. Ng.

"It has to be remembered, though, that all the evidence indicates that the events depicted on the videotape are at the earliest taking place in mid-April of 1985. The fact that a competent agreement, overall conspiracy might exist in April of 'eighty-five is certainly not indicative of such an agreement existing seven, eight, or ten months earlier."

Clancy nodded. The timing of all this seemed to be Ng's only weapon.

"It would indicate that . . . a lack of substantial evidence of the existence of that so-called conspiracy in the mid part, for example, of 1984.

"This is, I believe, particularly significant, because there is evidence here that one or more persons . . . and the name Charles Gunnar was mentioned prominently in this preliminary hearing . . . at a time when Mr. Ng was in Leavenworth prison and could have been no part of the disappearance of, say, Mr. Gunnar or other persons that, in fact, allegedly purportedly disappeared when Mr. Ng simply was not on the scene, not in California, but incarcerated.

"Relative to the Heale property and the burying in Tupperware containers of Paul Cosner's ID and other personal papers, and the gun that's been referred to, what is the purpose of burying these type of items, particularly an ID? A logical inference is to have such a thing handy if a person wanted to assume somebody else's name or identification. And obviously, in this case, Mr. Lake is Caucasian. Mr. Cosner was Caucasian. Mr. Ng, of course, is Chinese, and would have no real purpose for burying for future use to assume somebody's identity of . . . a Caucasian person, such as Paul Cosner.

"In addition, it's clearly established Mr. Ng lived in San Francisco. The Wilseyville property was owned by Lake's ex-wife's family. I . . . if Mr. Ng was burying things, it would be logical that he would be burying things where they were readily accessible to him.

"All in all, your honor, it's our position that the evidence is simply insufficient to establish probable cause in this case that Mr. Ng was connected with Mr. Cosner's disappearance and/or alleged homicide."

Oh no, Clancy thought, and looked at Sharon Sellito.

"I want to bring up another point, a distinct point relative to the Cosner disappearance, because it's important. It appears that even assuming, for purposes of argument, that probable cause might exist, the statutes in the California Penal Code, dealing with territorial jurisdiction over criminal offenses, would be such that a Calaveras County court simply, based on the evidence presented here, would not have jurisdiction over the offense involving the disappearance and the alleged murder of Paul Cosner."

What? Clancy thought. He's saying on one hand there's not enough evidence, and on the other that even if there is, Calaveras doesn't have jurisdiction.

"The territorial jurisdiction . . . the establishment of territorial jurisdiction must be established by a preponderance of the evidence. In this case, taking into account . . . the relevant code sections of dealing with homicide, the preponderance of the evidence on this record is that Mr. Cosner . . . went out to show his car to someone, that soon thereafter he was shot with a .22 caliber gun based on the criminalist Grzybowski's reviewing those .22 slugs.

"The District Attorney has a special use allegation in the complaint against Mr. Ng alleging the murder of Paul Cosner, alleging the use of a .22 caliber pistol. The preponderance of the evidence establishes that this happened in San Francisco. Of course, as the court is aware, in a homicide case, territorial jurisdiction can be conferred on the county where the wound is inflicted, where the death occurred, or where the body was found."

Clancy watched Sellito's profile. Sharon's face was a slight gray pallor. Her chin was set, her lips tightly pressed together.

Marovich continued, "The record here is devoid of evidence that, as to the disappearance and alleged murder of Paul Cosner, that somehow preliminary arrangements, preliminary acts took place in Calaveras County."

Clancy had begun taking notes of things she had to check. She would buy a copy of the final arguments from the court reporter, but she had to check out other things first—like the relevance of where Cosner was killed.

Now Marovich introduced a word that had Clancy scribbling again.

"It is particularly important, your honor, in that there's the issue of vicinage. That a person charged with a crime is entitled to be tried by a cross-section of the citizens of that particular county or district, as it were. That's a right included in the Sixth Amendment of the Constitution of the United States, made applicable by the state's Fourteenth Amendment."

Clancy wrote down "vicinage." *Sounds like a technicality to me.*

"Thank you, your honor, I would submit the Cosner argument. And Mr. Webster will continue the argument."

The judge said, "Mr. Webster. You may proceed."

Webster rose and walked to the front of the bench. "Your honor, first I'd like to go through the specific counts. We will be submitting a number of those counts."

Clancy took out her pen, then put it back. Webster was

clearly going for more technicalities. Then he launched into the thrust of his plea.

"As far as the District Attorney's argument regarding the showing of a conspiracy, an overall conspiracy between Mr. Lake and Mr. Ng to murder and obtain personal property, there is evidence to show that Mr. Lake was involved in the disappearance and murder of at least Mr. Charles Gunnar, and possibly someone by the name of Thomas Myers, and possibly someone by the name of Donald Lake, Mr. Lake's brother, during a time when Mr. Ng was not even in the state and was, in fact, incarcerated at Fort Leavenworth, Kansas.

"Not only was there evidence to show that Mr. Lake killed one Mr. Gunnar, there's also evidence that he used Mr. Gunnar's personal property and his ID. In fact, he was going by the name of Charles Gunnar for quite some time before there's any showing of any connection between Mr. Lake and Mr. Ng.

"There is obviously evidence to show that Mr. Lake and Mr. Ng were acquainted. But the first showing that Mr. Ng was ever connected with the Wilseyville property is sometime in mid-April of 1985. . . . Mr. Lake is the one who was a fugitive from justice. Mr. Lake is the one who was living under an assumed name or names, while Mr. Ng was living in San Francisco under his own name, working in San Francisco under his own name, was involved in a traffic accident in late April of 1985 in Bakersfield, California, driving an automobile, or a truck belonging to one of the alleged victims, and Mr. Ng waited around for twenty minutes to a half an hour waiting for an officer of the Highway Patrol to show up so that Mr. Ng could again give him his real name, his real address, his real phone number, rather than leaving the scene of the accident. I think all of this goes to show that Mr. Ng was not involved in any conspiracy with Mr. Lake until at the earliest, mid-April of 1985."

Clancy gave Webster another gold star. *It's the time sequence again. How long was Ng with Lake?*

"Mr. Martin indicated in his argument that the intent

to kill on behalf of Mr. Ng in this conspiracy is shown on the 'M Ladies' videotape where Mr. Ng says something to the effect of, "I'll get my weapon ready in case you try to play stupid." I would submit, when the court reviews that tape, that it should take a look at that weapon, which is a stun gun, as opposed to any kind of murder weapon."

Stun gun? Did I miss that? Clancy asked herself. Was it in the video transcripts?

"Mr. Martin referred to a statement by Mr. Lake evidently in the presence of Mr. Ng that, 'We have taken care of you'—'we,' meaning 'the Star Route Gang.' And I would submit that there is no proof whatsoever that there is any such gang or that Mr. Ng was a member."

Clancy checked her watch. The judge had imposed no time limit, but already Webster was through the main issues. The attorney walked quickly through his notes on the workers at the Dennis Moving Company. It was again a recital of how Ng could not be connected with property of the workers—his coworkers—in Wilseyville.

He finished with, "And so, your honor, in closing, in addition to Mr. Marovich's arguments regarding the Cosner count, I would indicate that there is not a sufficient showing to hold Mr. Ng to answer for either the Peranteau count or the Gerald count. We'd submit it, thank you."

The judge asked, "Mr. Martin, Ms. Honnaka, any rebuttal?"

"The People submit it, your honor."

Marovich rose. "Your honor, I would like to cite a case on vicinage. *People* v. *Jones,* 1973, 9 Cal. 3d 546, 108, Cal Reporter, 345."

"Mr. Webster," the judge said, "in terms of the stun gun in the tape, do you recall where, in terms of the transcript, that might be observed? Just near an area. You said when I'm going to get to my—"

Clancy smiled. *So the judge forgot that too.*

"It's in the last scene."

Marovich said, "Yes, your honor, and I believe this can be brief, and I believe it was prompted by the reference to the issue of what type of device Mr. Ng had in his hand, was it determined it was a pistol or a deadly weapon? It was a stun gun, the court's made that clear by the viewing."

The judge said, "It's consistent with a stun gun."

"It's consistent. That's fine, your honor. Relative to considering the entire tape and the transcript, I would like to make reference to several entries, page nineteen of the transcript, which is Exhibit Six, which would be line nine relative to . . . this is the Brenda O'Connor portion of the tape . . . Mr. Ng saying to her, 'Feeling better? Do you want some water?' and the tape reflecting, in effect, Mr. Ng obtaining a glass of water for her.

"On page twenty, line nine, in relation to a complaint from Brenda O'Connor, Ng indicating on the tape, 'Do you want some aspirin?' Both of these statements by Mr. Ng, I think it's important to point out for the reason, number one, we believe the inferences from that strongly negate the District Attorney's argument as far as intent to kill. Fact in the case, intent to act cruelly towards her, but particularly the intent to kill."

What's this? Clancy wasn't amused. Water? Aspirin? How about tearing her T-shirt off? How about slicing her bra off with a knife?

"Secondly," Webster said, "that type of language in the tape, on the face of it, being incongruous with other material on the tape, we believe, calls into question the entire, or the main thrust of the scenario throughout the tape as to the seriousness of the characters as far as their demeanor, as to whether they're exhibiting serious fear, or serious threats. We think those two lines are very relevant and call into question . . . the entire tape as far as the seriousness of the emotions displayed by the characters on the tape and the seriousness of the actions of the characters on the tape, drawing an inference in terms of whether the implication could be drawn, and we believe it could, that matters on the tape were, in fact, being considered seriously by the characters in terms of being reflection of genuine fear and genuine threats."

The judge asked, "Anything else?"

"That's all, your honor."

"Allowing reopening on rebuttal, Mr. Martin."

The prosecutor nodded and began at once. "Your honor, concerning page nineteen of the tape that Mr. Marovich mentioned, I would like to talk about another type of weapon that's depicted there and a clear inference that this defendant is taking some sort of action regarding that weapon. The fourth line from the top, Leonard Lake says to Brenda O'Connor, 'Slide them down and then sit down.' It is at this portion of the tape where it appears as though Leonard Lake is holding a pistol with what well could be a silencer on the end of it. Brenda O'Connor says, 'I'm too dizzy . . . just too dizzy,' at which point Leonard Lake helps her on the couch and it appears that he puts the weapon on the floor. He says, 'Slide them down. All right. Charlie, take this.' The People believe from the clear inference of 'take this,' is that he's picking up the pistol that Leonard Lake put on the floor. On page seventeen, the last two lines, 'You better believe us, Brenda, or you'll be dead.' Charles Chitat Ng states, 'Right.'

"People submit it."

Marovich said, "Again, your honor, the example—"

"No," the judge interrupted, "I'm—"

Marovich said, "It's incongruity to the statements of what we quoted and visually what's happening in relation to what the District Attorney has just cited as an example."

"Mr. Martin," the judge asked, "anything else?"

"Nothing further, your honor."

Clancy thought, It's over, it's finally over except for the judge's ruling.

THURSDAY, NOVEMBER 12, 1992, 5:30 P.M.

Clancy lay on the bed in her motel room and opened the paper. President-elect Clinton was already starting to choose his cabinet. Bush was still reeling from his defeat.

The front page of yesterday's *New York Times* had stories on New York State Chief Judge Sol Wachter resigning, on the FBI investigating William Sessions's decision to keep his post, and on the baseball owners stopping the San Francisco Giants' move to St. Petersburg.

Not much, Clancy thought. She closed her eyes and tried to visualize the courtroom she had just left. She could hear Judge Mewhinney's voice in her mind.

"The court will make the following finding: The issue before the court is whether or not pursuant to Penal Code Section 871 or 872 there is not or is sufficient evidence for a holding order as to the crimes charged in the complaints consolidated or any other crimes shown by the evidence.

"The standard is whether a reasonable person would entertain a strong suspicion that the offenses have, in fact, been committed, and whether Mr. Ng is guilty thereof.

"As to Case Number C-851094, as to Count One, a violation of Section 187 of the California Penal Code, a felony, alleging that between January first, 1985 and June fourth, 1985, that Mr. Charles Chitat Ng did willfully and unlawfully kill a human being, to wit, Kathy Allen, with malice aforethought and premeditation and deliberation, a violation of Section 187 of the California Penal Code, a felony, it does appear that that offense has, in fact, been committed. There is sufficient cause to believe that Charles Chitat Ng committed that offense in this county and state."

Over and over the judge repeated his decision, for the Dubses, for Bond, his wife Brenda, and his child, for Carroll, Stapley, Peranteau, and Gerald.

Nine times the judge repeated, "It does appear that the offense has, in fact, been committed."

There was a palpable rush of breath in the crowded room as each count was read and pronounced valid. When the Cosner indictment was pronounced and the judge said, "There is sufficient cause to believe Charles

Chitat Ng committed that offense. . . ." Sharon Sellito let out a sob.

Thank God, Clancy had thought at that moment. That woman needs the healing to begin. Only a trial would bring to light all the evidence, Ng's defense, the six hundred witnesses, the incredible amount of evidence carefully protected by so many law enforcement people on all levels—cities, counties, states, and federal.

At last it was over. The spectators rose to empty out into the sunshine. But not before Judge Douglas Mewhinney, after seven years, rang down the gavel the last time he would in this case.

Charles Ng was to be bound over for trial.

The date was set for January 12, 1993.

Chapter Twenty-six

THE PRELIMINARY HEARING, THAT QUAINT California idea that everything that's already public knowledge might not convince a judge that a trial should proceed, was over, in the Ng case, in November of 1992. It was over for the relatives of the victims, who had spent whatever savings they had on an improbable vacation site in the fall of 1992. For them it was another step in the quest for finality.

On January 12, 1993, the trial was scheduled to begin. Thomasina Boyd Clancy had enough cynicism in her nature to know that cases this big seldom come off on schedule. Yet she was back in California that Monday morning, in San Andreas, just because she sensed, trial or no trial, there was quite a story here. She thought, It's a story about issues of feminism and pornography and . . .

No. It was about an outraged citizenry. I've seen it in the streets of that small town of San Andreas. I've seen it in the people I've met over the weeks of the preliminary hearing. I've seen it, in the beginning, back seven and a half years ago, in the frustration and the dogged persistence of the cops who sweated out the initial investigation.

This is the one case I've come across, she thought, in which I really have no story. Sure, I can trump up the usual side angles about the law. Or I can try to outdo the tabloids on the sexual angle. Or I can count down the months—maybe the years—to the actual trial. Her cynicism again came to the fore.

What's happening today, January 12, 1993? she repeated to herself. The parking lot of the Government Center was unusually bleak. She stood with Matt Hedgers outside the courtroom. They had just listened to a comical exchange between Judge Perasso, the defense attorneys and the prosecution.

They had heard that Ephraim Margolin, representing Ng on his Marsden motion to dismiss Webster and Marovich, would argue to reinstate Garrick Lew and Michael Burt. They had heard the prosecution talk about multiple trials, about new layers of "preparation" if a change of venue were granted.

Matt said, "There weren't too many highlights to the preliminary hearing, at least for a local reporter. Everyone around here knows the facts of the case backwards and forwards."

"I read some of your articles, they were excellent."

"Take out the quotes and they'd be flat. Thank God for Sharon Sellito."

Clancy nodded knowingly. She had also gotten mileage from the zingers Paul Cosner's sister had fired off. She said, "I remember when Sharon said: 'I think he should be marched around Calaveras County and be forced to tell where all the bodies are, and then he should have a quick trip to the gas chamber.' "

Matt smiled. "She said, 'He was a very good murderer, but a lousy shoplifter.' "

Clancy thought, We all use different weapons to handle our grief and anger. Sharon's tool was black humor. She glanced around the courtyard. "Maybe I'll do a follow-up piece, just before the trial starts, something along the lines on where everyone is. Ballard dead, Nutall now the sheriff. Cricket waiting for her chance to testify. And of course she wasn't charged with anything."

"Don't forget to get in Cricket's father."

"Why?"

"He was quoted in the papers complaining about the

way the investigators left his property in a shambles. Then he had the gall to wonder aloud if any motion picture company might be interested in using his property as a backdrop to a movie."

"Why bother? The bunker's gone. Without that, all you need is any nondescript house in the mountains. Lord knows, there's enough of them."

"A lot of unanswered questions."

"The trial will uncover those details." Clancy paused. "Speaking of the trial, why wasn't a change of venue requested before now?"

"By who? They can't even figure out who's going to defend, let alone where."

Whatever happened, Clancy thought, to the terrible swift sword of justice?

She walked to her car, turned and watched the white van drive by. There was an unmarked lead car and an unmarked rear car. They were taking the prisoner back to New Folsom Prison, back to administrative segregation, back to maximum security, back to a solitary cell.

Guilty? Innocent?

That is up to a jury to decide. The American system of jurisprudence moves slowly when a life is at stake—Ephraim Margolin has burned that into my memory.

Without thinking about it, she followed the white van. The caravan of cars meandered north on Highway 49, going through the lush countryside.

Clancy kept a good hundred yards to the rear of the vehicles.

Back to Folsom, she thought, and remembered her depressing tour. She had seen the bleak four-by-eight-foot cells, the cold walls, the gray deadness, the terrible sound of metal on metal as cell doors were slammed closed.

What did Ng's lawyers hope to accomplish? To keep him out of San Quentin's gas chamber? To get him life without possibility of parole? Or did they really think they could get him exonerated?

That's their job, she realized, just as trying to get Ng a

reservation in the Death Watch Cell was the prosecution's.

The white van and its two-car escort turned off Highway 49 and headed toward Highway 50.

Back to Folsom.

What would I do if I was faced with living the rest of my life in a cage, thought so dangerous that I was segregated even from the general prison population? Never to see an ocean, never to see a river, never to see a city.

She smiled as she realized the answer. *I'd do what Leonard Lake did.*

Author's Note

OF ALL THE EXTREMES IN THE CASE OF Leonard Lake and Charles Ng, none is as interesting, in the end, as a fantastic leap of legal argument taken by Ephraim Margolin for the defense.

The reader will recall that Margolin had been placed on the horns of an ethical dilemma. In a capital case of this kind, the best strategy of the defense is usually delay. Yet he was convinced that Ng's original attorneys were better prepared, without the delay inherent in bringing in new attorneys, to present the defendant's case.

Thus it happened that, in a small county courtroom of a rural community, Margolin came before a judge and presented an argument based on an analogy with theoretical physics. Sometimes a case is so extreme, he said, that the normal rules do not apply.

The Ng case, Margolin concluded, is a megacase. It is so overwhelming that even the defense tactic of delay must be abandoned. The cause of justice would best be served by ignoring the traditional ideas of what disqualifies a defense counsel.

That argument, accepted by the presiding judge, was appealed to the California Supreme Court and rejected, 4–3. Yet in subsequent cases it was successfully used by other defense attorneys to break up large indictments into manageable segments, often bringing about rapid trials and judgments acceptable to both prosecution and defense. "Megacases" has now become part of legal language.

In the view of the authors, the Lake-Ng case suggests, by its very complexity, similar broad conclusions about the death penalty, about victims' rights, and about society's rights. At the time this is written, Mr. Ng has not had the benefit of a trial in California on the multiple murder charges brought by the people of two counties. The following conclusions do not depend, however, on Mr. Ng's guilt or innocence—merely on the evidence that is now a matter of public record and that is presented in this book.

Like Mr. Margolin, we would like to reach for an analogy outside the law. In mathematics, an effective way of finding the truth is to look at extreme cases. The philosopher Immanuel Kant employed a similar idea in ethics: an action is morally wrong which, if everybody did it, would lead to disaster for society. What we have in the Lake-Ng case is such an appeal to an extreme example.

Consider the death penalty.

The debate over the fairness or the necessity of the death penalty rises to a fever pitch before and after a well-publicized execution, then subsides. The arguments are familiar. The pro faction cites the need for finality for victims, the right of the state for retribution, and society's concern for reasonable self-defense. The con side points out the position of other "civilized countries," the inequity and capriciousness of how the death penalty is applied, and how killing by the state only institutionalizes and contributes to violence.

The Lake-Ng case offers a compelling argument of a new kind, against the death penalty. Again, by analogy to mathematics, this argument emerges because of the extreme character of this case.

In late 1992 the present Attorney General of California, Dan Lungren, debated this issue with the attorney for the late Robert Alton Harris—the man whose execution in mid-1992 marked the return of California to capital punishment. Are we a violent society? Yes. Is the anger directed at the alleged murderers like Ng a case of simple revenge? No. Is all killing wrong? Ask a World War II veteran or a cop who returns hostile fire. Such issues can be sorted out and brought to some reasonable resolution.

The California Poll at the time of the Harris execution showed strong support for the death penalty. Yet in this poll, when the option of an absolute life sentence without possibility of parole was posed, opinion changed drastically. The public was about equally divided on capital punishment. The public does not believe the courts when they sentence someone to "life without possibility of parole."

Why should the public believe the courts? A "ten-year sentence" often amounts to two years and nine months. "Life" turns out to mean twenty years. Parole boards change; judges die. A new governor is elected who may be inclined to pardoning.

Consider how the extreme delay in the Lake-Ng case bears on the question of believing the courts. In the course of researching this book, we talked to prosecutors, defense attorneys, attorneys for defense attorneys, public defenders, law professors at Stanford University and the University of California. Without exception they agreed that the possibility of killing an innocent man is a driving factor in the delay of bringing a defendant like Ng to trial. Surely judges fear reversal on their denial of defense motions. Surely it's in the financial interest of court-appointed attorneys, even if only unconscious, to rack up week after week of expensive hourly rates. In a single defense action in San Mateo County, California—the "Billionaire Boys" case—the taxpayers paid $3 million in fees between 1986 and 1993. The extradition procedure and preliminary hearings in the Ng case cost a similar amount.

Yet it's neither money nor fear of lost prestige that drives judicial decisions. It's simply this: no judge can admit that any delay is excessive when a man's life hangs in the balance.

The prosecuting attorney for Calaveras County warned, before the preliminary hearing for Ng, that a trial might not happen for a decade. The enormity of the crime meant an unprecedented number of documents, involving some six hundred witnesses.

What if there were no death penalty?

Defense attorney Ephraim Margolin points out that he has visited several clients in federal or state penitentiaries "where death seems preferable." He also agrees with the general lines of the argument that, paradoxically, the possibility of a death sentence robs some defendants of an early verdict.

The accused has a constitutional right to a "speedy trial"—this to avoid imprisonment without cause. Does society have a right to speedy justice—society in the persons of victims and victims' relatives, society in terms of taxpayers? Year after year, the time that it has taken capital cases to go to trial has lengthened. In the Ng case, the five or more years lost in the extradition battle in Canada exacerbated the situation. Regardless, Ng's predicament represents the extreme. The crimes he is accused of are of such magnitude that we, the people, must forgo swiftness of justice and must pay millions of dollars in court costs that might well have gone to more worthy needs of society.

Perhaps the Lake-Ng case can restore some sanity to this process, by its very extraordinariness. If the public-opinion polls are right, we won't demand the death penalty as long as life without possibility of parole really means something. Then we could bring people like Ng to trial as quickly as they seem to want it. We could spare ourselves this needless cost and grief. We could grant the relatives of victims a sense of closure. We could defend ourselves against society's enemies without killing them. And we could leave open, just enough to make it a hope, the doors of justice for those wrongly sentenced.

ABOUT THE AUTHORS

Joseph Harrington was born and raised in San Francisco and, like his father and grandfather before him, was for many years the proprietor of a bar and grill under his own name in the City. He and Robert Burger became interested in the Lake-Ng case when they assisted on a report for the San Francisco Police Department: *Juvenile Crime and Adult Responsibility.* He has been writing full-time since 1986. He lives with his wife and family in the Mother Lode country of northern California.

Robert Burger was born in Pizenswitch, Nevada of a pioneer '49er family. While a partner at the Burger, Felix & Wood advertising agency in San Francisco, he authored or collaborated on more than thirty nonfiction books. He has taught writing courses at the University of California and other universities. He and his wife live in the San Francisco Bay Area.